CASE MANAGEMENT

CASE MANAGEMENT

POLICY, PRACTICE AND PROFESSIONAL BUSINESS

DI GURSANSKY
JUDY HARVEY
ROSEMARY KENNEDY

Columbia University Press
New York

Columbia University Press
Publishers Since 1893
New York   Chichester, West Sussex

First published in 2003

Copyright © Di Gursansky, Judy Harvey and Rosemary Kennedy 2003

Set in 10.5/12 pt Times by DOCUPRO, Canberra
Printed by South Wind Production (Singapore) Private Limited

10 9 8 7 6 5 4 3 2 1

CONTENTS

TABLES AND FIGURES

TABLES

FIGURES

ACKNOWLEDGMENTS

We primarily wish to acknowledge one another. This is not to deny the invaluable contributions to our work of families, colleagues, practitioners and students over the years, nor is it meant to be self-congratulatory. We want to celebrate the delights and resolvable frustrations of collabatory work where each person contributes generously, readily assumes responsibilities for their own and others' work and interests, is respected, concedes and learns. We also wish to remark on the obstacles which attend this way of working. Despite all the contemporary rhetoric about teamwork, individual activity is often easier and certainly so much more easily understood, measured and rewarded within organisations. Many case managers will already have come to this conclusion. In particular, we are keen to emphasise that genuine collaborative activity can result in products which are greater than the sum of several solitary efforts combined. This book would never have been conceived of, planned or written by any one of us working alone.

INTRODUCTION

This book is not easily categorised and may not satisfy any number of familiar groupings. It attempts to overview case management across countries, disciplines, fields of practice, professions and client populations. This aim is ambitious but important, as so much experience of and writing about case management takes place in regional, disciplinary, professional and practice silos. Thus, for example, the practice knowledge of nurses may not benefit social workers; health and human service workers may be unaware that they share experiences; case managers in the United States and Australia may be uninformed about each other's problems and solutions; those relying on psychological explanations of their work worlds may be ignorant of sociological revelations; and case managers in aged care may not appreciate what might be learned from their contemporaries in correctional centres. This book, then, is a sort of *cadastre* or register of the extent of what is known of case management. It aims for unique breadth and scope.

Let us put some flesh on this declaration of commonality. The custodial case manager who is coordinating and monitoring a package of drug and alcohol and anger management services for a prisoner shares many of the risk concerns and service constraints of the community nurse case manager who is similarly seeking and managing a range of services such as meals provision, cleaning and home nursing designed to support an aged person in their home in the community. Likewise, the policy-makers crafting a case management approach to service delivery with homeless people or in child protection or disability could learn a great deal about data management and individualised budget management systems from their counterparts in acute health managed care. Case management in mental health—which may, for example, require a social worker to negotiate a complex web of social security, housing and employment services with and for a client—will involve the same issues of discrimination, a heavy case load and service eligibility restrictions which typify the experience of, say, a psychologist case manager working to rehabilitate injured employees.

This is not a 'how to do' case management book. It does not detail specific case management programs. It is not a social policy or law book, nor is it a book on the sociology of the professions. It is also not a book on career development. It is neither a specific human service nor a health book. But a little bit of each of these things characterises it. What it is designed to be, to use Moxley's (1996) categories, is a normative, a prescriptive and a critical commentary on case management directed at advanced students in the health and human services, case managers and others with a vested interest in the practice of case management. It aims to help them understand the broad context, nature and commonalities of case management work, to stimulate fresh thinking about improving practice, and to emphasise the necessity for active engagement by workers if they are to sustain or develop reasonable levels of work satisfaction and effectiveness.

WHO WE ARE

As authors, we have between us qualifications and professional identifications in social work, law, social policy and psychology, and practice experience in rehabilitation, public welfare, juvenile justice and mental health. We have all, for many years, been designing and teaching subjects in a wide range of professional and interdisciplinary human service programs. Through these diverse backgrounds and experiences, we have formed the conclusions which have culminated in this book but which continue to evolve. We are mostly located in the human services, and this will be evident—as will our Australian perspective. However, we share a commitment to looking and working across borders of any kind and we hope that this too is evident. Our ideological positions beyond those already mentioned must be declared, even though these too will reveal themselves. Our most fundamental concern is the priority of and outcomes for the service user. For this reason, we are most interested in promoting practice which produces positive results for clients. While we appreciate that many work systems present major obstacles to good practice, we do not think that workers are ever excused from aiming for better outcomes with clients. No matter how bad the workplace or program is, we believe the case manager can have some positive impact for clients, even at the most minimal levels. The challenges posed by these statements and their feasibility are discussed in the chapters which follow.

We are neither apologists for nor proponents of case management. Its various manifestations may be better or worse than traditional and parallel approaches to service delivery; however, the comparisons might be made. Case management is simply a challenging fact of contemporary health and human service worlds which demands analysis and response from all who are involved with it. Informed and balanced responses are what we would hope to promote. If—as is likely in future—new and more fashionable terms replace case management, the principles underlying it will probably remain and thus an understanding of it can add depth to a critical appraisal of its successors.

QUESTIONS OF LANGUAGE

Three matters of language must be addressed. One concerns case management itself; one concerns who it is directed at; and another relates to health and human services. What is meant by case management will be the subject of a number of later considerations, but the introductory point is that we have taken a broad approach in this book and also included material from care management and managed care in our commentaries. These three approaches are not synonymous, and none is a single entity, but they have some common historical and policy roots. In addition, they share the rhetoric of individualised service delivery. Much of the discourse and learning in any one of these areas has applicability and lessons for the others. Again we aspire to draw in and cross-pollinate knowledge from different arenas.

The second question of terminology is what to call the person or people for whom services are delivered. 'Client' is the term commonly used in the human services and now more universally. 'Patient' is the health term. 'Consumer' and 'customer' are newer general names with managerial origins and implications that we will revisit but, as

Sheppard (1995, p. xii) says, they are redolent of 'popping into Woolworths for some toys'. 'User' is also an increasingly evident label, but again Sheppard (1995) makes a point in warning that this is a colloquial term of abuse. We would add that it is now regularly used in relation to substance abusers. All of these terms carry historical, professional and ideological significance and there is no entirely satisfactory way to resolve problems of language in this area. We are most familiar with the word 'client' and tend to use, rather than endorse, it sometimes along with 'service user' and 'consumer'. We do not use the word 'patient' because it implies 'being done to by others'. While this may reflect our own professional acculturations, it is also true that the term is exclusive to the health sector. When referring to groups of clients, we commonly use target populations, recognising that this too carries connotations of managerialism and the New Right ideologies.

In relation to health and human services, we again take an inclusive approach. Health includes primary, secondary and tertiary services—both private and public—and related insurance systems. Human or community services 'may include the full range of government and non-government services which are active in and responsible for the development and provision of social welfare' (Wearing 1998, p. xiv). More specifically, like Mehr (1995), we include juvenile and adult corrections, child and family welfare, social services, mental health services, disability services, rehabilitation services, public health and general support and crisis services. Definitional niceties are not of great concern here. We are more interested in encompassing any health or human service field where the introduction, experience and practice of case management may add to the public store of knowledge about this phenomenon. There are other arenas where case management, or derivatives of it, are being adopted—such as in the legal and court systems—and we do not attend closely to these. Our ambition to embrace as much territory as possible must have some practical outer limits and we have set these at the increasingly blurred edges of health and human services.

ORGANISATION OF THE BOOK

The book is arranged into several parts which we think encapsulate emerging and new configurations of energy and concern under case management, and which together permit a comprehensive cataloguing and overview of the phenomenon. The three main parts represent what we believe is an original and more complete way of conceptualising case management and its practice. There is much already written on case management and we have attempted to avoid duplicating material about which there is consensus or extensive description. As we wish to extend rather than replicate understanding of case management, we mine existing information for imperatives and implications and we pursue linkages and themes across previously impervious borders. Within each of the three main parts, significant and often neglected points extracted from the literature contribute to the structure of the chapters.

Part I attends to case management as policy. It aims to answer questions about the several histories of case management, whether or not case management is really different from what went before, what the international policy trends around case management are, and how it has been applied and researched in many countries and fields of practice. Chapter 1 details the contextual forces which have resulted in the widespread adoption of case management, what the term might mean and the several different policy foundations of case management. Chapter 2 uses three case illustrations to explore further the policy and program contexts of case management, variations in application of the approach, and implications of shifts in service delivery through case management. Chapter 3 looks closely at the distinctiveness of case management as an approach to service delivery and attempts to unravel the varied and conflicting assertions about whether or not it is something new or different. To digress slightly at this point, throughout the book we maintain that there are some features which distinguish case management from traditional approaches to service delivery. However, it is rooted in the same ground as these traditional approaches and shares many of their characteristics. For this reason, much that we say draws on and has general relevance to the health and human services but its application to case management is always our main concern.

Part II turns to the practice of case management. It seeks to go beyond descriptions of how case management 'is done' to identification of important practice variations and critical and emerging practice challenges. Chapter 4 does outline the process of case management; this material has been covered previously and extensively in other books but it is returned to here with a focus on the distinctiveness of case management and the implications for practice. Chapter 5 looks at the impact of the many variations of case management on case manager roles, responsibilities and functions. Chapter 6 details and analyses re-occurring practice demands and ethical dilemmas around information and resource management.

Part III is concerned with the 'professional business' of case management—that is, what the phenomenon means for the identity, preparation, work practices and futures of the traditional health and human service professions and for individual workers. Chapter 7 investigates what the management component of case management actually means, especially for workers. Chapter 8 looks at who case managers are, the professions most involved with case management, questions of contested professional territory and implications of case management for the professions. The focus of Chapter 9 is on preparation for case management through education and training. Chapter 10 attends to the ways in which case management practice is regulated and how various formal and informal regulatory forces impact on workers and their decision-making.

Part IV, 'Reflections', is an attempt to bring the book's content together.

ENGAGING WITH THE REALITY OF CASE MANAGEMENT

As stated, this book is directed at those concerned with the practice of case management and we are preoccupied with better quality case management practice. Thus we attempt to unite a number of recurring themes in the book around these two interests. Throughout the following parts, there are constant refrains about sameness and difference, continuity and change in relation to case management and other approaches to service delivery; about contradictions and paradoxes; and about a cacophony of diverse voices espousing and pursuing different elements of case management policy, practice and professional business. The resultant maelstrom partly reflects our efforts to encompass many different perspectives, but it also characterises the realities of case management. Always, in threading our way through the material, we attempt to draw out the implications for practice, the practitioner and others concerned with practice.

Do we lay too much at the feet of the individual and the case manager in particular? It is common knowledge that people faced with demanding, discordant and clamorous environments often seek out safe havens where familiar and simple messages prevail. Why should anyone venture out into the clamour that we try to depict here? Because it exists, because it is fascinating, potentially enlightening and empowering, and because some degree of improved service delivery may result from confronting it. At the very heart of the concept of case management lies recognition of service complexity and the need for coordination of relevant but fragmented services. Avoidance of complexity and diversity is hardly a sound foundation for good case management practice. We hope that readers of this book are persuaded that there are advantages in opening up to the disorder that is the world of case management. We also hope that they are prompted to extend and perhaps alter their thinking about how case management service delivery might be improved for better client outcomes.

PART I

CASE MANAGEMENT AS POLICY

1

THE DEVELOPMENT OF
CASE MANAGEMENT

In a recent text on case management in the human services, Austin and McClelland (1996, p. 1) argue that the case management approach has become all-pervasive in service delivery. They echo the Cole Porter refrain, 'everybody's doing it', to highlight the breadth of its application. Many other writers endorse the view that case management has become a preferred service delivery approach in the human services and health sectors, attesting to its dominance and adaptability across diverse settings (e.g. Rose 1992b; Moxley 1997; Woodside and McClam 1998; Holt 2000; Huber 2000). Indeed, case management was the 'buzz word' of the 1990s (Netting 1992, p. 160) and its currency is being maintained at the start of the new millennium.

Despite the continuing popularity of case management as a vehicle for service delivery, the debates about what it is, who needs it and under what conditions it is best provided are recurring themes in the literature and on the international conference circuits. The term 'case management' evokes a sense of understanding that is more elusive than is generally acknowledged. There is a perception of shared wisdom about case management that permeates the discourses and distracts us from the level of critical analysis that is sorely needed to develop knowledge and practice. Without deconstructing or teasing apart the ideas about case management, we do not establish precise knowledge about the various manifestations of the approach in diverse practice settings. What is, or is not, identified as case management is often determined by the commentator's own position in the field. For example, the community care practitioner may see little common ground with the practice of case management in a prison environment, in managed care or case flow management in court administrations. However, from each of these settings, commentators would claim authority to speak about case management and its practice. This first part of the book examines the conceptual basis and the context for case management as an international phenomenon in service delivery. It is asserted that case management now pervades policy statements, program development and practice in the human services and health sectors. We support the view that it is through the context of service delivery that the nuances and diversity of the approach are best understood (Burns et al. 2000; Austin 2001). It is the broad application of case management that has created conditions that are redefining the nature of professional practice, service provision and consumer expectations.

Any claim to produce a single history of case management defies the reality of its diversity and multiple applications. Depending on the commentator's discipline base, orientation to the approach and experience, the perspectives on history vary. To echo a theme from Popper (cited in Tripp 1976), 'there is no history . . . there are only many histories of all kinds of aspects of human life'. The exercise of searching for a single and continuous development of case management inevitably leads to simplistic analysis and detracts from our understanding of the complex and parallel processes that have contributed to a shift in service delivery approaches in the human services and health sectors.

With a critical eye, it is possible to discern a number of trends and issues that have contributed to the emergence of case management since the 1970s. In this chapter we will overview early historical accounts of case management documented in the nursing and social work professions. We will canvass the problems that arise from a quest for definition or typology of the approach. An analysis of contemporary developments of case management will demonstrate the diverse agendas that are served through its application. We would argue that, for various stakeholders, the rhetoric of case management has served different purposes and that the shifts in the culture of service delivery have yet to be fully explored. It is beyond the scope of this book to pursue this path. However, in the final section of this chapter, we will discuss the characteristics and principles underpinning case management, an approach to service delivery that is reconstructing practices and service provision.

ACKNOWLEDGING DIFFERENT TERMINOLOGY

In the Introduction, matters of terminology were raised. Here it is relevant to comment on some of the variations in nomenclature that apply to case management itself. In this book we generally adopt the term 'case management' as it is the one used most frequently at an international level. However, different terminology does prevail in particular countries and/or program contexts. For example, in UK community care policy and programs, the preferred term is 'care management' (Sheppard 1995; Burns and Perkins 2000). The adoption of the term 'care management' addresses the frequently voiced criticism that the emphasis on 'case' management detracts from the personal nature of services being offered. The consistent use of the term 'care management' is peculiar to the United Kingdom, but this term and other variations can be found in programs around the world.

Within programs, alternative terms such as 'case' or 'care coordination' and 'service coordination' are applied most often where service provision is focused on brokerage or service management. Here the coordination task is paramount, and the activities of the case manager are directed towards ensuring that the services deemed necessary in the assessment process remain responsive, effective and cost efficient for the client. When specific terms like clinical case management, team coordination, strengths or empowerment approaches are referred to, we are likely to find the case manager involved in more intensive activities, with clinical specialisation being incorporated into the case manager's responsibilities. Examples of these clinical or specialised case management roles are frequently found in mental health, diagnostically based services in health, community based services and institutional settings. Terms such as critical or clinical pathways, risk or disease management, life care planning and managed care are synonymous with service provision in acute health and insurance based medical and injury management (Newell 1996; Weed 1999; Huber 2000) emphasises that many of these procedures are 'algorithmic' and are driven by systemic and clinical needs for demonstrable outcomes, quality improvement and cost containment. In acute health situations, for example, the case managers are focused on responding to variance from the clinical pathway to capitalise on gains from improved practice or to rectify individual or recurring incidents that require responses beyond the predicted pathway. In these circumstances the case manager is expected to maintain a monitoring role in terms of efficiency, risk management and cost containment (Cohen and Cesta 1997, pp. 158–9). The agenda here is not to list all of the possible variations of the terms that might be found under the rubric of case management. It is fair to say that the term remains both ubiquitous and ambiguous (Rothman 1991, p. 520; Solomon 2000, p. 421). The goal is to alert readers to the fact that the terms are applied interchangeably, that variations do exist and different agendas in relation to outcomes are often accommodated within the notion of case management.

CONFRONTING PROBLEMS OF DEFINITION

Definitions of case management abound. To be consistent with our own analytical stance, we endorse efforts to provide descriptions of particular applications in definitional terms. It is through specificity that understanding of the different perspectives on the approach can be acquired. However, to leave the issue of definition aside would abrogate responsibility to scope developments and understanding of case management. We do not intend to present a 'model' *per se*, as this path is reductive analysis and does not facilitate the exploration of variations in application and context.

It is possible to discern at least two broad emphases in definitions found in the literature. First, there are those definitions that can be described as generic. They focus on the process, tasks and functions involved in practice without locating the particulars of the approach in terms of target population or setting. In this style of definition, key words and phrases include individually tailored services, coordination, linkage, service network and efficiency, and cost effectiveness. Several examples are presented here:

> Case management is a set of logical steps and a process of interaction within a service network which assume that a client receives needed services in a supportive, effective, efficient and cost effective manner. (Weil et al. 1985, p. 2)

> A process of tailoring services to individual needs. (Ovretveit 1993, p. 15)

> Case management is widely viewed as a mechanism for linking and coordinating segments of the service delivery system . . .

to ensure the most comprehensive program for meeting an individual client's need for care. (Austin 1993, p. 16)

Second, there are definitions that designate case management as clinical or advanced practice. Definitions of this type are likely to detail coordination responsibilities and clinical tasks for the case manager. In these circumstances, it is likely that the target population will have complex and ongoing needs and that personnel will have professional backgrounds relevant to treatment strategies. The following definition is illustrative of the clinical or advanced practice:

> Forming a relationship between the case manager and the patient; the use of the case manager as a model of healthy behaviour and as a potential object for identification; and active intervention in the patient's daily life to structure a mutually tolerant environment. (Harris and Bergman 1988, cited in Raiff and Shore 1993, p. 86)

Kanter (1989), and more recently Burns and Perkins (2000) and Marshall and Creed (2000), elaborate the breadth of responsibilities of a clinical case manager in mental health settings. Kanter's definition is detailed here as his practice orientation was widely endorsed with the initial shift to community-based service delivery in that sector:

> A modality of mental health practice, that in coordination with the traditional psychiatric focus on biological and psychological functioning, addresses the overall maintenance of the mentally ill person's physical and social environment, with the goals of facilitating his or her physical survival, personal growth, community participation and recovery from or adaptation to mental illness. (Kanter 1989, p. 361)

Although there is no intention to pursue the idea of one or more 'models of case management', it is acknowledged that this is often the language of practice. Examining 'the models' presented in the literature is illustrative of the diverse applications of the approach but does not produce clarity about it. Making sense of the many descriptions led to efforts to create some classification of the applications of the approach. For example, Austin (1992, p. 402) argues that the range of case management 'models' can be classified as a continuum. Kanter (1989), using a similar approach in the specific context of mental health, suggests that the extremes of such a continuum are analogous to the role of travel agent and travel companion. The travel agent coordinates, attends to detail, monitors and is a resource to be drawn on to assist with changed itinerary needs. The travel companion stays with the person for the whole journey, engages in the journey and shares the client's experiences. In case management terms, the continuum extremes are aligned with program arrangements that are systems oriented, where the case manager is a more distant resource, though by no means inactive in setting up and maintaining the set of resources needed to support the client. At the other end of the continuum, we see the case manager as travel companion, engaged more intensely to support complex needs and higher risk populations.

As with all efforts to create conceptualisations across diverse contexts, where different professional and human service personnel practise, the inevitable blurring of boundaries poses many analytical challenges. We would also want to put one caveat on the preceding commentary in relation to the recent developments in managed care. In the literature, the terms 'case management' and 'managed care' can be used interchangeably, confusing the fact that the first is an approach and process in service delivery and the latter is policy and business strategy to control health care use (Cohen and Cesta 1997; Rossi 1999). The developments in managed care refocus service delivery in health care in very specific ways and we will explore this aspect of health care policy further in Chapter 2.

In spite of the necessary discussion of definition, agreement on it should be of less concern than the task of understanding the nature of practice generated by this service delivery approach. Key characteristics are the critical issue, and the task in each context is to seek precision about each application of case management. We shall return to this task later in the chapter and in more detail in the practice section, but before addressing the breadth of application, both the beginnings and contemporary trends of the approach are summarised.

THE BEGINNINGS OF CASE MANAGEMENT

Case management is seen to have its origins in the early practices of the social work and the nursing professions, primarily in the United States (Bower 1991; Murer and Brick 1997; O'Connor et al. 1998). This does not mean that the practices associated with the beginnings of case management in these professions might not be paralleled in other areas such as the United Kingdom, Europe and Australia. As a consequence of the US leadership of case management in the 1970s, the literature has been dominated by North American commentary, with an understandable focus on wide-ranging contemporary issues.

In the social work literature, the first efforts to coordinate public human services are identified with activities of the Massachusetts Board of Charity in 1863 (Weil et al. 1985, p. 4). Subsequently, case coordination 'to promote cooperation in charitable work' (Kennedy 1985) became a critical component of the practices developed through the internationally linked Charity Organisation Societies and the Settlement Houses in the late 1880s. The beginnings of case management are identified with the use of methods to determine need that were promoted through both of these organisations (Heffernan et al. 1997). It is also common to link the work of Mary Richmond, recognised as a founder of the social work profession in the United States, to the early history of case management and social work. Mary Richmond promulgated a model of case coordination and social investigation for direct service practice (Netting 1992, p. 160). In this period, cooperation between organisations, and careful documentation of work with individuals and families, was designed to more effectively coordinate services and ensure gatekeeping of resources (Weil et al. 1985; Wood and Middleman 1989, p. 159; Burns et al. 1995, p. 353; O'Connor et al. 1998). Two explicit intentions of more scientific or systematic practice were to manage fraud and ensure efficient use of resources (Austin and McClelland 1996, p. 3)—notions that resonate with contemporary calls for efficiency and accountability in terms of service provision.

In a similar way, the nursing profession identifies the beginnings of case management in private duty nursing, institutions and early public health practices (Bower 1991; Murer and Brick 1997; Hawkins et al. 1998; Huber 2000). Lillian Wald, who founded the Henry Street Nurses Settlement in 1895, is named as the first American public health nurse and case manager (Huber 2000). She developed a role for the public health nurse as the link between a family's social, economic and health needs and the services the individual needed to become or stay healthy (Woodside and McClam 1998, p. 44). In addition, her practices were recognised as contributing to cost containment, leading to the principles being adopted by insurance companies.

Regardless of the early beginnings of case coordination, and these early forms of case management, it is generally agreed that by the 1970s case management, as we know it, emerged in response to a number of factors. An understanding of these forces for change provides a context for the adoption of case management as the preferred service delivery approach.

THE IMPERATIVES FOR CHANGE

It is widely acknowledged in the literature that multiple factors have contributed to conditions that created the opportunities for new approaches to service delivery. Case management in the United States in the 1970s is specifically documented, and is associated with a policy shift from institutional care to community care (Rose 1992b, p. 6; Enos and Southern 1996, p. 27; Holt 2000, p. 10). Deinstitutionalisation posed new challenges for service delivery. Practitioners were no longer able to draw on the self-sufficient resources of the large institutions (Applebaum and Austin 1990). Institutionally-based care had been central to service provision in areas such as mental health, aged care, disability and for children in need of care, and it is in these fields that case management was first implemented. Institutional care had been the traditional response for those needing long-term care or protection. Within the enclosed environment of the institution, those in need of care and their families were offered assurances of safety, comprehensive services and permanency. In addition, the institutional environment provided an economy of scale in the provision of care. Resources were arranged to limit the need for residents to move outside of the institution, and to ensure standardised care and routine in a secure environment. The offering of asylum or safe places, in such areas as mental health, established a key role of professionals as the arbiters of access to these resources (Leff 1997, p. 7).

Advances in medical technology in the postwar years created new opportunities for people with chronic health issues to be supported in the community. In particular, the new psychotropic drugs significantly altered the prognosis and management of those with severe mental health problems. In addition, the potential for rehabilitation of the elderly, those with chronic disability and others facing complex health issues was significantly improved. The interest in rehabilitation was given impetus with the demobilisation of military personnel and the pressures for reconstruction under peacetime conditions (Walsh 2000,

p. 26). Although Walsh is referring particularly to the United States, the service developments in rehabilitation for this population were evident in all the Western Allied countries. Over time, these services were extended beyond ex-service personnel to the wider civilian population.

But technology was not the only force for change. The shifts to new bases of service delivery were sustained by a combination of trends (Walsh 2000, p. 27). In Western industrialised countries, the consumer rights movement developed in the 1960s and 1970s, alongside the demands for civil rights, recognition of women's place in wider society and demands for independent living (Lewis and Glennerster 1996, p. 2; Holt 2000, p. 9). The case against asylum and institutional care had rested on a powerful combination of explicit arguments relating to efficiency and general resource implications of maintaining reasonable standards of care (Means and Smith 1994). In addition, in the 1960s, all forms of institutional care came under scrutiny in the face of various reviews that highlighted human rights abuse (Goffman 1961; Leff 1997; Jack 1998). Consumers began to assert demands for greater independence and services that reflected individual need and choice. Families sought more positive outcomes for family members with high care needs—whether they were aged family members or those with physical or mental health problems.

Several factors contributed to redefinitions of the role of the state in relation to welfare services. In the 1970s, the 'oil crisis' precipitated world economic pressures and governments were confronted with the reality that assumed levels of growth could not be sustained (Pierson 1994; Midgely 1997, p. 135; Saunders 2000). Microeconomic reforms in Western countries presaged realignment of government priorities and responsibilities that were driven, in part, by emerging demographic trends. Increasingly, governments were facing population trends that would extend demand on services to a heavier level, it was argued, than the productive sector of the economy could bear.

In Western industrialised countries, governments endorsed the importance of family responsibility, individual measures to protect against changing life needs, competitive and market strategies to enhance choices and quality of service provision. For those countries that had endorsed the notion of welfare state principles, the shift away from collective to individualistic strategies has seen a major realignment in service provision. Bryson (1992, p. 227) argues cogently that: 'Recent changes in policy directions and in the implementation of programmes are underpinned by a change in the leading political philosophy, from political liberalism to economic liberalism . . . a favouring of individual rather than collective activity.'

Case management has provided a framework that could be endorsed by a range of stakeholders who might challenge traditional service arrangements. It was indeed a timely notion that many interests could accept and endorse while accommodating very different agendas. What could be more attractive to consumers, their families and advocates than a service delivery approach based on assessed need and constructed to meet individual needs? What could be more attractive to service providers than funding that recognises different service arrangements and encourages efficiency, flexibility in service design, potential for an increasing deregulation of the workforce and worker accountability for outcomes? What could be more attractive to funders than an emphasis on efficiency, accountability, outcomes, cost containment, maximum use of all resources and challenging traditional organisational boundaries? 'Like an idea that finds its perfect moment, case management has spread exponentially across all human services' (Furlong, cited in Davis 1997, p. 230).

CONTEMPORARY DEVELOPMENTS IN CASE MANAGEMENT

Most writers agree that the contemporary applications of case management were well established in the United States by the 1970s, and had been adopted internationally by the 1980s (Rose 1992b; Austin and McClelland 1996; Ozanne 1996). Case management became something of a mantra and a panacea for service delivery difficulties (Gursansky and Kennedy 1998). Initially, case management was linked to policies of deinstitutionalisation and community care (Challis et al. 1993; Lewis and Glennerster 1996; Ozanne 1996; Baragwanath 1997; Rothman and Sager 1998; Challis 2000). It was Austin (1993) who argued persuasively that case management developed out of dysfunctional delivery services that were operating in the interests of providers rather than service users. The need to support clients in the community highlighted the complexity of the service mix, barriers to access and lack of continuity in care. The concept of the case manager holding responsibility for coordination, acting as a 'boundary spanning' agent and as a key contact for the client (and carers) was promoted to address complex service delivery needs (Moore 1992). Ironically, what was also promoted as an agent for system integration and increased collaboration around the needs of individuals diverted attention from the structural dynamics that have perpetuated fragmentation.

But there are other discourses of case management that are not embedded in community care policy. The literature is replete with examples of case management programs and models that have been applied to diverse populations. To illustrate this point, we will refer to a selection of these programs that identify case management as their *modus operandi*. In child welfare, the approach has been utilised in alternate care (Steering Committee for the Review of Commonwealth/State Service Provision 1997) and in child protection services (Murphy-Berman 1994; Zlotnik 1996; Halfon et al. 1997). The acute health system has adopted case management as it confronts increasing pressure to contain costs and meet demand (Loomis 1992; Cohen and Cesta 1994; Berger 1996). In clinical settings, diagnostically focused services are adopting case management models for people living with HIV/AIDS (Roberts et al. 1992; Brennan 1996), for managing people with terminal illness (Polinsky et al. 1991) or, as further examples, those people with burns, cancer, transplants and diabetes (Rossi 1999). Case management is offered to Holocaust survivors (Fern and Marks-Gordon 2001). There is a well-established and distinct history of case management in the insurance industry as it relates to claims for personal injury, complex medical rehabilitation and the more recent development of managed care (Henderson and Collard 1992; McClelland 1996; Huntt and Growick 1997; Schamess and Lightburn 1998; Blanch 1999; Frager 2000; Erdmann and Wilson 2001). And so listings could continue as we identify developments in community corrections, prisons and court administration (Enos and Southern 1996; Clay 1999; Healey 1999; McCallum and Furby 1999) and labour market programs (Hagen 1994; Kirner 1995; Stuart and Thorsen 1996; Eardley and Thompson 1997; Gursansky and Kennedy 1998).

In addition, the approach is being transposed into different cultural contexts where notions of assessment, individualised service delivery, contracted service provision and informal care pose particular challenges for implementation. Limited systematic research has been undertaken in the implications of cross-cultural adaptation of case management, although a number of writers stress the importance of case managers being adequately prepared for these situations (Raiff and Shore 1993; Rogers 1995; Este 1996; Roessler and Rubin 1998).

The implementation of case management with Indigenous communities and individuals poses another set of questions about the relevance of the approach. For example, what is the place of individualised service arrangements in communities and family structures constructed on a broad kinship base? What is the meaning of contracting in social structures built on mutuality and cooperation? What are the consequences of individualised service arrangements where sharing resources, reciprocity and exchange predominate over acquisition? The list of questions could be extended and some might also be relevant to the current commodification of case management in eastern European and Asian countries.

A further trend in case management is being reported, primarily in North America. Although there are examples of case managers holding funds for individuals, the devolution of resource allocation has not been widely applied. In most circumstances, case managers access funding through agency procedures. However, there are innovations being piloted that locate cash to consumers (Consumer Directed Long Term Care Programs), enabling them to purchase and manage their own support services. In these circumstances, the case managers' roles become those of facilitators and educators of the traditional case manager (Kunkel et al. 2000, p. 110). This innovation is referred to here, in part at least, to highlight the dynamic nature of the concept and the extent to which major changes in practice can be absorbed under the rubric of case management. The question for another time is whether the consumer-directed programs signify another major shift in human service provision.

We have already alerted our readers to the limitations of classifications and simple definitions in relation to case management. Forcing programs into categories detracts from recognising distinct and pertinent differences. However, having made this point, we offer a visual presentation of the diversity of case management applications to illustrate broad areas of application, acknowledging that there is inevitable overlap between and across programs. Despite the common terminology associated with the approach, it is hard to compare case management in prisons with case management as it is practised in mental health or aged care. It is difficult to reconcile case management in labour market programs with case management in acute health care. It is difficult to compare case management in the disability sector with case management practised in the area of workers' compensation or under managed care. All these programs might be labelled case management, but the varia-

Table 1.1 **Schema of case management applications**

Community care	Institutional based care	Target population
Aged care	Prisons	Rehabilitation (injured workers)
Mental health	Acute health care	Guardianship–trustee programs
Disability	Supported accommodation	Settlement programs
Child welfare	School-based programs	HIV/AIDS
	Court services—case flow	Managed care
	management	Addiction services
		Labour market programs
		Vocational rehabilitation
		Teenage parents
		Emotionally disturbed children
		and adolescents

tions within and between them mask significant differences which are not commonly acknowledged. The point that we want to emphasise is that community care does not equate with case management; managed care does not equate with case management; supported accommodation programs do not equate with case management. Each of these provides an example of a setting in which case management has been applied. Case management has provided a rubric, recognisable label or banner for diverse and complex changes to service delivery, professional practice and the responsibilities of all stakeholders in health and human services. As Austin (2001) has maintained, the context determines the style and presentation of case management.

THE SUSTAINABILITY OF CASE MANAGEMENT

Contemporary developments in case management now span four decades and are evident on all continents of the globe (Africa— Ivantic-Doucette and Maashao 1999; Japan—Ikegami 2000; Israel— Lowenstein 2000; Hong Kong—Chi and Wong 2001; Halevy-Levin 2001; Lemire and Mansell 2001; Bolivia—Montevilla-Vargas 2001; Canada—Silin 2001). The adaptability of the approach is evident in Table 1.1. The multiple faces of case management represent colonisation of the concept by a variety of stakeholders with very different agendas:

> The second phase of case management has colonized and capitalized on the generally progressive underpinnings of the

first (meaning here the applications that linked to the shift to community care), and its use or application of that language has not been contested. (Gursansky and Kennedy 1998)

Dill (1995, p. 110) provides a critical interpretation of this progressive phenomenon, arguing that case management's sustainability and adaptability rest in its organisational ambiguity and cultural meaning. Enshrined in legislation that ensured its perpetuation (Applebaum and Austin 1990; Dill 1995; Austin and McClelland 1996; Austin and McClelland 2000), the rhetoric of the approach has also been captured and permeated in policy direction and programmatic formulation. The individualisation of service delivery has proceeded relentlessly over the last 30 years, espoused and endorsed as variously meeting the goals of practitioners, consumers, carers, service providers and policy-makers. Understandably, each of these stakeholders has viewed the approach in terms of their own positioning. Like the chameleon's capacity to change colour in different environments, the variations in the forms of case management have been accepted with remarkable tolerance, perhaps because of the lack of understanding of their significance. The concept of tailoring services around the individual has legitimated the dismantling of established service arrangements. It has reshaped the nature and focus of professional relationships in the human services by emphasising the management of the situation rather than the provision of care through therapeutic intervention. In fact, the case management approach has in many settings created a distinct occupational identity: the case manager, who coordinates a range of service providers to work in collaboration around the consumer.

The coordination of services for the individual has meant support for case management from consumers because, on the face of it, they have the opportunity to assert their needs as well as being more actively involved in the planning and ongoing management of their situations. Choice and the responsibility for creative use of all potential resources has implied that considerable power is given to the consumer and/or their carers, as plans are put in place. The practice may not always meet the promise of case management, but the rhetoric suggests a level of collaboration that redresses perceived imbalances of power in many professional relationships. The explicit emphasis on cost containment and accountability has proven attractive to policy-makers, providers and purchasers of services.

For a range of reasons, then, this service delivery approach has proven to be a bonanza for policy reformers, service providers and, to some extent, consumers and carers. The responses of professionals involved in the human services and health sectors have been more variable, but their critiques have had limited effect on the burgeoning growth of case management. In part, their critical stance has been undermined by a lack of clear analysis about the approach and careful research about practice and outcomes for consumers. As is so often the case in the human services, the doing of the work obscures the analytical task that is critical for development of practice.

THE ENDURING CHARACTERISTICS OF CASE MANAGEMENT

Despite all the diversity evident in definitions, practice or program applications, it is possible to argue that there is a significant degree of consensus about the characteristics of case management. It is also possible to argue that the approach is not the exclusive domain of any one professional group. These characteristics are synchronistic with all health and human service professional practice. There will be limited discussion here of these characteristics as they are more appropriately reviewed in the practice section of the book. However, they are tabled here as part of the context-setting exercise that we are pursuing.

The characteristics of case management, detailed by writers across a range of disciplines and settings, reflect remarkable agreement about the focus of practice (Orme and Glastonbury 1993, p. 32; Davies 1994, p. 114; Challis et al. 1995, p. 5; Austin and McClelland 1996, p. 6; Huber 2000, p. 524). It is reasonable to claim that outreach, screening and intake, comprehensive assessment, care planning, service arrangement, monitoring and reassessment are the accepted core characteristics of the approach. Table 1.2 illustrates each characteristic and the focus of activities that relates to each.

Table 1.2 reflects the promise that is explicit in the rhetoric of case management. Under ideal conditions, the case manager has legitimate authority to respond to individualised need with customised service arrangements. The case manager will negotiate with the service providers that the client prefers and maintain a monitoring brief to ensure that the plans can be modified to respond to changing client needs. In addition, the case manager advocates for change for individuals and

Table 1.2   Core characteristics of case management

Characteristic	Focus of the activities
Outreach	Identifying the most appropriate clients; disseminating information for referrals; establishing the target population for any given service or program.
Screening	Using initial intake procedures to determine eligibility and the most effective targeting procedures.
Comprehensive assessment	Utilising assessment tools to determine levels of risk and individual need and to specify desired outcomes in partnership with the client and appropriate others such as informal carers and specialist service providers.
Care planning	Developing a care plan based on the information established through the assessment stage and in consultation with the client and caregivers. The case manager is expected to draw on a range of services needed for the individual and if necessary create new service arrangements to achieve this goal.
Service arrangement	Contracting of services to operationalise the care plan and negotiating with informal caregivers. The selection of service providers is to be determined in consultation with the client and reflecting their preferences.
Monitoring	Maintaining oversight of the situation to ensure the case manager can respond promptly to changing circumstances.
Reassessment	Reviewing needs and care plans where variations in the individual situation. In addition, the experience of the case manager may prompt advocacy for the individual client and a wider population.

populations as evidence of barriers to effective service delivery is identified.

PRINCIPLES UNDERLYING CASE MANAGEMENT APPROACHES

As a template for service delivery, case management accommodates a number of principles that appeal to various stakeholders and have proven to be adaptable over time, across settings and in different countries.

Reiterating a theme of this chapter, we argue that the rhetoric of case management promotes its value as an approach to service delivery on the basis that it focuses services on individual need, maximises the use of resources from informal networks and existing services and provides consumers with choices about services. In addition, in case management, the service arrangements with consumers and the various providers make explicit the outcomes desired and formalise the accountability of all parties involved in service provision. The principles underpinning case management are detailed below and the italicised keywords identify the particular quality of the principle that has perpetuated its popularity with all stakeholders.

- Service delivery is designed around the individual and their needs (*tailoring of services, needs-based*).
- Consumers and carers are actively involved in developing case plans (*individualised, consumer-driven planning*).
- Consumers are offered choice about the services they use and who provides the service (*choice*).
- The care plan is specified in terms of objectives and responsibilities of all parties and expressed as a contract (*contractualised* and *accountable*).
- Services required by an individual are drawn from a range of providers in response to particular needs (*boundary spanning, seamless service delivery, service integration, efficiency*).
- Where necessary, services are created to meet consumer need, considering formal and informal options (*service development*).
- Outcomes are specified, allowing for monitoring by purchaser and consumer (*accountability, quality measurement*).
- Case managers are expected to review service arrangements and to respond to changing circumstances (*responsiveness* and *timeliness*).
- Case managers are expected to establish a service package that provides the best value for the money available, building on both informal resources and formal services (*cost effective*).
- The service arrangement has specified timeframes ensuring continuity of care that relate to the needs of the client and outcomes of the contract for service (*time limited, outcome-oriented*).
- Knowledge gained from working with clients and service systems is used to advocate change at individual and systems levels (*evaluation* and *advocacy*).

AMBIGUITY PREVAILS

Discussions about case management abound in the literature of human service and health professionals, and in the rhetoric of service providers and practitioners. However, despite all efforts to describe and categorise, there has been limited analysis of the approach. This is a policy-driven and management-focused approach that has gained currency because its intent has appeal to different stakeholders. The concept tantalises many, but it remains elusive. It might be argued that there is much to be gained from the smokescreen that case management creates because the illusion of systemic remedy averts the critics from the inherent contradictions that plague contemporary human service and health delivery systems (Austin and McClelland 2000). In the next chapter we will examine the policy context that has sustained case management and stimulated its adoption in programs and settings without specific policy direction. The endorsement given to case management in community care—its adaptability to multiple agendas—has established its paramount position in service provision.

2

POLICY TOOLS AND
PROGRAM STRATEGY

The focus of this chapter is on the policy context of case management and its incorporation into programs which thereby institute new practices in service delivery. We have explored the history of case management and the difficulties of definition, and introduced conceptual frameworks through which the approach can be examined. All too often, the focus of discourses about case management is on the minutiae of practice, neglecting critical analysis of its central positioning in contemporary health and human service delivery. Certainly, a significant number of writers do pursue these broad perspectives and we will draw on their work in this chapter. However, we postulate that the demands of practice distract from the task of critique. The questions that are generated from a critical perspective pose dilemmas for those in front-line roles and, furthermore, these are difficult to address at this practice level. Understandably, many keep their attention on practice issues and avert their vision from the complex and demanding landscape of policy.

We will now turn to that very landscape: the policy environment in which case management is located. Implicit in much of the discussion that has preceded this chapter is a view that the sustainability of case management is a reflection of its adaptability to many agendas: 'The genius of case management is its extraordinary versatility, adapting to a wide range of programs, in a variety of settings, serving diverse client groups' (Austin and McClelland 1997, p. 119); 'A public policy masterstroke' (Austin and McClelland 1996, p. 275).

However, it has essentially remained a 'top-down' strategy for the restructuring of service delivery. Inevitably, the approach is reshaped through the actions and interpretations of practitioners and service users (Lipsky 1980; Bar-On 1995), a theme pursued in more detail in the later chapters of this book. The point being made here is that the appropriation of the term for a range of purposes has resulted in its wide application internationally and its iteration through policy statements and in program development. The rhetoric of case management has seductive appeal to many stakeholders. This position is not intended to promote either a conspiracy theory or a grand plan to explain its popularity. Both its popularity and sustainability might be considered serendipitous or unintended consequences of the polymorphous quality inherent in the concept, which has created opportunities for a new service delivery approach.

These diverse factors were alluded to in Chapter 1, and they are elucidated here. There is much evidence that the changing economic, social and political conditions of the 1970s gave cause to challenge the dominant views about the role of government in human service delivery, the presumption that resources were available for continuance of welfare state policies, and expectations of citizens about their rights as service users. From the perspective of service users, providers and funders, these conditions proved conducive for new strategies in service delivery.

The initial task of this chapter is to table concepts fundamental to analysis of case management applications in the context of policy and program development. Initially we will overview concepts about policy. To some readers, this may seem like a detour from the declared agenda for the chapter. However, we have in mind the diverse backgrounds of practitioners and managers who are involved with case management and assumptions that are made about shared knowledge and experience. To this end, we have decided to briefly discuss key concepts relating to social policy, policy process and the notions of welfare state policies, as each has bearing on the developments of case management in contemporary policy contexts.

Subsequently, three policy contexts in which case management has been implemented are reviewed. We take the point made by Austin (2001) that context is the definitive issue in any examination of case management. Our selections focus on different target populations, strategies for implementation and agendas of key stakeholders. The examples also demonstrate international patterns of application. Here the diversity that is symptomatic of the development of case management over the last 30 years is illustrated. In many countries, case management has been embedded in government policy. Equally, however, it is important to note that there are contexts in which case management has been introduced without formal policy sanction. The shift to a new service delivery approach at program level often gives insight into the role, authority and resourcefulness of organisational leadership.

MAKING CHOICES: RATIONALE FOR POLICY ILLUSTRATIONS

It is beyond the scope of this book to provide detailed case studies. We are, in fact, indebted to those who have systematically reported on policy and program developments incorporating case management. For the purposes of this exercise, selections from the literature will be used to highlight applications of case management in community care, in programs for the long-term unemployed and in health care.

There is a rationale for each choice. The first selection, community care, has the longest history of case management and is the most systematically evaluated both in the United States and the United Kingdom. It provides a valuable illustration of the case management approach incorporated into policy and endorsed internationally. In aged care, mental health and the disability sector, community care policy is dominant. Here the focus is only on aged care where case management has been a mechanism for diverting the frail aged from high-cost institutional care and where this policy direction has been endorsed by stakeholders, consumers and professionals—albeit for different reasons. It is evident that a significant number of the issues that arise in this sector are equally applicable in disability and mental health service delivery.

In the 1980s, the issues of long-term unemployment plagued many Western industrialised nations. Case management was incorporated in policy and program responses and this will be the second example used. Labour market programs have been the centrepiece of government responses to politically sensitive policy and resource allocation principles. In implementing case management, governments can be seen to reshape service delivery by promoting a new service mix and contracting out programs. Through this exercise, both the responsibility of government for unemployment benefits and the expectations of citizens have been redefined.

The final area for attention will be health care, where case management is applied in institutional settings (hospitals) and other health care service arrangements. In the ongoing reform of the health care sector, we see case management adapted to streamline acute care both within the institutional context and through the extended service arena of managed care in the United States. Case management is also applied in specific service programs to support target diagnostic populations and in home-based services. There is clearly overlap in service provision between community care arrangements and health care, but this will not be the focus of the case illustration. Here attention will be given to aspects of the health sector where business agendas of efficiency, outcomes and cost containment are explicitly articulated in case management, and more particularly in managed care service arrangements.

For the purposes of analysis, each illustration will be discussed in terms of three broad criteria:

- policy or program context;
- critical features of case management in the setting; and
- implications of the shift in service delivery.

KEY ELEMENTS OF THE POLICY CONTEXT

Any discussion of case management and its place in policy and program development will take us into the terrain of social policy, policy process, discourses on the welfare state policy and the changing role of the state as service provider. Each of these conceptual frames of reference is located within a value orientation that is contested and dynamic. The intention here is to alert the reader to the context within which these terms are utilised in the literature.

SOCIAL POLICY

Distinguishing social policy from other policy areas inevitably leads to boundaries based more in conceptual territory than in reality or practice (Hill 1993). For example, to separate economic policy from social policy ignores the reality of the resource base needed for service provision. Distinguishing trade policy from social policy underplays the social implications of shifts in international tariffs and quotas. The social consequences of trade policy on agricultural communities in Europe, North America and Australia provide palpable evidence of the interconnectedness of policy. However, making this point does not negate the value of clarifying terms.

So how might social policy be defined? The literature is replete with definitions and theoretical discussion of social policy. Graham (2000, p. 19) argues that social policies are cultural constructs which reflect dominant values, ideology and incorporate responses which are the inheritance of the past. In other words, social policies are dynamic, value based and negotiated through the political processes of each nation. They reflect a given society's views about social need and social responsibility and the roles expected of the state in maintaining social life (Gil 1992; Burch 1999; Graham et al. 2000). And, as Levin (1997, p. 1) points out: 'the role of central government in the social policy fields is a particularly interesting one to study, because it allows us to explore the interaction between government and society, to see how ministers and officials perceive and respond to circumstances in the "real world"'.

Critical analyses of social policy lament its non-responsiveness to changing social conditions. Some writers argue that policy trends have sustained national unity, culture and family life rather than being responsive to changing values (Williams 1989; Bryson 1992). In particular, more recent shifts in social policy directions in Western industrialised nations affirm traditional values despite the use of contemporary slogans of 'individual responsibility', 'families first' and 'personal choice' over government intervention. The slogans belie the extent to which recent governments have clawed back the gains made through what Dominelli (1997, p. 47) names as the 'feminist emancipatory project' and more recent claims for recognition of cultural diversity from immigrant, refugee and Indigenous populations.

To avoid the inevitable limitations of a search for a single definition, a number of writers prefer to identify social policy through the issues it addresses (Levin 1997). Gil (1992, p. 24), for example, speaks of social policies as 'guiding principles for ways of life, motivated by basic and perceived human needs'. In the postwar expansion of programs identified as welfare states—or at least in the tradition of this consolidated approach to social programs to support vulnerable populations—the main areas of government activity are focused on income maintenance, health care, housing, employment strategies and education. The combination of programs adopted and the mix of service provision reflect dominant views about the role of government and cultural values of the community in question. Pierson (1994, p. 1) argues that the enormous postwar expansion of programs became an integral part of all advanced industrial democracies. However the welfare state was constructed, the social policies introduced extended the level of government intervention as the provider of social assistance for citizens. In Pierson's view, the welfare state became synonymous with an era of big government. Mullaly, cited in Graham (2000, p. 12), provides an inclusive statement on social policy parameters when he asserts that: 'Social policy deals with major social issues that generally relate to notions of social justice, social equality, human rights and freedoms, empowerment and human authenticity, progressive redistribution of wealth, full employment, medicare, criminal justice and mutual aid.'

POLICY PROCESS

As previously argued, social policy reflects choices about the type of society that is desired. The task of developing policy involves complex processes and a diversity of actors (Edwards 2001). Key considerations in policy process are motivational, opportunity-based and linked to resource capabilities (Levin 1997, p. 65). Graham (2000, p. 125), writing on the Canadian context, asserts that social policy development in the new millennium will be influenced by the environmental imperative, the political and economic context of globalisation, social welfare retrenchment, social rights of citizens, costs and responsibility for welfare. In other words, the capacity of governments to shift policy direction, to introduce new arrangements and to respond to changing social demands will depend on complex variables, some beyond their immediate control.

The policy-making process inevitably brings together planning and implementation in a dynamic relationship to achieve desired or declared objectives (Hill and Bramley 1986; Bridgman and Davis 2000; Edwards 2001). And, as Gil (1992) has emphasised in his work on policy analysis, any policy brings intended and unintended consequences that provoke further responses. This, then, is the dynamic of the policy process.

WELFARE STATE AND WELFARE POLICY

The concepts of welfare states and welfare policy have been central to the development of social policy since World War II: 'In all advanced industrial democracies, the welfare state was a central part of the postwar settlement that ushered in a quarter of a century of unprecedented prosperity' (Pierson 1994, p. 3). The welfare state embodies notions that governments will act to address social and economic consequences of vagaries in the market economy (Mishra 1984; Bryson 1992; Pierson 1994; Denney 1998; Graham et al. 2000). In fact, there are many reasons why welfare is a concern of governments, including political pragmatism, as a strategy for productivity, social stability and integration (Goodin et al. 1999, p. 21). The social reforms of the postwar years in advanced industrialised countries did not lead to uniform adoption of a welfare state model. The form varied significantly between countries, with greater commitment to comprehensive models in the United Kingdom and Scandinavia and more residual approaches in the United States and Japan (Bryson 1992, p. 36). To reiterate a point made earlier, the policy mix that develops in any given country reflects established values, desires and capacities of governments to implement a coordinated and planned approach to welfare policy.

CHALLENGES TO THE WELFARE STATE

Pressures on the welfare state emanate from many sources but commentators generally acknowledge that these intensified in the years following the first oil crisis of the early 1970s (Bryson 1992; Graham et al. 2000). Challenges to welfare state ideology and welfare policy were driven by fiscal pressures, demographic changes, expectations of extended services and budgetary pressures (Pierson 1994, p. 180). With these pressures came political challenges from conservative parties and business interests questioning welfare state policies and perceived 'big government'. In the face of economic pressures, the demands to free market forces, limit government intervention and mobilise the workforce through incentives for participation gained ascendancy. By the 1990s, the advanced industrialised countries were forced to address the full impact of globalisation, changes in economic organisation, realignment of long-standing political blocs, industrial relations and capacity to provide services.

Since the 1980s, there has been a continuing discourse about the welfare state in crisis (Mishra 1984; Offe 1984; Johnson 1987; Bryson 1992; Saunders 2000). Despite the remarkable endurability of much that is associated with the welfare state and welfare policy, the implications of demographic pressures, costs of service provision (affordability), cynicism about effectiveness and ideological differences with the principles underpinning notions of comprehensive state service provision continue to reshape expectations and the mechanisms through which welfare provision is maintained (Graham et al. 2000; Saunders 2000). Pierson (1994) applies the concept of retrenchment to explain the realignments in service provision. In his view, even the most conservative governments (like those of Thatcher and Reagan) have been unable to move back from all welfare state policies because of expectations established through welfare state policy. Greater efficiency, choice, smaller government, lower taxation and entrepreneurialism have been the promotional strategies for retrenchment and shifts in service provision since the late 1980s. Governments have become increasingly business oriented in their approach to managing government, policy development and public sector reform (Gaebler 1996; Weller 1996).

In the face of diminishing resources, contested views about the role of government in service provision and fragmented service arrangements, new policy reforms were promulgated (Hassett and Austin 1997, p. 9). We have already discussed the shift to community-based service delivery (community care policy) in the 1970s. Service integration or seamless service delivery were the banners for more effective and efficient service provision, though there were various ways in which they were interpreted by different stakeholders (Hassett and Austin 1997, p. 13):

> For some it means doing a better job of coordinating across human service programs and organizations. For others it involves the physical integration of services networked together. For still others, service integration refers to the fundamental restructuring of human service organizations to improve service delivery at the neighbourhood, county and regional level. (Austin 1997, p. 1)

While we can demonstrate planned policy incorporating case management in a variety of sectors, it is equally important to acknowledge its application without formal policy or program specification. Already a number of arguments concerning the sustainability of case management have been put forward. These include the usefulness of the idea for a number of stakeholders, cultural shifts in expectations about service delivery and the spread of the idea as an often-repeated mantra that establishes a life unto itself. We are working on the premise that the inclusion of case management in policy has been fundamental to its continued popularity and wider adaptability.

THE CASE ILLUSTRATIONS

We will now turn our attention to the case illustrations. The selection of community care allows for consideration of one of the earliest policy directions that incorporated a case management approach. The implementation of care management during the Thatcher years illustrates the use of policy to dictate desired changes in service delivery. A later policy response involving the application of case management is illustrated through Australia's *Working Nation* strategy, developed for the long-term unemployed. The third illustration presents a more complicated story. The growth of case management within the US health care system does provide examples of case management being integrated into public health services. However, the incorporation of case management as a strategy within clinical service for critical pathway management, for clinical management of specific populations with complex needs and in private health provision has not been policy based. Here, the development of case management has been sponsored by business or corporate agendas. When health care is traded as a commodity on the stock exchange, case management is likely to be an explicit tool for cost containment and efficiency. These variations in application will be discussed in the third case illustration.

CASE ILLUSTRATION: COMMUNITY CARE

In this illustration, we will not spend time detailing the rationale for the shift to community care that is seen in Western industrialised countries from the late 1970s through the 1980s. As we have outlined in the preceding chapter and the introductory sections of this chapter, imperatives for change in policy direction are associated with concerns about standards of care in institutions, increasing levels of demand for care, escalating costs and stronger claims in the area of consumer rights.

Policy and program context: community care in the United Kingdom

Community care is the policy arena in which case management has the longest history as the specified and primary approach to service delivery. In the United States, it began with demonstration projects in the early 1970s (Austin 1996, p. 74) at a time when long-term care was nursing home-based. In light of fiscal and demographic pressures, this could no longer be sustained as the predominant mode of service provision. Case management became the key component of long-term care from the outset of the shift to community care. Coordinating fragmented services, based on individual need and with people being supported within the community, was the *raison d'être* for its widespread adoption. Within a similar timeframe, the first case management experiments were introduced in the United Kingdom (Davies 1994, p. 5). In Australia, the first initiatives were in the disability and aged care sectors through the federally-funded Community Options Program in the mid-1980s (Davies 1992; Ozanne 1996). By the late 1980s, similar initiatives had been documented in European countries and in Canada, and there was emergent interest in New Zealand (Davies 1992).

As previously argued, case management has been popular because the concept has some ambiguity, enabling different stakeholders to identify the aspects most congruent with their agendas. Within the parameters of a case management approach, service users can be empowered and encouraged to be active participants in their own care planning; the case managers can be held accountable for effective and efficient service provision that is both outcome-based and meets the agendas of management and funders; and, finally, case managers can be affirmed as skilled professionals and offered new employment options. Each of these positions is contentious and they are all revisited in subsequent chapters.

Critical features of case management in the setting

Challis, Darton and Stewart (1998, p. 1) argue that community care has been a long-standing policy objective in the United Kingdom for all client groups; however, impetus for a major policy shift strengthened in the late 1980s after the publication of the Griffiths Report and the subsequent White Paper, *Caring for People*. The definition of community care as promulgated in the White Paper is: 'Community care means providing the services and support which people who are affected by problems of ageing, mental illness, mental handicap or physical or sensory disability, need to be able to live as independently as possible in their own homes, or in homely settings in the community.' Lewis and Glennerster (1996, p. 8) maintain that the impetus was the 'haemorrhage in the social security budget' as people used this route to access private care (that is, residential care) and the goal was to redirect existing resources and increase access to community-based services.

The 1990 *National Health Service and Community Care Act* established the basis for the shift to community care. Implementation proceeded in 1993, with a key objective being 'to make proper assessment of need and good case management the cornerstone of high quality care' (Lewis and Glennerster 1996). Under the auspices of the Conservative Party, the policies 'signalled a shift in ideology from the post-war consensus on health and welfare service delivery to a new ideology dominated by neo-liberal or right wing views of economic and social relations' (Baldwin 2000, p. 23).

Care management (the term finally preferred in the United Kingdom) was the tool used to address the task of coordination based on individual need—that is, 'adapting services to need not fitting people to existing services' (Sheppard 1995, p. 5). Local authorities, charged with the implementation of new service arrangements, were encouraged to purchase services from the independent sector, leading the way for a mixed economy of care or quasi-markets (Ovretveit 1993, p. 11; Baldwin 2000, p. 23). Consequently, social service departments were encouraged to move from their roles as traditional service providers to those of gatekeepers and resource managers. In many ways, the social service departments had been slow to respond to shifts in service delivery and management of resources already introduced into hospitals and schools (Lewis and Glennerster 1996, p. 12). Now government policy was directed at extending reforms, in its goal to hold public expenditure, increase collaboration between health and social service departments, shift old practices and engender creative partnerships in service provision.

Implications of the shift in service delivery

The development of community care in the United Kingdom provides an example of national policy directed at reform of long-standing public-sector practices and service arrangements. The new policy of the 1990s was built around a presumption of effective collaboration between health and social service departments and personnel to plan and coordinate service arrangements based on individual need (Baldwin 2000; Gray 2000, p. 87). It rested on suspicion of the postwar welfare state principles that were seen to foster paternalism and professional dominance and inefficient management through local government authorities (James 1994, p. 12). New strategies were seen as essential to promote self-reliance and individual responsibility in clients and to challenge the power base of the professions embedded in welfare state bureaucracy (James 1994; Sheppard 1995; Wilmot 1997).

The Personal Social Services Research Unit (PSSRU) reports of research findings from the Kent Community Care Project and subsequent trials in the United Kingdom support the view that, where case management approaches were used, positive community placements could be sustained and inappropriate institutionalisation avoided (Davies 1992, p. 97). However, evidence suggests that replication of these outcomes was not sustainable as full policy implementation proceeded (Gray 2000, p. 87). As has been asserted previously (and will be again), case managers cannot compensate for inadequate resources.

The new policy represented a major shift in culture for organisations and practitioners. Many of the existing personnel in social service departments came from social work backgrounds with established practice orientations towards individualised intervention, viewing individuals and their needs through a systems framework and working collaboratively with other professionals. However, the changes heralded in community care policy challenged professional dominance and autonomy, and focused on management of complex situations, redefining the role of the incumbent care manager. Sheppard (1995, p. 5) notes the wording of the Griffiths Report in relation to this: 'not all social care need be the concern of social workers'. This issue will be explored in more detail in Part III of this book.

Care management is identified as the mechanism for more effective and efficient service arrangements. The extent to which declared objectives are successful will be evaluated differently from the perspective of various stakeholders. For example, the fact that there has been a reduction in institutional placements is acknowledged and perceived as positive by government and local authorities. However, the quality, flexibility and options available for alternate care arrangements remain a concern for front-line staff, service users and their carers. Nocon (1998, p. 55) cites research by Robertson and others which powerfully demonstrates these different perceptions of carers who record concern about the adequacy of basic needs, gaps in or restrictions on service availability: 'If basic needs are not being met, "putting in help with meals, with shopping, with cleaning or with getting dressed etc makes a mockery of care".'

As Davies (1992, p. 123) argues, effective outcomes from case management strategies in community care policy depend on a shared vision of new service arrangements by all providers and staff. In addition, effective outcomes are only achieved if there are partnerships between service providers to build collaborative potential and address structural barriers for seamless service delivery. The organisational conditions for new service arrangements require appropriate account-ability measures, devolution of responsibility to facilitate flexible and responsive service delivery and investment to establish the basis for long-term capacity. Finally, Davies emphasises the need to review and adjust at each level of implementation. This overview presented by Davies captures the enormity of major realignment of service arrange-ments under community care policy.

CASE ILLUSTRATION: PROGRAMS FOR THE LONG-TERM UNEMPLOYED, AUSTRALIA

Policy or program context

Although high unemployment levels have been a recurrent issue since the 1970s, the complicating aspect has been their persistence despite economic recovery and increased numbers of jobs (Eardley and Thomp-son 1997, p. 1; Edwards 2001, p. 137). Unemployment policy has been a central concern of all OECD governments since the 1980s. Eardley (1997, p. 1) argues that 'intractable problems of long-term unemploy-ment in recent years have led a number of countries to look for new ways of providing employment assistance to job seekers'. Reducing levels of unemployment is a complex process, politically sensitive and significantly costly in terms of budget commitment to income maintenance.

Internationally there have been major policy initiatives to address entry and re-entry to employment. In the United States, welfare to work programs were introduced in the late 1980s through the *Family Support Act* 1988 (Perlmutter and Johnson 1996; Eardley and Thompson 1997, p. 31). The JOBS program, for example, was designed to reduce welfare dependency and increase self-sufficiency. This was a national policy initiative to be implemented at state level with case management identified as the preferred service delivery approach (Hagen 1994; Perlmutter and Johnson 1996, p. 184). These latter writers indicate that some 49 states have in fact utilised a variety of forms of case management in the programs. Across Europe (for example, in Belgium, France, Denmark and the Netherlands) labour market programs that target support to long-term or difficult-to-place unemployed people have been introduced and they offer individually oriented support to achieve placements. However, Eardley's research indicates that systematic case management is not part of these policies and programs (Eardley and Thompson 1997, p. 10). He also notes that, in the United Kingdom, greater individualised assistance has been instituted to improve placement outcomes and to monitor activity effort. But policies 'stop short of full scale case management' (Eardley and Thompson 1997, p. 19). In Canada and New Zealand, individualised assistance also features in labour market programs. But it was in Australia that case management was the centrepiece of a national policy for labour market reform (Kirner 1995, p. 49; Eardley and Thompson 1997, p. 56; Gursansky and Kennedy 1998, p. 17).

During the 1993 Australian election campaign, the government declared that employment policy would be a priority if it was re-elected (Edwards 2001, p. 138). Commitment to employment policy reflected a number of forces for change in this area. Internationally, the OECD was promoting an 'active society' approach to unemployment, encouraging policy effort to seek employment rather than guarantees of support to the unemployed (Cass 1995, p. 19; Eardley and Thompson 1997, p. 57). Nationally, Australia faced the highest levels of unemployment since the Great Depression (Edwards 2001, p. 138) and the government had already moved towards reform as a result of the Social Security Review of the late 1980s. Against this backdrop, the newly elected Keating government espoused major reform detailed first in the Green Paper (Restoring Full Employment) of 1993 and formalised as a policy statement in May 1994 in the White Paper, *Working Nation* (Eardley and Thompson 1997; Edwards 2001).

Critical features of case management in the setting

In *Working Nation*, programs case management formed a central element in the restructuring of service delivery arrangements. Embedded in the policy was the notion of the Job Compact, expressed as a reciprocal obligation between government and the long-term unemployed person. The government commitment was to guarantee placement, and in return the unemployed person was obliged to accept any reasonable offer (Eardley and Thompson 1997, p. 61). The consequence of failing to respond would mean loss of income support for a determined period.

Minister Ross Free, speaking about *Working Nation*, declared case management to be 'one of the important new service delivery strategies', based in a partnership between a jobseeker and an individual case manager as a more efficient means of finding employment (Free 1995, p. 10). Joan Kirner, the newly appointed chairperson of the Employment Services Regulatory Authority (ESRA), stated that 'case management is the essential connector in generating employment requirements, employment needs and the community's needs for a skilled and cohesive society' (Kirner 1995, p. 49). ESRA's role was to establish standards for the proposed case management system of labour market programs; training was to be instituted and performance monitored.

Through *Working Nation* programs, employment services were reconfigured creating a competitive model of services that included the restructured government employment service (Employment Assistance Australia, or EAA) and contracting out to community and private-sector organisations (Eardley and Thompson 1997, p. 63). This is not the place for a detailed discussion of the shift to contracting out and competitive markets in the human services and health, and principles of contestability; however, it is important to note here the significance of this major realignment of service provision in Australia.

As a result of the policy shift, resources were directed to training existing personnel involved in employment services. Standards set by ESRA established systematic practices for working with unemployed people in more personalised ways, and evaluating outcomes. Although some research into the impact of case management was commissioned, Eardley (1997, p. 88) points out that continuing policy changes and the relative newness of case management as the key service delivery strategy made evaluation of the effectiveness of case management difficult. This position is affirmed in national research into women's experience of case management under labour market programs undertaken in 1996 by Carson et al. In this research, the findings found no positive correlation between the case management status of the respondents and the employment outcomes reported by them (Carson et al. 1996, p. 20). The key factor that was most often identified by the women as the positive aspect of the labour market program was the personal qualities of the case manager.

Implications of the shift in service delivery

Case management has been the vehicle to promote individual responsibility and to shift the expectations of the unemployed and the wider community about the way in which assistance will be offered. Sanctions were built into policy reinforcing compliance and case managers' responsibilities included monitoring of individual commitment to their obligations. Despite the changes to the programs with the election of a new government in 1996, the principles of individualised service delivery remain and income support continues to be defined firmly, though it is now expressed in terms of mutual responsibility.

The original policy espoused in *Working Nation* paved the way for wider applications of competitive markets in service provision formerly seen as the traditional domain of government. In that process, both non-government and private providers have been drawn into different relationships with government through service contracting and a government-supported regulatory authority (Edwards 2001, p. 162). Within government, the policy represented a major initiative in a 'whole of government' approach that emphasised the complementary roles of various segments of government.

The Australian reforms generated through *Working Nation* further legitimated the value of case management as a service delivery approach. The specification of the service delivery approach in the contracting process potentially systematised the practices of diverse service providers. The original implementation proposals incorporated extensive training for personnel to support case management and to change old practices. As a great majority of personnel being designated to the case management role had extensive administrative or field experience, training was identified as a major element for shifts in practice.

Working Nation may represent a high point in the articulation of national policy incorporating case management—at least in the Australian context. The vision was expansive, but whether its full potential was achieved is more difficult to assess because of changing political agendas, limited capacity to resource comprehensive implementation and the problems of embedding the range of evaluation strategies needed (Edwards 2001, p. 170).

CASE ILLUSTRATION: CASE MANAGEMENT IN THE US HEALTH SECTOR

The third sector to be examined here is health care. It is with some trepidation that we have made this choice because it is a complex and multifaceted environment for service delivery. Even the most cursory examination of health care systems internationally illustrates significant variation and it is an area of specialist knowledge. However, we have maintained this selection because health provision is a fundamental service in all industrialised countries. In addition, the development of health services in the United States provides examples of diverse applications of the approach and this is useful to the task we have set.

The complexity of health care systems means that there are multiple histories of the approach as it has been used for many reasons to redress problems in the system. In contemporary health care systems, for example, we see case management approaches applied in rehabilitation, insurance schemes, primary health within institutions and community-based, managed care and specific diagnostic client populations (Berger 1996; Newell 1996; Havas 1998; Matorin 1998; Roessler and Rubin 1998; Rosenberg 1998; Rossi 1999 and Huber 2000). Case management is an increasing and integral activity for professions identified with the sector, particularly for nursing and social work health professionals (Murer and Brick 1997; Hawkins et al. 1998; Vandivort-Warren 1998; Cohen and deBack 1999). But this is also true for physicians as they are drawn into new constructions of partnership in health care (Agich and Forster 2000, p. 189; Shapiro et al. 2000, p. 71).

The agenda here is not to detail all aspects of the US health care system, but rather to highlight case management in its various applications as a tool in public policy, as a strategy for streamlining clinical practice, as a basis for coordinating particular client populations with chronic service needs and as a mainstay of health management systems. In the US health system (in itself a disputed notion), the dominance of private health insurance must be emphasised. Adherence to case management is pervasive not as government policy but as a management tool to maximise cost-effectiveness and the sustainability of business enterprise. This has led to questions about the validity of case management in such settings and the appropriateness of some human service professionals involving themselves in the role. The latter point is illustrated in one of the debates in Gambrill and Pruger's (1997) book about controversial issues in social work (Gordon and Kline 1997) when a contributor to the debate asserts that 'concern for client well-being is filtered through a series of questions and administrative restrictions that have little to do with the client's suffering and more to do with the economic security of the clinician and the managed care company'.

Policy and program context

In reviewing the literature about the US health system, one consistent theme emerges. It is that health is 'fraught with complications' (Cohen and Cesta 1997, p. 3), 'lags behind the rest of the world' (Rosenberg 1998, p. 3), 'with a system never centralised or exclusively government controlled' (Huber 2000, p. 14). McClelland (1996, p. 205) observes 'that whereas many countries introduced government control over the financing and sometimes the delivery of health services, the United States has followed its own unique service delivery path based on private health insurance'. As a consequence of this heritage, the current health care system is fragmented, complex, uncoordinated and expensive. Furthermore, it is inequitable in terms of access, offering the best to those who can afford it, while many citizens remain without access to the most basic cover (Cohen and Cesta 1994, p. 111). Rosenberg (1998, p. 3) quotes Levine, saying that 'families are and will be under increasing pressures to pay more direct costs; provide more hands on and often more complex care; undertake greater burdens for longer times and forgo more educational, career and social opportunities'.

Havas (1998, p. 75) argues that powerful interests have opposed the development of a national health care policy on the grounds that it would be un-American and further the growth of big government— the ultimate trigger for broad-based electoral support. As a result of these barriers, reform has been averted and the existing pattern of services remains entrenched. Both McClelland (1996) and Rosenberg (1998) overview historical trends in reforms that have led to the present managed health care arrangements. Early reliance on private health insurance and prepaid group practice models to reduce the uncertainty of consumer payments to health providers and subsequent tax exemptions for employer-paid health benefits established patterns for contemporary health care.

More recent health policy reforms have been driven by a number of factors, including escalating costs, demographic indicators of increasing demand and the need to establish strategies for vulnerable populations. Key areas of reforms have been health insurance for the elderly (Medicare) and social security recipients (Medicaid) in 1965 (McClelland 1996, p. 206; Murer and Brick 1997, p. 2). In 1981, an amendment to the *Social Security Act* allowed for case management services to be covered under Medicaid (Murer and Brick 1997, p. 6). Hospital reimbursement strategies were devised to contain costs but, in the face of continuing high costs in acute health, the *Health Maintenance Organisation Act* of 1973 was introduced to promote competition and thereby encourage cost containment. These are the preconditions for managed care and a health care system dominated by business principles and market strategies.

Critical features of case management in the setting

Case management is embedded in the various subsystems of health care and is specified through policy and program design. As has been detailed previously, case management has an established history as a service delivery approach in long-term care for the aged, people with mental health issues and specific diagnostic groups. Case management in these situations was promoted as a service delivery strategy to coordinate these populations with policy shifts from institutional care to community care. Case management continues to be a cornerstone of service delivery in these sectors, but there is inevitable overlap with health system-specific case management arrangements and the introduction of managed care into these same domains.

So the first critical distinction we want to make is between case management and managed care. Managed care has in fact become synonymous with the US health system and case management has been subsumed in a similar way (Austin and McClelland 2000, p. 7). McClelland takes the position that the links are detrimental to the legitimacy of case management and that, in the context of managed care, the approach is substantially focused on cost containment issues (McClelland 1996, p. 204). But what is managed care? It is a term applied to a range of policy initiatives that have addressed the resourcing of health care. It incorporates the federal policy directions that have stimulated competition through private insurance, employer health care benefits and publicly managed health care programs. Managed care is said to be the 'systematic integration and coordination of finances performed by health care plans that try to provide their members with prepaid access to high quality care at relatively low cost' (Huber 2000, p. 551) and 'a system that provides the generalized structure and focus for managing the use, cost, quality and effectiveness of health care services: an umbrella for several cost containment initiatives that may involve case management' (Cohen and Cesta 1997, p. 32). In these circumstances, government policy has created a regulatory environment to mandate competition and provide the incentives for the providers to contain costs (Austin and McClelland 2000, p. 7). The very same competitive pressures are incorporated in the principles of public health programs (Berger 1996, p. 148), with case management endorsed as an appropriate service delivery strategy. Case management has been adopted as one of the strategies to achieve the dominant fiscal, administrative and resource allocation agendas of a managed care approach.

Within institutional health care settings, case management has been developed in a number of ways. Teams and allied health professionals have been incorporated into case management models through the development of critical pathways (also known as critical paths or multidisciplinary action plans) that focus on expected outcomes of care as a day-by-day progression in the hospital and as a continuing treatment plan post-discharge (Cohen and Cesta 1997, p. 167). 'A patient assigned to a clinical path is expected to meet certain present goals regarding his or her medical status or ability to perform certain functions at a specified point in time' (Newell 1996, p. 177). The case manager—and in acute settings, nursing has played a key role in this position—monitors and triggers responses to variance from that pathway. Here the case management process is directed at quality of care, efficiency and cost-effectiveness, a critical concern for hospitals with capped funding arrangements.

Implications of the shift in service delivery

In the context of US health care, questions need to be posed about the efficacy of case management as it is applied specifically to cost containment agendas. The traditional focus of case management as driven by notions of partnership, empowerment, client needs, choice and flexibility in service arrangements can be dissipated within the discourse of managed care. The emphasis on market-driven principles in health provision does not inevitably mean abrogation of social responsibilities, but the risks are higher. The fact that managed care approaches are being applied broadly to health care poses challenges for vulnerable populations. Standards for case management are generated through the range of professional associations developing around it but the contradictions for practitioners are widely acknowledged (McClelland 1996; Newell 1996; Cohen and Cesta 1997; Schamess and Lightburn 1998; Huber 2000). 'The fundamental ethical dilemma of risk-based methods of reimbursement stems from the fact that the practitioner is paid more for offering less treatment' (Frager 2000, p. 252).

Case management in managed care could be said to transform traditional professional practice, redefining key responsibilities of the practitioner and the relationship to the client. More attention will be given to this theme in later sections of the book. Here we would reiterate the previously mentioned danger that equating managed care with case management potentially undermines its legitimacy and reframes public perception of professionals involved in service delivery.

In the US health system, the commentaries used to research this case illustration confirm the problem of imposing strategy without addressing the core structural problems in health care. For historical, philosophical, cultural and political reasons, the task of major reform has been subverted. Regulatory arrangements have been introduced by successive US federal governments despite the evidence that many citizens remain unable to access adequate care under these policy arrangements. It is possible that, despite this evidence, these strategies will have appeal in other countries struggling to manage the expanding resource needs for health care systems.

Case management emerged in the 1970s in response to particular service delivery needs but, as these case illustrations show, it has been reshaped for diverse agendas and with significant consequences for all stakeholders. In the following sections, the nature of those consequent changes to practices will be examined through the experience of clients and professionals.

3

SEARCHING FOR DISTINCTIVENESS

The issues often raised in exchanges with human service practitioners and students confirm what is evident in the literature. Despite at least 30 years' experience with the approach internationally, there is still confusion about and limited confidence in the construct of case management. In other words, one of the recurring questions presented to us is whether case management is really any different from 'ordinary practice'. Certainly the very best and established practice traditions of both the nursing and social work professions emphasise holistic approaches to intervention and collaboration and systemic interventions to maximise opportunities for change. As documented in the previous chapter, there are strong links between early casework practice in social work and the processes used in primary health and home nursing (Weil et al. 1985; Cohen and Cesta 1997).

However, common ancestry is not the basis of equivalence, and since the late 1990s commentators have acknowledged that the diversification of, and new developments in, service delivery approaches have necessitated a rethinking of what case management is and where it fits. Austin (1990, p. 400) asserts that one of the myths about case management is 'that it is just plain, old fashioned social work'. The voices echoing the theme of difference in case management, or recognition of new professional responsibilities for health and human service professionals, have strengthened with the diversification and ever-increasing applications of the approach (Vourlekis and Greene 1992; Raiff and Shore 1993; Austin and McClelland 1996; Cohen and Cesta 1997; Moxley 1997; Compton and Ashwin 2000). In commenting on the significance of a shift to care management in the United Kingdom, Sheppard (1995, p. 61) states that it 'represents a particularly profound shift in practice, not simply because of what it means for the individual social worker in their relationship with clients, but because of its impact on the autonomy and control of practitioners'.

Later chapters examine in more detail the nature of practice and the professional challenges that arise for practitioners as they confront the demands of an approach that sets them the task of integrating, coordinating and maintaining cost-effective service arrangements based on individual need. We take the position that establishing distinctiveness unshackles thinking about the case management approach from traditional paradigms. Through that process, the critical tasks for future development of case management and service delivery options will become clearer. As we argued in the previous chapter, it is problematic to equate case management with any professional group *per se*, or to assume that a case management program in one setting is analogous to all others.

THE TASK AT HAND

In an effort to advance the idea of the distinctiveness of case management, two lines of argument are pursued. First, case management is discussed from the perspective of the organisation. Here we are interested in establishing the distinguishing characteristics of case management and traditional service provision in health and human services. The following questions drive this meta-comparative analysis:

- What are the key organisational arrangements under different service delivery approaches?
- What are the issues in terms of resource allocation, service mix and workload?

Second, the characteristics of professional practice in traditional casework and in case management are explored. For the purposes of the exercise, we are building on the work of two writers who happen to come from human service and social work backgrounds. In part, the decision to refer to these particular pieces of work reflects our own backgrounds, but it also has been difficult to identify the articulation of these issues in other specific professional discourses. With the exception of the nursing profession, with its acknowledged early practice links with coordinating care for individuals and their families, the other professions being drawn into the case management role usually acknowledge it only as a manifestation of recent policy and program developments. Understandably, some of the newer allied health professions have been more clinically focused and it is only with these contemporary developments that case management has emerged as a professional employment option for them.

Before proceeding, it is important to return to a point made in the previous chapter regarding recent developments in the health sector. It is acknowledged that, within the nursing discourses, attention is given to a distinctiveness between different service delivery approaches—in this context, case management and nursing case management. For example, Newell (1996, p. 179) argues that in case management—which is also synonymous with the term 'critical pathways'—treatment outcomes are emphasised, certainly incorporating individual needs but equally recognising the providers' management of the treatment regime. This is contrasted with nursing case management, in which the dominant focus of service provision is individualised in all aspects. In highlighting human service concerns in our analysis in this chapter, we remain conscious of similar preoccupations in other professional groups, of which nursing is a prime example.

With these parameters in mind, let's turn to a closer examination of these two perspectives.

ORGANISATIONAL DIMENSIONS OF TRADITIONAL AND CASE MANAGEMENT APPROACHES

At an Australian conference on community care in 1990, Ozanne presented a paper that proposed a set of dimensions for comparison of traditional or existing service arrangements with those that are consistent with the case management approach. The major thrust of her argument was that there is a shift in the management of service delivery as case management is implemented. In her words, 'case management, as a specific approach to service delivery . . . is not well understood and although it incorporates components of previously existing service arrangements, it differs from them in a number of important ways' (Ozanne 1990, p. 186).

Ozanne specifies nine key organisational tasks or dimensions that she argues are essential to service provision. The dimensions include organisational authority and sanctions that establish the conditions for service provision and define the parameters for interagency relationships. In addition, specification of system and target populations further identifies the boundaries and capacity of any given service. The issue of resourcing is addressed in terms of service provision, caseload management and duration of any service to the client population. These are key determinants of the scope and style of service delivery and they are defined through organisational policy as well as funding specifications. Ozanne also attends to the core technologies of the service delivery approaches, and it is within this dimension in particular that the blurring of language and descriptors can be seen to contribute to misunderstandings about case management. The last dimension for comparison is the issue of worker autonomy and accountability.

Although Ozanne's paper was presented a decade ago, the issues raised through the comparative analysis remain relevant to a contemporary examination of case management. We have used her dimensions, but have modified the content of her table to incorporate more recent knowledge about case management. Ozanne's phrase 'traditional service arrangements' is used interchangeably with 'casework', and with 'therapeutic' and 'clinical intervention'. It is accepted that these latter terms are being used imprecisely, but they all denote direct service delivery to the individual and therefore can be described as traditional.

Ozanne's analysis—and our adaptation of it—relies on stereotypical or archetypal conceptions of traditional individual practice and case management. This conceals the commonalities between the two approaches, which have been well described by Rothman and Sager (1998, pp. 16–20). Adopting these basic conceptions skirts an evaluative commentary which may be similar in many respects for both. In addition, it disregards the many variations of programs within both the casework and the case management approaches. However, it is precisely because this exercise puts to one side the many obscuring claims for sameness that it advances understanding of the construct of case management.

It is useful to elaborate further on the key areas discussed within Table 3.1.

Table 3.1   Organisational dimensions of case management

Dimension of comparison	Case management approaches to service delivery	Traditional service arrangements
Authority and sanction	Derived from policy and program specification to operate at the intersystem level	Derived from one specific agency auspice or legislative authority
Client targeting	Targeting those with complex, multiple problems and at risk of institutionalisation or recurrent referral	Targeting in relation to specific agency service focus and/or populations identified in the legislative mandate
System targeting	Inter-organisational–intersystem focus on the coordination of a complex and fragmented range of services from different agencies to meet individual client needs	Intra-system focused— delivering the available services of one agency to the target population, who might need to seek assistance from multiple agencies to address all needs
Resourcing	Increasing pressure on resources, enforcing prioritisation	Increasing pressure on resources, enforcing prioritisation
Caseload controls	Caseload control in response to complexity	No specific caseload controls but time spent with client tends to be increasingly rationed because of increasing demand
Service mix	Coordinated, using a range of services from government- and private-sector services and informal resources of family and community	Services limited to the range offered by one agency; consumers may need to negotiate services from several agencies
Duration and intensity of contact	Variable according to service contract and target population; emphasis on achievement of specified outcomes matching service contract and program goals	Variable according to organisational mandate and practices; service coverage discretionary and open-ended

Table 3.1   Organisational dimensions of case management (*cont.*)

Dimension of comparison	Case management approaches to service delivery	Traditional service arrangements
Core technology	Individualised service delivery. Reliance on the implementation at a relatively high level of core tasks which are also identified with traditional casework practice—namely screening, assessment, care planning, monitoring, resource mobilisation and resource development; these tasks are performed by a practitioner who is skilled in both interpersonal and inter-organisational negotiation	Individualised service delivery; focus is on the expert services provided by the agency
Case manager autonomy and accountability	External (to self) accountability for the delivery of the appropriate mix of services to meet client needs and responsibility to take decisions and ensure compliance with care plan. In some cases, the case manager will have authority to manage the budget for a given individual	Limited external accountability. Workers are usually responsible to supervisors who authorise service arrangements and expenditure

AUTHORITY AND SANCTION

As discussed in Chapter 2, in the Australian context case management continues to be sanctioned and legitimised in policy and the scope of these policies has been extended significantly in the 1990s (Wearing 1998). For example, case management is the service delivery approach specified in policy relating to supported accommodation or homelessness services, community-based aged and disabled care services, alternate care for children, corrections, mental health, Family Court services, and labour market programs. Similar directions are evident in the United States and the United Kingdom, where policy initiatives have specified case management in community care (Challis et al. 1990; Ovretveit 1993; Sheppard 1995), managed care in the health sector (McClelland 1996; Huntt and Growick 1997; Schamess and Lightburn 1998; Frager 2000), the mental health and disability sectors (Intagliata 1992; Cnaan 1994; Rapp and Kisthardt 1996), aged care (Applebaum and Austin 1990; Austin 1993) and public welfare (Zlotnik 1996). And, as illustrated in recent publications, applications of case management are also evident in Europe, New Zealand and Asia (Applebaum and White 2000).

Case management is commonly described as a flexible, planned and individualised approach to service delivery that provides consumer choice and maximises the efficient use of formal and informal resources in service provision (Moxley 1989; Vourlekis and Greene 1992; Davies 1994; Moxley 1997; Roessler and Rubin 1998; Woodside and McClam 1998; Rossi 1999). The service plan developed for any individual consumer is expected to be outcome-oriented and cost-effective. Current policy directs both the application of case management and the broad outcomes to be achieved. Through the generic application of a case management approach, an emphasis is placed on a more systematic set of practices and on outcomes rather than on prescription about input factors such as the backgrounds of staff. From a policy perspective, which personnel undertake the case management functions is less important than the issue of the provider's capacity to demonstrate achievement of measurable results.

The policies that dictate the service delivery approach intend to realign the territory and authority of organisations or agencies (Raiff and Shore 1993; Sheppard 1995; Austin and McClelland 1997). The case managers are directed to inter-system collaboration rather than intra-organisation servicing. It is case management's perceived superior capacity to eliminate multiple entries and duplication of assessment, together with its efficiency across a service delivery sector, that has led to the approach being enshrined in policy. This organisational authority differs from that of traditional service delivery arrangements where a single service or population-specific service operates. There may be statutory legitimisation of a service for a whole population, but the single agency approach acts as if its more limited service parameters are non-permeable. If the agency does not provide the full range of services needed by the client from that population, then a referral might be made to another agency, or the client might be left to negotiate any other services needed. The original case management policies were specifically introduced to address these barriers for clients with complex needs.

CLIENT TARGETING

Case management has been used to target particular populations, particularly those at risk of high-cost institutional care, or excessive usage of health, legal, income maintenance or other service assistance. Moxley (1997, p. 246) endorses the view that client targeting will persist, as case management is directed at the needs of the most challenging client populations who will be the future enterprise of human services. Case management has been used to restructure service delivery systems for a variety of purposes. This has included efforts to systematise service delivery, increase accountability and individualise service delivery in response to complex situations and in recognition of client 'difference'. In more traditional service arrangements, clients were serviced if they fitted within the scope of target population and activity relevant to the agency in question.

SYSTEM TARGETING

One of the declared objectives of the case management approach is to create seamless service delivery and to maximise all resources available in any given situation. The notion of seamless service delivery has challenged organisational ownership of clients and exclusivity in specialist agencies. In addition, there has been an emphasis on the value of cooperation across organisations and sectors. Rather than only offering those services that are available through the single agency, the case management approach has fostered service arrangements which can be resourced from a range of service providers. One of the major criticisms of more traditional approaches has concerned individual agency ownership of clients, multiple agency assessments and unsatisfactory negotiations to establish services for clients with compound needs (Sheppard 1995).

RESOURCING

This topic presents one of the most fertile sources of debate about case management. The rhetoric has never matched the promise of the 'new' service delivery arrangements, and it is argued that in its recent forms it is resource-driven rather than need-driven (Cnaan 1994; Challis et al. 1995; Austin and McClelland 2000). Early pilot or demonstration projects in community care had the advantage of robust resourcing (Austin and McClelland 1996), but this level of funding has seldom been maintained in ongoing funding arrangements (Kubisa 1990; Orme and Glastonbury 1993). By the late 1990s, human service resourcing was being tightly controlled. The increasing commitment of governments to market and user-pay principles has seen the dismantling of much service provision offered by the state. While governments remain committed to funding service provision, in the quasi-market conception of health and welfare, they prescribe activity and recipients more narrowly (Sheppard 1995; McClelland et al. 1996; Hugman 1998b). Thus case management services may be developed at the cost of more traditional individual services. However, whether the argument is fallacious or not, the language of case management allows for it to be seen by policy-makers as a cheaper option, and it does explicitly refute service duplication and inefficiency.

CASELOAD CONTROL

In practice, caseload control has been difficult to maintain in most settings and in any approach to service delivery, inclusive of case management (McClelland et al. 1996). Even under traditional approaches, fluctuations in resources led to rationing of services (Ozanne 1990). However, through the rhetoric of case management, it has been asserted that stronger inter-agency collaboration, by leading to a greater use of informal, contracted and inter-agency resources, would inevitably create cost-effective practices. In theory, the complexity of client problems should determine caseload limits in case management services. In more traditional individualised services, existing professional practices, industrial factors and the service type offered would be significant in caseload fixing. While the practical difficulties with caseloads in both service delivery approaches might be very similar, the discourses are quite different.

SERVICE MIX

Under more traditional service delivery approaches, a single agency supplied services within its mandate, and clients dealt with whatever combination of agencies was necessary to meet their needs. More often than not they experienced difficulty in accessing all of the required services. Case management was promoted because of its potential to address these issues.

There are impediments to the realisation of this potential. First, there have been minimal effective intra- and inter-organisational protocols established. For example, there have been difficulties in establishing cooperation where there are already high demands on an agency, or where a potential client population falls into what Moxley (1997) would describe as an 'undesirable population' and resource exchange is not consistent with the demands perceived. There are clashes of cultures and rivalries and competition between agencies (Wearing 1998). In many cases, the move to case management is nominal rather than substantive. There are still numerous consumer examples of multiple assessment and organisational and professional boundaries limiting access to effective service planning and provision. Further to this point, it must be noted that broad-based policy statements prescribing the case management approach often are not underpinned by detailed specifications of services or agencies which are to be caught within the scope of the policy or by essential service agreements (Gursansky and Kennedy 1998).

However, none of these obstacles weakens the rational appeal of case management and its professed potential to produce more effective use of services across agencies and the community.

DURATION AND INTENSITY OF CONTACT

Case management is presented as providing continuity of care in complex and chronic situations. The intensity and duration of contact may be specified in service agreements, with providers being expected to match level of service against schedules of risk management or dependency in long-term care. Commonly, predetermined outcome measures will determine when a case is to be terminated. Generally, the scope and character of the case manager's role are dictated by the program's financing (Austin 1996, p. 83). It could be argued that all human service delivery has always been shaped by budgetary and program parameters. However, with the implementation of case management, there has been a shift in the way in which case decisions are addressed. In traditional service delivery, the practitioner had considerable discretion about the way in which work with the client was performed. The locus of decision-making about matters such as duration and intensity of contact was more directly with the worker. In these circumstances, cases could remain open for extensive periods of time without active intervention occurring, or cases could be reopened in response to recurring crises.

CORE TECHNOLOGY

The effectiveness of case management relies upon a number of factors, not least of which is the range of technological coordinating and management skills required of the case manager. These contrast with the specialist direct service skills offered under more traditional approaches. When dealing with complex social situations, the effectiveness of the case management service plan that is developed and monitored depends significantly on the sophistication of the assessment and the knowledge, creativity and persuasion skills of the case manager. As case management has been adopted as a core service delivery approach in the human services over the last decade, organisations have reconstructed the roles of existing personnel. All too often the assumption has been made that the workers will be able to adapt to new demands with limited or no strategic preparation when in fact 'entirely new sets of skills and knowledge' are required (Hugman 1998b, p. 176). The attention to training about case management within undergraduate and postgraduate professional education is random, and within industry there is much to suggest that policy redirection has not led to serious retraining of staff (Kennedy et al. 1998; Kennedy et al. 2001). However, while there are problems with the way in which workforces have been prepared for case management, if anything these problems highlight the demands and accountability emphasised by the systemised intervention of the case management process. These issues will be pursued in Part III of this book.

It is relevant to note here—leaving more detailed discussion for the practice section—that the very nature of case management suggests that there would be much to gain from advances in information technology to support practice. In reality, the resources and expertise to implement high-technology assistance for case managers have been slow to eventuate, although there are particular sectors that have made significant progress in this area, such as health and aged care (Pilisuk and Sullivan 1998). However, despite changes in service delivery, most case managers rely on technology that has changed very little, and many face serious accuracy and reliability problems with the information technology systems that are available to them (Glastonbury 1997).

ACCOUNTABILITY: AUTONOMY OF THE CASE MANAGER

The final dimension of comparison in the table presents a distinction between case management and traditional service delivery on the basis of the autonomy and accountability of the practitioner. In traditional service delivery arrangements, the caseworker's line of accountability is to a delegated person within the agency. In theory, the practitioner will be imbued with a sense of primary professional responsibility to the client. Often clinical supervision and professional support are provided through senior staff from the worker's discipline or profession. However, in a case management approach, emphasis is placed on the assumed commitment of the practitioner to the funding body and organisational objectives. Supervision is more likely to be linked to the monitoring of effectiveness and funder-determined outcomes. The contracted nature of servicing and the specification of outcome and management responsibilities of the case manager accentuate new levels of accountability constructed on management principles rather than on those of discipline or professional practices (Wolk et al. 1994; Bar-On 1995).

The case manager may well have reporting and accountability responsibilities to several agencies and managers involved in funding and service provision. There are debates about whether or not the purchasing and provision functions of service delivery should be split (Hadley and Clough 1997). How this service question is determined at policy level will impact on the complexity of the reporting and accountability requirements and the purchasing flexibility and autonomy of the case manager.

PRACTICE DIMENSIONS OF TRADITIONAL AND CASE MANAGEMENT APPROACHES

The second perspective we explore is linked to the preceding discussion, but extends the analysis more specifically to the construction of practice under traditional service provision and the case management approach. Rothman and Sager (1998, p. 16) present a framework to compare and contrast the characteristics of clinical practice and generic case management—or the new paradigm—in terms of a number of components, including worker practice mandates, aims and focus. They claim, in respect of the distinctiveness of case management, that 'it is when the components are used fully and in close interplay that the configuration represents something unique' (1998, p. 15). In most respects, their framework affirms our modifications of Ozanne's earlier work, and in some cases overlaps with it. Rothman and Sager's conceptualisation, reproduced here in Table 3.2, allows for examination of the changes in traditional practice that flow from a case management approach.

GOAL OF INTERVENTION

The first point of distinction highlighted through the table is linked to the traditional clinician's objective of 'curing' the problem presented by the client. Implicit within this idea of cure is an assumption about the expertise of the clinician and their capacity to fix the difficulties. The construction of case management as an intervention designed to create an effective set of services to support the consumer is predicated on collaboration with many parties, and with the consumer having a central position in the process. The policy arenas where case management has been implemented often address the needs of consumers that will not be resolved in a way that might be understood in terms of a cure. Rather, they will continue in situations where risk must be managed and positive outcomes may be conceived of as improved quality of life and containment of costs. The issue of costs does not

Table 3.2 Traditional practice versus the new paradigm

Traditional clinical practice	The new paradigm
Cure: elimination or reduction of original impairment	Enhancement—optimisation: enables clients to maintain themselves satisfactorily in the community with the original impairment
Delimited, short- to medium-term duration of service	Continuous, long-term duration of service
Helping in depth, focused needs	Helping in breadth, multiple needs
Practitioner is primarily a direct service provider (micro orientation)	Practitioner is substantially a linker to community support resources (micro–macro orientation)
Primary focus on client insight, emotional growth, personality development	Primary focus on developing client coping skills to function in a community setting
Single helper	Multiple helpers; practitioner as coordinator of a helping system
Agency or institution as locus of help provision	Community as locus of help provision (community-based service)
Practitioner authority is clear and sanctioned (fixed boundaries)	Practitioner authority is unclear and variably sanctioned (fluid boundaries and boundary-spanning role)
Eventual self-sufficiency for client; practitioner disengages	Partial self-sufficiency for client; practitioner maintains connection
Case termination or discharge	Ongoing monitoring and reassessment

Source: Rothman and Sager (1998, p. 16).

feature, to any significant level, within the traditional clinical practice discourse.

DURATION OF CONTACT AND CASE TERMINATION

If the perspective is a cure, the period of intervention can be determined at the point of 'recovery'. These conditions do not apply in the same way in case management where, across an extended period (in theory), the duration and the level of intensity of case management should vary. If we look at a long-term prisoner who is being case managed, it is not difficult to see that, once an appropriate plan is in place, the level of involvement of the case manager might vary.

Similarly, a person with a severe disability who is being moved into the community will need intensive contact to ensure that assessment and planning are comprehensive, but over time involvement levels will fluctuate. While Rothman and Sager (1998) correctly emphasise the flexibility of both the nature and the extent of case management contact, it is our contention that, increasingly, there are practical constraints on this flexibility. The inadequacy of resources and contemporary suspicion of any service that might engender dependency often place severe limits on desirable fluctuations in intensity and on the length of time over which case management is offered. It is quite common now for case management programs to stipulate limits on the amount of service offered and/or the maximum length of time in the program.

WORKER ORIENTATION IN INTENSITY OR DEPTH AND FOCUS OF CONTACT

There is also a distinction between the focused 'helping' of the clinician and the more broadly based 'helping' of the case manager. For the clinician, the helping role is determined by their field of expertise, and in any given client situation there may be a range of other clinicians also involved with the client. The case manager will be dealing holistically with the consumer's situation and working with a group of providers, perhaps including specialist clinicians, to establish and deliver a comprehensive service or care plan. The traditional clinician works directly with the client to help bring about changes in the client's psyche and behaviour. While some case managers also do this, most are oriented towards the client's improved functioning in the community through the use of available community support services.

The management aspect of the case management role emphasises the sharing of responsibilities, combining of resources and adaptation around the client. The expertise of the case manager is linked to coordinating and management tasks. However, this is not to deny that there are case management models sometimes called clinical or advanced ones (Kanter 1989; Raiff and Shore 1993), and sectors like managed care (Frager 2000) in which the specialist clinical knowledge of and direct service provision by the case manager may predominate in the service delivery equation.

NUMBER OF HELPERS

The individual clinician operates within a relationship with the client and assumes mostly sole responsibility for a positive outcome or resolution of the problem. Other expertise is drawn on only at the instigation of the clinician and is based on his or her judgment that it is warranted. This is personalised service, private and shrouded in the mystique of professional autonomy and expertise as described by Pithouse (1987). In contrast, the case manager is expected to work in partnership with the consumer and to draw on all available resources to achieve the desired outcome. Depending on the model of case management and the setting, the case manager may have more or less personal contact with the consumer. In these different orientations, micro versus macro perspectives are important. Rothman and Sager (1998) distinguish this difference between traditional clinical practice and case management in terms of the number of 'helpers' (single versus multiple helpers). The very existence of multiple helpers demands different skills from the worker as case manager.

LOCUS OF HELP PROVISION AND WORKER AUTHORITY

Another dimension of contrast is in the arena of practice. Traditional clinical practice locates the clinician within the boundaries and mandate of the agency. In contrast, the case management approach sets the community as the arena of practice with the agency as a resource and administrative base for the practitioner. When the case management is operationalised through an institutional setting (for example, in health), the case manager is expected to link services and ensure effective transition back to the community. The traditional clinician's organisational mandate will largely determine the population being served, the resources available and the conditions for access to service delivery. However, by definition, the case manager is required to move beyond the confines of agency and to respond creatively to the consumer's situation and context. In the former circumstances, the boundaries of the practitioner's authority are more clearly defined. In contrast, for the case manager they remain fluid in order that the desired service outcomes might be achieved. Netting (1992) refers to this characteristic of case management as a *boundary-spanning function*. This is a vexed issue because authority is in practice mediated by a number of factors, including the social status of workers and their clients (Rothman and Sager 1998) and power over budgets (Friedman and Poertner 1995).

EVALUATING THE EXERCISE

A number of points can be drawn from the preceding discussion. First, it can be argued that the assertions made about case management and casework being one and the same are difficult to sustain. In addition, such assertions detract from efforts to conceptualise the particularity of the various manifestations and demands of the case management approach. Second, the practitioner operating in the case management approach will draw on skills and knowledge that are also used in traditional clinical practice. But other demands are placed on the case manager because the intervention process depends on collaboration with a range of service providers, other professionals, informal networks and private providers, beyond the extent envisaged even under the best systems-oriented casework. The emphasis on the management of service delivery for any given client clearly distinguishes case management from traditional casework.

Finally, it is fair to say that case management is significantly embedded in policies that are reshaping the nature of service delivery, the relationships between practitioners and their employer organisations. Expectations of the case management approach have not been properly established for all parties, be they consumers, carers, practitioners or organisations. It is little wonder that we view this elusive approach in its different guises with either a sense of confusion or with an unfounded confidence that is based on an ignorance of its true nature. As we move now to explore practice, the nature of that different approach will be elaborated on.

PART II

CASE MANAGEMENT AS PRACTICE

4

THE PRACTICE OF CASE MANAGEMENT

The fundamental intervention process conducted across the health and human services frames a wide spectrum of service delivery approaches, of which case management is one. Core elements of the process—intake, assessment, planning, implementation, monitoring and evaluation—define the structure within which a variety of different theories, tactics and activities can be accommodated and programmed to suit a number of target groups, intervention purposes and organisational demands. Although implemented differently in a dynamic process, the core elements provide the framework within which a number of systematic practice approaches lie. While conforming to this structure, individual case managers do things differently according to their client base, the organisational context and their own skill base. Bower (1991) explains the same blend of case management activities and the clinical reasoning process that forms a framework for nursing case management. Work with frail elderly clients living in the community, for example, requires a particular adaptation of the core functions (Naleppa and Reid 2000). Institutionally based case managers, like school counsellors, custodial officers and physiotherapists, implement the functions very differently from case managers working in the community from an agency base that can provide no direct service. Practitioners engage in client and context-specific activities (Raiff and Shore 1993; Rothman and Sager 1998) which are goal-dependent and rely on their skill and knowledge of particular client populations. All, however, move through the phases of intervention, so these are considered as a foundation upon which to place the nuances of case management practice and from which to begin to understand its wide and diverse application. It is not the intention of this chapter to labour this practice framework. The core elements of intervention are presented comprehensively in standard practice texts such as those for social work which also detail the guiding practice principles (e.g. Hepworth et al. 1997; Miley et al. 1998; Sheafor et al. 2000). Components of case management reflect traditional social work practice (Greene 1992; National Association of Social Workers 1992a) and its conceptualisation reflects traditional social work concepts like 'the person-in-environment perspective, the social-interactionist orientation, the systems basis of generalist practice, and the social ecological framework' (McClelland et al. 1996, p. 258). Currently, there are health and human service practice texts—mostly from the United States—devoted to detailing the case management process (e.g. Bower 1991; Rothman and Sager 1998; Woodside and McClam 1998; Holt 2000; Summers 2000). Most present the basic phases of the intervention process and address the practice components in each phase. How case managers implement the process and apply techniques depends very much on the context in which they work and the kind of client with whom they work.

Pursuing the discourse in an earlier chapter where case management was compared and contrasted with traditional casework, we reflect here on some distinguishing features of case management as a generic concept by looking for what is emphasised in the literature about case management practice. Using the intervention framework, we shall consider what is being promulgated as case management practice. The six contiguous but overlapping stages are presented in the sequence in which they commonly occur; for each we will draw out the particular challenges and priorities for the case manager.

THE PRACTICE FRAMEWORK: CORE ELEMENTS OF THE CASE MANAGEMENT PROCESS

INTAKE

This phase is essentially about attracting and screening potential users of the service, determining eligibility and appropriateness, and providing information about the agency. Use of forms and the formality of the process differ markedly across various organisational settings.

Authors disagree about the relative importance of this preliminary stage of the case management process. Some (e.g. Summers 2000) essentially ignore it, some (e.g. Raiff and Shore 1993; Woodside and McClam 1998) incorporate it in the assessment phase while others (e.g. Weil et al. 1985; Applebaum and Austin 1990; Rothman and Sager 1998; Holt 2000) break the intake phase down into distinct components, establishing its significance to the practitioner. The task of creating awareness of services and of targeting clients and client groups is a characteristic one for the case management service agency (Siefker et al. 1998). Case management is an approach designed to service highly vulnerable client groups who may be ignorant of, or resistant to, the services available to them. As well as diligently noting clients' proficiencies in a screening process (Weil et al. 1985; Greene 1992), it is often necessary for case managers to implement effective ways to attract and direct clients for whom their services are intended. Engagement is a distinct function of strengths-oriented community support programs (Kisthardt and Rapp 1992) and studies in the United Kingdom have shown that engagement of clients with a mental illness living in the community depends upon assertive outreach (Ryan et al. 1999). Weil et al. (1985, p. 31) nominate 'client identification' and 'outreach' as intake components and highlight the responsibility of intake workers to be 'aggressive and creative'. Rothman (1991, p. 522) acknowledges that outreach work involves going into the community, to 'search for and encourage' clients to enter services. This access function is pursued more substantially by Rothman and Sager (1998, p. 208), who identify three components: 'need assessment and client identification', 'outreach and social marketing' and 'channelling'. The case manager's responsibilities in relation to both providing access and soliciting clients are evident from descriptors such as these. Where services experience over-demand, the responsibilities are to screen against eligibility criteria and to be knowledgeable about alternative services to which potential users can be referred.

Intake: particular challenges for the case manager

The notion of marketing is not a traditional one for health and human service workers, schooled as they are to respond to rather than initiate situations. In order to fulfil intent, both agencies and case managers need to clearly understand eligibility criteria (Welch 1998) and be an active marketing force (Siefker et al. 1998). Potentially, case managers have a very important role to play in ensuring their agency's orientation and receptivity to particular clients so as to ensure that the best use is made of their time and that their service reaches those for whom it is intended. Later chapters attend to the notion of workers influencing their environments. The emphasis here is on the need to coach service providers as well as clients to ensure a good match. This commercial aspect of the stage is often neglected and can be partly responsible for inequities, inappropriate referrals, time wastage and, ultimately, poor client outcomes for the agency.

There are two predominant reasons why intake is often not practised as fully or as energetically as it should be. First, those services an agency advertises and those clients an agency accepts or seeks to attract are more often dependent on economic and efficiency factors than on criteria more germane to the stated enterprise. Systems characterised by competing interests and 'creaming' of clients tend to overlook those who are more difficult to reach and help. Second, many agencies are over-stretched and exhaust their worker resources dealing with a capacity caseload. Despite these and other contextual impediments to good intake practice, there are pragmatic and direct ways to improve the service orientation.

Intake: some practice priorities

Intake does not have to be an extensive process. An active, well-considered intake and engagement process which creates an appropriately screened and prepared client base propels service users smoothly to the individual assessment phase. It would seem particularly important to explain the nature of the case management process and the role of the case manager to potential service users. Bower (1991, p. 18) calls this the 'interact' stage of nursing case management, emphasising the development of relationships between those involved as the key component. Kisthardt and Rapp (1992, p. 113) insist that in order to engage, the case manager 'must plainly and simply reeducate the consumer regarding the unique nature of the case management process'. Clients, their carers and family members would have more realistic expectations and experience less frustration with more careful schooling in the nature of the case management process, particularly the envisaged extent of contact with their case manager, the level of authority that the worker may need to exert and, in many cases, the prospect of more than one case manager. Armed with some under-

standing, members of the client system would feel truly empowered and able to contribute usefully to their management.
Databases are critical. The compilation and maintenance of a dynamic directory of complementary and alternative services can save untold time and frustration. Establishment of clear, well-understood eligibility criteria, the development of user-friendly intake forms and the subsequent establishment of an accessible database can transform both the management of clients (Rapp et al. 1998) and the agency's potential to target and use its service to best effect. Information management is a key issue to which we will return later.

ASSESSMENT

Described as the 'bedrock of the helping process' (Sullivan and Fisher 1994, p. 65), assessment is the information-gathering phase, during which the worker ensures there is a sufficient information base from which to make decisions about how to work with and help a service user. It is a two-pronged process involving both establishment of the facts and the application of a disciplined analysis. Many agencies employ a condensed assessment process prescribed by targeting, resource and priority parameters. As far as possible, information about the client and their social functioning should be sought from all necessary sources using a variety of methods (Sheafor et al. 2000) and this information is then carefully examined, placed in context and appraised. A structured, disciplined approach to assessment is essential, planned and organised so as to reap better decisions leading to improved client outcomes. As an ongoing process, assessment features throughout to maintain a perspective on client response to intervention and their progress. Assessment is collaborative, dependent on the active involvement of the client and a focus on client strengths during the process (Kisthardt and Rapp 1992; Saleebey 1992; Rapp et al. 1994; Sullivan and Fisher 1994; Miley et al. 1998). It is generally accepted that a professional and comprehensive assessment phase is in itself an intervention which can lead to constructive outcomes in terms of increased understanding by clients of their situation, awareness of the resources available to them and the acknowledgment of their motivation and commitment to change. Whatever its extent, in specific practice contexts assessment requires great skill and an orientation to practise conducive to the fostering of mutual trust and a working partnership.

Assessment: particular challenges for the case manager

Weil et al. (1985) discuss the complexity of the assessment process for case managers and conclude that professional training is needed for its effective management. Critiquing community care management contexts in the United Kingdom, Welch (1998) expresses concern that assessment is commonly misunderstood and too diffuse. Assessment of a client's social functioning includes consideration of capacity which is more difficult to discover in vulnerable client populations. In-depth assessment can be thwarted by sequential, cross-agency assessment processes. Debates about who conducts assessment often exist and involvement of the client can be inconsistent: a long-term mental health client's informal networks are often scattered or depleted and their previous and current involvement with diverse formal agencies may be the only information available, obstructing attention to aspects of their more positive functioning. Similarly, the availability and viability of resources for such clients is not easy to establish. Dealing with a user's current and potential service network can be very demanding, requiring perseverance, assertion and negotiating skills during the assessment phase. Holt (2000, p. 35) refers to assessment as the 'central' element in case management programs and this level of significance is undeniable in an individualised service delivery approach. Care and attention to detail are required as well as the discipline to focus on pivotal issues that have potential for change.

If the client–worker relationship is a core feature of a particular case management program, it can be cemented during assessment if staff continuity permits. Time and energy must be invested to cultivate working relationships with highly vulnerable clients living in the community in order to achieve continuity of care and successful outcomes (Cleak and Serr 1998; Issakidis et al. 1999; Burns et al. 2000). This applies to the more severely disadvantaged in any client group: the long-term unemployed, the chronically infirm and mentally ill, parolees, the young and homeless, perennially fostered children, the aged with dementia. The assessment phase can be quite protracted to accommodate this development. Workers and agencies cannot expect to apply a fast, efficient assessment process with all clients and must differentiate those who require more concerted effort from those for whom a proper assessment is not contingent upon an effective relationship. This differentiation of responses to individual clients presents quite a challenge in some contexts. Despite the established importance of individualised and comprehensive assessment procedures, for many case managers the process is streamlined, somewhat mechanistic and antithetical to the notion of individualised service. This is particularly so where workers are constrained by restrictive standard assessment procedures and packaged formulations of service delivery.

Assessment: some practice priorities

Even in programs where assessment is separated from service provision, there is no doubt that efficient management of assessment information gleaned in an ongoing process is paramount. Strong encouragement to develop computerised systems (Rapp et al. 1998) is endorsed for those multi-problem clients with extensive and diverse agency contacts. Such systems can help to avoid multiple, repetitive assessment, enable effective multidisciplinary teamwork and control information flow that can easily transgress confidentiality and ethical boundaries. They will also encourage workers to document information in a disciplined and readily accessible manner. Instead of being restrictive, such procedures—when used compatibly with more traditional and subjective interviewing methods—can aid and abet effective assessment. While accepting the reality of a limited assessment process in some contexts, practitioners can make imaginative use of categories of information to render them less restrictive and more conducive to sound planning.

Rothman (1998, p. 52) adopts Moxley's (1989) broad framework to consider aspects of the assessment process. The four categories of that framework do serve to highlight significant tasks for the case manager. They are: the nature of client needs; the client's capacity to address these; the contribution of informal supports; and the contribution of human service agency supports. The last two of these emerge as distinctly useful to explore in order to understand some of the case manager's priorities in this assessment phase.

The contribution of informal supports transpires perhaps as the single most sought-after resource area in case management planning. With widespread scarcity of services, many workers depend to varying—but usually quite large—extents on the availability of informal support. It is quite sound to embrace informal support given current community care policy directions, but it is a common misconception to think that it comes cheaply. Care must be taken not to presume the existence or quality of support from concerned, involved kin or neighbours. Familial or friendship obligation, resistance to change or worry about alternatives may cause informal carers to overstate their capacity to provide care despite the enormous strain it imposes. It is not sufficient merely to establish who provides or accepts responsibility for a person's care; its worth as a resource needs to be assessed in terms of the relationship between those who provide and receive the care, analysed from an historical, current and future perspective (Holt 2000). Purposeful assessment of the calibre of informal supports is accompanied by an investigation of strength and capacity in specific terms of what and how much development and nurturing is required. All too often it is merely the support's existence which is established.

The creation of informal resources is a direction to pursue when working with clients whose informal support systems are depleted or non-existent, such as those that fall into Moxley's (1997, p. 239) 'undesirable' population category. A full assessment of a client's situation includes consideration of potential informal resources where they are needed, to clarify the type and extent of work that would be required in their creation and whether or not the case manager can provide it directly or indirectly.

Assessment of the contribution needed from formal supports is crucial, and realistic planning for change accommodates assessment of the availability and accessibility of those services. All too often what is offered is what exists and/or the case manager is constrained by the unavailability of resources when identifying what is needed with a client. This is an area fraught with frustration and the lament of 'insufficient services' abounds. Hudson (1994, p. 153) aptly describes the relationship between assessment of need and availability of resources as a 'conundrum' which signals again the contentious issue of resource management and the onus on the practitioner to develop, know and influence services prior to planning. It is an issue we return to repeatedly.

PLANNING

Goal-setting is the logical outcome of the assessment phase and merges into the planning stage where the broad goal areas are operationalised.

On the strength of a substantial and comprehensive assessment an effective service plan can be constructed. A plan provides direction and focus for both the service user and worker, and is the result of collaboration between them (Weil et al. 1985; Rothman and Sager 1998; Sheafor et al. 2000). Formulating a plan together is a dynamic process in which involvement from the client and carer(s) is encouraged in an effort to tailor it to have idiosyncratic meaning and to provide a sense of purpose. The key components of the planning phase are goal-setting and the development of a series of activities for both client and worker that will lead to achievement of the objectives and thereby the goal. Planning involves troubleshooting, confrontation and a mixture of idealism and pragmatism in working with the client to create a plan of action that is accepted as an achievable challenge.

Case management is usually implemented in the context of increased accountability measures, and case managers need to be very clear about planning, given that most service provision is tied to tangible outcomes (Woodside and McClam 1998). Theoretically, a sound plan has to be definitive, clearly structured and documented (Rothman and Sager 1998). For some practitioners, this is quite a departure from their established procedure and does present challenges in a culture that can work against 'pinning down' both the process and intended outcome for a client. Tangible, articulated plans can be seen as mechanistic and clinical to a worker who wants to operate intuitively. It is a pity when plans are considered restrictive because thoughtful effective planning reflects flexibility and dynamism, accommodating intuition and different perspectives. Case managers accommodate both inter-organisational and intra-organisational purposes when formulating plans for intervention. Within their own agency, plans are effectively a contract between the agency worker and the client, and can be used to monitor and evaluate worker performance and service effectiveness. As such, they should be used to structure contact with the client, in case conferences, in collegial discussions and in work performance sessions. They establish priorities, timeframes and allocate responsibility. As a readily accessible record of intent—both of the client and of the services—they can be used to direct and persuade service providers to become involved. A good sound plan is evidence of clear thinking and mutual commitment and can be used to influence the provision of services and sustain motivation.

Planning: particular challenges for the case manager

Let us consider for a moment the actual goal-setting process which Holt (2000, p. 49) identifies as one of the most difficult. Most text instruction urges workers to ensure that goals are defined in behavioural terms from the client perspective—that is, to make sure it is a client goal, not a worker goal (Hepworth et al. 1997; Miley et al. 1998; Sheafor et al. 2000). Some discipline is required on the part of the case manager, who assumes a lot of responsibility and coordinates many services; it is easy to set your own worker goals (for example, 'secure a nursing home placement for Mr S' or 'protect baby M from further harm'), but they need to be nested within client-based ones to reflect the onus upon clients to take responsibility and work towards their own change. One way our examples could be stated as broad client goals is 'Mr S to prepare for transition to nursing home' and 'Ms P and baby M to live independently', so that under each goal a series of objectives and associated activities can be devised. That goals have to be achievable is obvious, but it is in the area of goal achievability that some plans stumble. Clear goals can increase worker power and show achievement, but they can also act as a disincentive. Many outcome-based programs using case management force inappropriate goals on to the users of their services: employment programs for the long-term unemployed with very little chance of securing employment, for instance, can insist that acquisition of a job is the outcome for all recipients of the service. Client resistance is reduced (Holt 2000) and commitment enhanced when plans are premised on the accomplishment of equally tangible but much more achievable goals, such as 'apply for a number of jobs' or 'serve as a volunteer at the local youth club'.

Objectives, or sub-goals, are the steps to be achieved on the way to goal accomplishment. They should be client based and are best documented sequentially and logically so that subsequent objectives can rely on the achievement of previous ones. As well as plans often being constrained by the availability of services (Sullivan and Fisher 1994), there is a tendency to formulate provision of specific services as objectives rather than this being the change in the client the services are meant to promote. This translates into a predominance of restrictive and repetitive planning in some practice contexts.

Planning: some practice priorities

From a case management perspective—especially those situations where the role is predominantly one of service coordination—it is tempting to mark client progress by the receipt of successive services. This is, we suggest, one of the fundamental practice issues in case management that has ramifications across many stages of intervention and across various diverse programs. It is highlighted here as a planning issue because it is at this stage that the parameters of what is envisaged for a client are set. Meaningful outcomes are critical to the service user, but many plans lack creativity and vision because they reflect nothing more than a range of services. In some Australian prisons where case management has been implemented, for example, a prisoner's progress is planned and charted according to completion of a series of core, set programs (such as drug education, anger management and literacy). These are perfectly acceptable and probably appropriate directions, but what is set as an objective is the prisoner's attendance rather than the prisoner's response to these programs in terms of any changes to their attitude, behaviour or cognition. Case plans for the elderly receiving community-based support services lack lustre if they document mere provision of specific services, such as carer support programs, periods of respite, home nursing and domiciliary care tasks, without any reference to other—perhaps less obvious—needs such as companionship, training or the fostering of family support. Plans that address a range of social functioning areas as well as specific services are potentially more valuable.

IMPLEMENTING PLANS

This is the most 'visible' phase (Sheafor et al. 2000, p. 437), and the one which encompasses service coordination—one of the most fundamental defining characteristics of case management (Libassi 1992; Murer and Brick 1997). To facilitate change in individual client situations, workers ensure things happen according to devised plans. For case managers, this predominantly entails linkage with various service providers, the advocacy needed to ensure the availability of those services (Walsh 2000) and continuity of change efforts (Hepworth et al. 1997). Whatever the setting and nature of the program, the service coordination is the critical characteristic that reflects case management activity in this phase of intervention.

Implementing plans: particular challenges for the case manager

Amongst others, Weil et al. (1985) and Rothman (1991) concentrate on the tasks of resource identification in their rendition of the planning phase, highlighting that what is programmed and intended for a client is inextricably linked to the services and resources available. Stroul (1995) highlights the challenge to create resources where none exist. Particular tensions emerge for agencies and case managers involved in identifying, creating and maintaining effective resources, and in keeping up-to-date records of these. Implementation of plans crosses organisational boundaries: resources need to be found and juggled without allowing constraints and inadequacies to overshadow what can be achieved. It is a fine balancing act, one which relies on the ability to 'oscillate swiftly and easily between many different and often conflicting roles' (Campbell et al. 1994, p. 11). Linking clients to resources often requires creative work to overcome obstacles posed by the demands or limitations of the service providers and those posed by the user. Again, effective planning will have sifted these out and addressed them, but the activities required of the case manager to ensure the successful acquisition and receipt of services can be diverse—indeed monumental—in the current context of sparse resources.

Implementing plans: some practice priorities

Case managers simply must establish a connection to the array of services that pertain to the current and potential needs of their client base so that they can both involve users in the most appropriate services (Ryan et al. 1999) and ensure that the services do what is intended. This is what is meant by coordination. It is usually insufficient merely to link clients to these resources, albeit with clear prescriptive referrals. Implementation demands much more effort on the part of the case manager to ensure that things happen as they should, when they should. The nature of the role can take a dramatic shift here from one of individual collaborative planning involving a small circle of people to a much wider one where the case manager has to exert quite a deal of authority to influence and direct the acquisition and maintenance of what is needed (Stroul 1995). Control over resources is critical (Rife et al. 1991; Austin 1993) and must stay in focus for development if it is lacking. The challenge is to stay true to the notion of collaboration (Patterson 2000) amongst a range of disparate professionals and service providers. It is too often the case that providers of discrete services work in isolation without a complete picture of a client's cocktail of services—or, indeed, a conception of their guiding plan. Paucity of information and lack of collective involvement can lead to overlapping, skewed and mismatched services and a regrettable loss of efficiency. Inter-agency coordination and advocacy are key intervention activities (Rothman 1991) and nowhere are they more critical than in the implementation stage. To achieve a functional level of collaboration and mutual cooperation amongst service providers requires the worker to engage in activities specifically designed to inform and discipline service providers. Collective activities such as dissemination of plans, regular bulletin-type updates and case conferences come to mind, all involving decisive, clear leadership and management. Issues of power and management tasks are addressed later in the book.

MONITORING

After establishing inter-agency collaboration while services are implemented, an ongoing constructive review of those services is implemented in which it is important to incorporate client feedback about the progress being made (Intagliata 1992). Dependent upon an ongoing relationship between worker and client, this should be structured into the plan of action. Effective monitoring that reaps the most for the client is contingent upon an authoritative stance from the case manager. This is often problematic as the mechanisms may not be in place to detect or influence the quality of services (Netting 1992). Hudson (1994, p. 154) observes that 'great tact' is required to establish and sustain the communication links with other professionals that enable scrutiny and set some accountability measures in place. The resistance from service providers fearful of relinquishing control to a case manager reported from Holland (Willems 1996) has general relevance. Certainly diplomacy skills should emerge from the bundle of those needed to ensure the availability of information required to assess the quality of services. Conflict management, negotiation and assertiveness skills all figure in the profile of a good manager, and the professional development we focus on later in the book addresses these areas. A case manager's profile and position within an agency are often not regarded as significant, so they do not readily attract attention or receive information. The case manager who needs to establish credibility across the range of professionals and service providers has to plan strategically and expend time and energy to effect personal and professional impact. Without this regard from those they seek to influence, case managers cannot successfully advocate for their client—a role that has 'taken on significant meaning in the field of case management' (Murer and Brick 1997, p. 39).

ADVOCACY: A PARTICULAR CHALLENGE

Expanding opportunities for clients faced with inequities and social injustices by upholding their rights is acknowledged as a fundamental responsibility of human service workers, and is particularly critical given the emphasis on consumer participation and empowerment outcomes of advocacy work (Payne 1995; Miley et al. 1998; Woodside and McClam 1998; Hyduck 2000, p. 183). The need to redress inequities is more pronounced when dealing with the most vulnerable, disadvantaged groups and advocacy is recognised as a critical component of case management practice (O'Connor 1988; Raiff and Shore 1993; McClelland et al. 1996). It is described as a quite specialised activity for the case manager; for Rothman (1998, p. 176), it is 'determined and forceful action' which pervades much of the intervention process. For Sunley (1997, p. 88), it is one of the most important case management functions, contingent upon the passion, determination and commitment of the practitioner. The tasks associated with achieving positive change for underprivileged clients are arduous in a competitive, under-funded human service arena, so there are a number of obstacles to the successful execution of advocacy. In many settings there is inherent role conflict for the practitioner, who is simultaneously representing the client with certain needs and the agency with tight cost restraints on its services (Austin and McClelland 1996). It is frequently an angst-ridden task when the worker encounters hostility and resistance to change from insular professionals and services that are stretched to the limit. Intense and sustained advocacy is an apparently neglected aspect of case management activity because case managers either do not perceive it to be part of their role and/or because they lack the resources to operate as valuable advocates. In fact, Rose (1992a, p. 271) goes so far as to suggest that, when workers are dealing with clients in dire need of a case management service, the denigration of advocacy is 'the most common form of betrayal'.

Advocacy is not well understood or practised across a wide range of services (Bateman 1995) and, like counselling, is somewhat diluted by a rather generic practice conceptualisation. It is important to draw attention here to the bipolar nature of advocacy, comprising the representation of individual clients (case advocacy) and that of a collective of clients with similar problems and needs (cause advocacy) (Raiff and Shore 1993; Miley et al. 1998; Rothman and Sager 1998). It seems that more case managers are willing and able to embark upon case advocacy which essentially ensures that clients are linked to resources initially denied them. It also seeks to maintain the viability of service provision when that is threatened. Case advocacy is often confused with less complicated routine brokerage activities. It is contingent upon the ability of the case manager to influence those who have the capacity to improve clients' lives. That influence is so much more effective if the case manager has recourse to a sound plan for the client and documented evidence in the form of reliable case notes.

The less widely practised part of the function is cause advocacy, which requires creative work on behalf of a group or collective of clients. For instance, if frustrated by the unavailability of a particular type of service or aware of the need to alter how a service responds to a particular type of client, agencies and case managers should consider carefully how best to change the perceptions, beliefs and practices that are reflected. Targets can be their own agencies, other organisations, political parties and community groups (Raiff and Shore 1993). Persuasive tactics such as lobbying, public meetings, submissions and petitions can be used, requiring a well-planned and structured approach from the case manager. Organisation of a public rally may be called for in order to harass a politician to consider an issue. Again, evidence and documentation should support the various activities: opinion may need to be formally canvassed and individual experiences integrated into a formal document in order to plea for the creation of a service. Unusual, clever alliances with businesses can be forged and collaboration sought between consumer and professional groups. There are many ways to make people change their minds and attitudes. Most of them rely upon an advocate who is prepared to be zealous, to speak up and persist. Sunley (1997) warns of the lack of interest in and support for staff poised to pursue cause advocacy in today's cost-obsessed organisations. Ideally, this resistance to structural changes within an organisation should add to the sense of injustice. At the very least, case managers should not erase the possibility from their repertoire of ways to help their clients.

Advocacy practice priorities

Two major practice issues emanate from this brief contemplation of the advocacy role. First, it is imperative for the case manager to engage in advocacy-related activities that promote client participation and ultimately lead to the enhancement of clients' ability to promote their cause and bring about changes to improve their lives. This may be a more painstaking, frustrating strategy for the worker than doing the work for the clients, but it is ultimately more satisfying and fruitful. It is tempting to take short cuts, however, and case managers do need perseverance. A study from Sweden shows that advocacy is essential, linked directly to client satisfaction with case management services (Bjorkman and Hansson 2001). Second, to be well organised and to keep good records is essential. The benefit of having access to documented evidence of what has transpired and what is planned for a client or group of clients is immeasurable; good advocacy is dependent upon good documentation. The availability of documented accumulated practice knowledge promotes practice wisdom. Once again, record-keeping is in focus as a crucial skill.

EVALUATION

Lamentably, evaluation is not accorded the attention it deserves from many practitioners. Evidence-based practice is the exception rather than the norm across a range of health and human services, including case management (Bjorkman and Hansson 2000). Murer and Brick (1997) highlight the lack of case management practice research whilst Kane and Rich (1991) observe that, in the United States, hardly any attempt has been made to link costs with outcomes. Currently, in the health and human services, much of what is promoted as evaluation can be viewed cynically as fitting a political rather than a practice agenda (Everitt and Hardiker 1996). Practice effectiveness can and must be differentiated from overall program success (Trevithick 2000) for the advancement of practice awareness and the development of techniques that work. The broader question that can be posed about the effectiveness of case management as a method of service is not addressed here—our intent is less ambitious and confined to the onus on the individual practitioner to answer systematically the question, 'How well did it, and I, work?' With its emphasis on economic efficiency and effectiveness, case management practice has a level of accountability that demands strict evaluative procedures. Given the confusion and resistance that hampers a good deal of what is practised under the case management moniker, it is imperative to use reflective techniques to improve what is done and how it is done. The concept of a 'reflective practitioner' as one who moves forward and develops is well venerated (Schon 1983).

A clear distinction exists between evaluation carried out during intervention and that conducted at completion or abandonment of a particular intervention plan (Miley et al. 1998; Rothman and Sager 1998; Holt 2000; Sheafor et al. 2000). Linked inextricably to the monitoring phase, formative or progress evaluation is used to inform and guide ongoing practice. Sometimes referred to as reassessment (Applebaum and Austin 1990; Rothman and Sager 1998; Holt 2000), it is a process where the worker continuously evaluates and adapts to keep a plan of action pertinent and dynamic. Summative or outcome evaluation is the measurement of goal achievement and identification of what contributed to the success or otherwise of the outcome. Thus it is a concerted attempt by the practitioner to consider the effectiveness of the methods and techniques used, as well as other client or contextual factors that have impinged on the outcome.

The particular challenge: doing it

In linking evaluation and reassessment functions, Rothman (1998, p. 171) lists some impediments to successful execution: lack of client motivation, loosely formulated goals, client resistance, unsteady client progress, uncooperative agencies, time limitations and work pressures. The last two of these would seem to be particularly pertinent to case management practice. Evaluations have to take account of the practice context (Trevithick 2000), and it is unfortunate that most case managers are functioning in inadequate systems. As well as an apparent resistance to self-evaluation in health and human service workers, contextual confusion often blurs the practice role and purpose. With factors such as these dampening incentive, the challenge for case managers is actually to conduct formal evaluation. Practice evaluation does appear to be the most dispensable task in a series of others that are more visible in the sense that there is more accountability associated with them. Most serious evaluation is for the practitioners' benefit and not seen to be of immediate relevance to clients and number-crunching managers.

Evaluation practice priorities

Evaluation techniques should be as objective and comprehensive as possible to avoid narrow, self-justifying evaluative outcomes. Sound and efficient formative evaluation is dependent upon skill and diligence in the monitoring and planning phases of intervention. An unambiguous directive stance is needed to investigate ongoing service provision and maintain its transparency. Goals that are clearly articulated, objective and sequenced can easily be discussed and measured. Consistent attention to client progress and assiduous checking of service provision leads to a cleaner evaluative focus on the more substantial aspects of intervention. Good record-keeping means that colleagues, clients and others can be involved more effectively in evaluation of their practice, which summons more objectivity. Acceptance of self-evaluation as the basis of professional development plans is made in ensuing chapters and emerges here as a critical, often neglected component of evaluation.

These criteria clearly apply to both progress and outcome evaluation, but it is the latter—which has more ramifications for the development of case management practice as an industry—that is more neglected. Miley lists four benefits of outcome evaluation which neatly encapsulate how important it is: continuous feedback; accountability; transferability; and professional development (Miley et al. 1998, p. 398). The enterprise will remain static unless knowledge is accumulated about practice outcomes. Diligence is required to overcome some of the obstacles and to assiduously evaluate outcomes and methods in order to develop practice wisdom.

REFLECTION ON THE CASE MANAGEMENT PROCESS

The characteristics that typify case management practice in each phase of the systematic intervention process have been identified in this chapter. This has built a generic perspective on case management practice that goes some way to distinguishing it from other forms of service delivery while acknowledging its sameness in structure. Some general case management practice emphases have emerged and some particular pervasive challenges have surfaced. We need now to appreciate more fully the contextual factors that affect how case management work is carried out in order to pursue these challenges and priorities in more detail. The next chapter takes a look at some of the persistent practice variations that have evolved in different applications of the approach.

5

KEY PRACTICE DIMENSIONS IN DIVERSE SETTINGS

Earlier in the book we modified Ozanne's (1990) dimensions of case management from an organisational perspective in a comparison with traditional service approaches. The priorities of the previous chapter emerged as key dimensions of practice and we want now to explore some of the articulated dimensions in more detail. To achieve analytical depth, we are obliged to consider practice variations in different applications of the service approach. Case management practice defies universal description because of the myriad ways in which it is applied across fields in different settings (Stroul 1995; Peterson et al. 1997). Tensions surrounding practice dimensions like the relationship between client and worker, degree of worker authority, level of advocacy and the effective management of information and resources are responded to in the context of the practice setting which determines organisational goals and dictates service priorities.

Consideration of how practice is applied in different typical settings will help to illustrate noteworthy issues which pervade all practice but which are especially challenging in terms of the particular context or direction to which we apply them in this analysis. A recognition of some broad categories of approach is useful before we broach these contextual practice issues.

BROAD CATEGORIES OF CASE MANAGEMENT APPROACH

A simple demarcation of client-centred and system-centred approaches has been considered by a number of American writers (Applebaum and Austin 1990; Rose 1992a; Moxley 1997; Rothman and Sager 1998; Geron 2000; Solomon 2000). Characteristics of practice can be sorted crudely according to the supremacy of particular goals. All case management approaches aspire to meet the dual objectives of individual needs and system goals (Geron 2000), or those to which Rothman (1998, p. 18) refers as community and policy 'impulses'. However, in diverse settings, they reflect these very differently. Practice is adapted to conform to these goal emphases (Rose and Moore 1995).

Moxley (1997) adeptly summarises the distinguishing features of the two archetypes and shows that defining them helps to focus attention on characteristics of practice. In response to criticism that both reflect paternalism, he proposes a third archetype, which he calls a 'consumer-controlled' approach to case management (1997, p. 10). Often referred to as consumer-directed practice, it is identified as ideologically different from other service directions (Kunkel et al. 2000) and touted as having the potential to overcome some of the current shortcomings in case management applications (Moxley 1997). It is worthy of particular attention.

We shall use these sweeping practice descriptors—client-centred, system-centred and consumer-directed—to highlight practice emphases in each of these three directions and trust that they are not taken too literally to typify mutually exclusive practice approaches. Any practitioner can be involved simultaneously in all three, but is probably steered more to one by virtue of a particular organisational context.

HOW TO SORT PRACTICE APPLICATIONS

In every country where it is practised, the number of different programs conducted under the label of case management is disquieting. Attempts to categorise case management applications are consequently diverse and sometimes confusing. Netting (1992, p. 161) observes that they can 'typically be classified according to target population, auspice, purpose, setting, and roles performed', whereas Geron (2000, p. 10) differentiates 'staff qualifications, caseload size, scope and duration of effort, relationship of care management to service delivery, and the

Table 5.1   The settings and associated practice dimensions selected for discussion

Practice location, population or direction	*Selected key dimensions*
Community-based settings	Case manager as generalist, broker or therapist and Relationship between client and case manager Level of organisational authority Authority to purchase services
Teamwork in service centres	Team membership and Individual authority
Managed care settings	Monitoring and cost containment and Information management
Social control settings	Monitoring and surveillance and Advocacy
Consumer-directed practice	Education, training, consultation and Availability of the case manager Advocacy

amount of authority vested in the care manager to authorize or purchase services'. There are many dimensions against which applications can be compared and contrasted, but applying relatively micro dimensions is complex in the face of so much diversity.

Rothman (1998, p. 18) emphasises that, to avoid 'conceptual chaos', investigation cannot be removed from the practice context (Stroul 1995). Conti (1999) suggests that consideration of practice-based models—those tailored to specific client populations—is the most instructive way to analyse practice. Service orientation, as well as the type, range and extent of activities, is shaped quite decisively by contextual factors such as the population to be served, the geographic location of the service and the organisational structure of the agency. The setting influences how the task is conceived and where practitioners direct their efforts.

PRACTICE ISSUES IN FOCUS

The process of sorting case management programs in terms of location and population does drive out some central issues. As we have already indicated, there is no pretence that these are not issues that generally pervade practice but they are brought into sharp focus when considered in a particular practice context. Five distinct contexts will be used to generate discussion of practice dimensions that are particularly critical in each context. These are then examined in order to arrive at a direction or imperative to improve practice within each context. To cover all the issues would require a much larger tome, so our focus has been fairly selective to achieve depth of analysis. We look now at some of the more critical issues encountered by practitioners working in particular settings. Table 5.1. shows the configuration selected.

PERSPECTIVE ON COMMUNITY-BASED CASE MANAGEMENT

A diverse array of services exists, catering for the needs of a very wide range of consumers and their carers living in the community (Murer and Brick 1997). The range of different approaches used in community settings is significantly dependent upon the nature of the target population (Solomon 2000). Within their capacity, case managers work differently with different client groups and can be identified by functional predominance as—amongst others—a generalist, a broker or a primary therapist (Weil et al. 1985; Perlmutter and Johnson 1996; Woodside and McClam 1998; Holt 2000; Solomon 2000).

The *generalist*, as a single source of contact, assumes responsibility for coordinating the care of a range of individual clients in a variety of settings across a professional network of services with those informal resources that can be applied. The actual provision of direct services by the case manager in this role can be a feature or not, depending on worker capacity and the availability of volunteers, aides and informal support.

The *broker* function is somewhat less expansive; it is one of linking clients with services and resources and ensuring appropriate delivery of those services. Operating primarily in these roles of getting things done by others highlights the need for organisational skills and readiness to manage others in a business-oriented way (Wolk et al. 1994;

Holt 2000). We visit this managerial component of the work later in the book: it is a role which some find alien and threatening.

The *primary therapist*, as the person who provides counselling or some other therapeutic service, can assume case management responsibility for a client—as happens for the mental health nurse who visits clients to administer medication and check on their welfare. The role can become much more, embracing a robust relationship with the client on the basis of which the nurse can manage other aspects of the client's life to improve social functioning.

Client-centred roles such as these feature predominantly in the coordination and provision of community support to the aged, vulnerable children, and adults and adolescents who are socially isolated, drug dependent and/or have physical or mental disabilities. In these scenarios, the role of case management has 'enduring relevance' (Ryan et al. 1999, p. 120) and tends to be well understood and respected (Moxley 1997). Practice here is comprehensively directed to meet the individual needs of recipients, where the case manager's activities can be seen as twofold: with the client, as a reference point, providing emotional or direct support; and with the service delivery system, organising, managing and developing services.

THE RELATIONSHIP BETWEEN CLIENT AND CASE MANAGER IN COMMUNITY-BASED SETTINGS

The relationship between a client and their case manager(s) is often identified as a key dimension of case management conducted in community settings (Applebaum and Austin 1990; Burns and Perkins 2000). Brokerage and generalist roles do not rely on an intensive relationship, whereas various other approaches—for example, more intensive ones with the mentally ill (Kanter 1992; Rapp and Kisthardt 1996; Walsh 2000)—do emphasise the degree of relationship established with clients and the necessity of limiting caseloads (Burns et al. 2000). Some would even argue that nurse case managers focus on interaction and relationship building with clients in acute and community health settings (Glettler and Leen 1996). A necessary component in planning for change is collaboration with the client (Naleppa and Reid 2000) and the client's increased participation in programs of care is proportional to the increased amount of time spent with the client system. A client has to be engaged to be involved. In diverse contexts, the time and effort invested by the worker in the relationship are the critical factors when it comes to breaking down resistance and denial in clients who abuse substances (Rapp et al. 1994); achieving the involvement of ostracised, mentally ill clients (Issakidis et al. 1999); providing emotional support to the long-suffering carers of those with dementia (Roberts et al. 2000); achieving kinship care of children (Scannapieco and Hegar 1995); caring for victims of AIDS who are culturally isolated (Ivantic-Doucette and Maashao 1999); or achieving a safer environment for children in families where the mother is struggling with addiction problems (Halfon et al. 1997). A related factor is the extent and availability of informal resources and support. Sometimes the case manager's time is better spent bolstering that informal support; however, it is symptomatic of the most vulnerable clients to have little or no tangible family support and work directly with them is often concentrated and demanding.

Summers (2000, p. 53) discriminates three levels of case management in community care contexts: administrative, resource coordination and intensive—akin to the minimal, coordinated and comprehensive levels of service identified by Weil et al. (1985) and Korr (1991) and contingent upon degrees of relationship. Others have suggested that various conceptualisations can be placed on a continuum that distinguishes the service management and brokerage activities from those which are clinical and therapeutic in nature (Solomon and Draine 1994; Peterson et al. 1997). Positioning on such a continuum correlates with the extent of the relationship between the case manager and the client system. Three dimensions come into play when considering relationships: time spent with the client; the scope of problems; and the longevity of the process (Applebaum and Austin 1990).

Within the reality of workload and resource constraints, it is often extremely difficult for individual case managers to decide how to apportion their time with clients. Astuteness relies on thorough assessment of client characteristics, carers and other informal resources and knowledge of formal services (Diwan 1999). It takes time to integrate resources effectively and to allocate the most valuable commodity—time. It is evident that the extent of the role played by the case manager is dependent upon the development of a sufficient relationship with the client in community care work. Practitioners must carefully assess threshold levels and make sure they are met.

LEVEL OF ORGANISATIONAL AUTHORITY IN
COMMUNITY-BASED SETTINGS

Practice in the community can be distinguished according to the level
of the organisation's financial power and the power it bestows upon
its case managers (Yarmo 1998; Holt 2000). Opportunities, caseloads,
range of work and incentives vary from place to place, particularly
across sectors. Child protection work, for example, is usually a public
welfare mandate, and a practitioner's contact with a family may be
minimal in conducting an initial risk assessment and referring families
to other private or non-government agencies for direct services. In
situations such as these, unambiguous delegation of authority avoids
dissipation of control and accountability. Responsibility for organisational and managerial tasks must be retained by a case manager who
is identifiable to all as such. Of course, this does not have to be just
one person, but problems often result when there are multiple case
managers (Baragwanath 1999). Accountability can diminish and, along
with clarity of task division, the responsibility to oversee and coordinate is easily lost. The disciplining and monitoring of service provision
require strong and evident management, but a case manager's level of
perceived and felt authority is at risk when monitoring is seen as less
specialised work. Stroul (1995) highlights individual case manager
authority as crucial to service outcome.

AUTHORITY TO PURCHASE SERVICES IN COMMUNITY-BASED SETTINGS

Across agencies, the case manager's control over the allocation and
distribution of financial resources to individual clients influences care
planning (Applebaum and Austin 1990; Kane et al. 1991) and directly
affects their capacity to attract, achieve and influence service provision
(Kubisa 1990; Austin 1993; Orme and Glastonbury 1993). It is argued
that financial autonomy provides more direct accountability (Cambridge 1992) and leads to increased creativity and resourcefulness
(Davies 1992). This source of power plays a critical role and deserves
the attention we direct to it in the next section. It is sufficient here to
emphasise that case managers who have some fiscal authority do not
have to resort to begging, pleading and cajoling to achieve services
for their clients. This aspect of the task can be costly and demeaning,
leading to the unfortunate situation where the goals in focus for some

workers easily become the securing of the service rather than the changes in the client the service was meant to trigger. Again, this loss of focus on the individual client leads to a diminution of the implementation and monitoring role, and any evaluation measures undertaken tend to look at the type and extent of service provision rather than the quality of service.

PRACTICE IMPERATIVE IN COMMUNITY-BASED SETTINGS: ABILITY TO INFLUENCE

A common imperative is indicated by consideration of these three key dimensions of community-based practice. Outcomes are limited by lack of opportunity to become involved and develop relationships with clients and by poor configurations of responsibility and authority that deplete worker capacity. In many settings, case managers exert little influence over how their roles are conceptualised and nurtured. Organisations need to ensure positions of authority for case managers (Friedman and Poertner 1995; Stroul 1995) and workers themselves have the responsibility to develop their standing and level of influence by involving themselves more strategically in their own and other organisations with which they have an association.

TEAMWORK IN SERVICE CENTRES

Service centres (Weil et al. 1985; Woodside and McClam 1998) respond to the needs of the aged and those with physical or developmental disabilities or the mentally ill who reside in, visit or attract outreach services from the centre. More or less institutionally based, some centres provide a comprehensive array of core client-centred services under one roof and host a range of professionals who form a team of case managers. The organisational structure affects how the case management role is perceived and enacted.

Community programs with the mentally ill that employ interdisciplinary teams to provide full direct services have been found to be superior in effectiveness to those which entail more brokerage (Craig 1998; Bedell et al. 2000). Burns and Perkins (2000) argue from the United Kingdom that both a team approach and a focus on the development of individual trusting relationships are important when working with the mentally ill. Assertive community treatment, used in the United States with the chronically mentally ill and with drug users (Inciardi et al. 1994), embodies these principles. In lauding the track record of assertive community treatment in the United States and Australia, and anticipating its widespread adoption in the United Kingdom, Marshall and Creed (2000, p. 195) proffer the 'intensity, versatility and cohesiveness' of the team as a main ingredient of its success. Rapp (1998, p. 180) identifies the benefits of the respective team approaches in both assertive community treatment and strengths models as 'backup, support and service-planning ideas', irrespective of whether or not the actual provision of case management service is a collective responsibility or that of an individual team member. Teams of case managers can be an effective way to integrate professional resources (Raiff and Shore 1993; Back 1999) and ensure best fit between client need and professional expertise (Ovretveit 1993). Sharing case management responsibility and different professional perspectives (Stroul 1995; Holt 2000) within a team revolves around an unequivocal type of network relationship. Other services are provided by colleagues in close proximity and in-house meetings or case conferences are usually held regularly to devise, monitor and evaluate plans for individual clients. There is mutual involvement across professions and one member usually assumes responsibility as the team leader, monitoring and controlling the work of others in the team. Members of a functional team have clearly defined roles and know what each member can contribute (Ovretveit 1993; Back 1999).

THE QUESTION OF INDIVIDUAL AUTHORITY IN TEAMWORK

Most organisations have a hierarchical structure and the position and perceived status of the case manager dictates their decision-making power and the impact they have on others who make decisions. Having little authority restricts how much difference a case manager can make (Yarmo 1998). Social workers are often not central to decision-making within an organisation (Bar-On 1995), so may engage in more direct client-centred work and fewer planning meetings than, for example, a psychiatrist who leads a mental health team. Their opportunity to influence decisions about service direction or to advocate for a group of clients may be relatively constricted. In other centre settings, the social worker, physiotherapist or nurse practitioner may be employed in more senior positions where they can influence service decisions more effectively. It is important for team members to promote a collective image (Back 1999) and to be seen—particularly by clients—as equal contributors (Ovretveit 1993). Unfortunately, it is quite a challenge in some work cultures for the dissenting voice to be heard. It may not be easy for the mental health nurse or social worker, for example, to assert their point of view if it contradicts that of the psychiatrist or doctor. This can affect the service by suppressing the range of activities, particularly in resource development and advocacy directions.

PRACTICE IMPERATIVE IN TEAMWORK: ABILITY TO INFLUENCE

A practitioner's level of authority within an organisation or as a member of a team has emerged in this discussion as a key variable. A lack of such authority frustrates the management of resources and restricts the extent of the case management role. Again, the imperative for practitioners is to enhance their standing and influence so as to serve their clients more comprehensively.

MONITORING AND COST CONTAINMENT IN MANAGED CARE SETTINGS

Although almost any application of case management assumes a cost-saving function which 'challenges the autonomy and authority' of workers in the health and human services (Weil et al. 1985), there is a distinct category of service approaches where the cost-saving function is omnipresent. Moxley (1997, p. 237) separates market-like frameworks of care—'the management of the economic costs of human services'—in practice terms from other approaches. There are settings in which the instruction to contain service costs within set parameters dictates the manner in which services are organised and delivered (Stroul 1995). The goals of the organisation can be seen to take precedence over individual client goals where what workers do is governed more by bureaucratic than professional imperatives (Braye and Preston-Shoot 1995). The work of case managers in hospitals particularly, as well as those in other outcome-based funding models of care like occupational rehabilitation and employment services, is affected dramatically by the system-dominated nature of the goals. The impact of the organisational context upon the behaviour of case managers is nowhere more obvious than in the area of so-called managed care, which is widely implemented in the United States, predominantly in the health sector. It is a blatant policy that imposes restrictions on nurse case managers in hospitals to control the costs of care to within set parameters. Case managers employed by these organisations act as gatekeepers, limiting unnecessary expenditure and making sure there is little or no deviation from planned care arrangements.

Glettler and Leen (1996) cite three major functions for the community- or clinic-based nurse case manager: interpretation, advocacy and surveillance. These all help the client to access information and make decisions about the best available services. They warn of the danger of compromising these benefits of case management in hospital-based care where the nurse case manager is required to 'serve the institution before the client' (Glettler and Leen 1996, p. 125). Rather than being seen as the providers of care, it is common now for nurses to be called managers of care (Daiski 2000) in both institutional and community contexts, responsible for implementing plans that reflect empirical formulas of response to certain ailments to streamline the care process. The focus is on the problem, not the individual client, and services to those with the same problem are dictated by the same plan. This is difficult for workers trained in—and wanting to offer—personal, individualised attention to clients (Orme and Glastonbury 1993). There is a similar focus on fixed outcomes and measurement in the rehabilitation and employment sectors. Case management of the long-term unemployed and those in occupational rehabilitation programs is often exclusively directed towards a return to work. Funding for employment programs particularly is usually premised upon successful job-finding outcomes which direct worker attention away from the social functioning deficits which beg to be addressed in the most vulnerable, multi-problem client who is unemployed.

Case managers in these roles monitor clients' efforts to get ready for work and control the services for which they are eligible. The number of visits made to a psychologist or physiotherapist in a rehabilitation program is strictly limited and the number of job applications submitted by an unemployed person is carefully monitored. Responsible for the coordination of clients' care in terms of adherence to the care plan, nurses exercise a similar surveillance and control function over service providers and family members (Daiski 2000).

Austin and McClelland (1996) highlight the role conflict for case managers in managed care settings who are trying to function as both a client and a system agent controlling costs; the risk is that the advocacy role is all but excluded by the predominance of this gatekeeping function (Netting 1992; Sunley 1997; Yarmo 1998). Just as in community settings, the position of the case manager in the organisation, or their level of training, affects their capacity to advocate: they can easily be ignored or intimidated by a specialist. The importance of sensitively developing relationships with physicians in order to strengthen the nurse case manager's role has been emphasised by Netting (1999) and it is crucial for others who are confined in system-centred contexts to manipulate their capacity to exert influence over service providers. One way of achieving this is to use information systems to advantage.

INFORMATION MANAGEMENT IN MANAGED CARE SETTINGS

The management of information in these settings has been highlighted by Moxley (1997) as a critical aspect of the work. Both good recording practices and good information systems are required. Efficient maintenance of up-to-date and comprehensive records is dependent upon sophisticated computer systems and how patterns and costs of care are monitored and kept within bounds (Rafferty et al. 1995). The extent of recording required on some systems is often viewed by workers and clients alike as restrictive. It is seen as compromising nurses' expertise and their potential to make clinical decisions for the improved well-being of clients in hospital. Nurses have become most proficient in a range of information management systems and, as we point out later in the book, other professionals have a lot to learn from the way the nursing profession has adapted to the case management role in managed care organisations. Documentation of diagnosis, ongoing recording and outcome monitoring have overtaken some of the other tasks to which nurses were once accustomed. Some professional issues surround this use of nurse time, but it is an unequivocal demand of the organisation to which the profession has adapted. Proficiency in establishing and maintaining good records means there is more time to attend to the neglected aspects of client care. Access to quality information can strengthen any worker's capacity to influence and more properly advocate on behalf of clients for unusual digression from an overly restrictive plan.

PRACTICE IMPERATIVE IN MANAGED CARE SETTINGS:
ABILITY TO INFLUENCE

With so much emphasis placed on surveillance and control through information management, those practitioners who are proficient in the documentation and retrieval of pertinent, focused information can use it to influence service provision. Levels of client autonomy—particularly vulnerable in market-like frameworks—can more effectively be protected by a case manager who uses information systems well and can influence how the organisation treats the clients.

MONITORING AND SURVEILLANCE IN SOCIAL CONTROL SETTINGS

Another work context where the case managers are agents of the system rather than working primarily in a social support capacity for their clients is the area of social control, where it is argued that society is the client (Holt 2000) and the work is the management of those deemed 'undesirable' (Moxley 1997). Falling into this category is work in institutional settings such as prisons or centres and lock-up facilities for the seriously demented or mentally ill who are perceived by society as a threat. To varying degrees in the countries to which people flee from persecution and oppression, asylum seekers are seen as a threat and removed from society so their prospective case management would also fall into this category of social control. The predominant goal is to protect society. Even when placed in community settings, on parole or in structured group homes, the main emphasis is on controlling client behaviour and keeping it within certain limits set by society, as in work with the homeless, the drug-addicted and others who threaten and offend society at large.

Particularly challenging is the almost inevitable conflict that arises for case managers who are accountable to the community for the compliance of their clients whilst trying to develop constructive relationships with them premised on the fundamental human service principles of self-determination and empowerment. The surveillance or monitoring component of the work is a priority and this does contaminate the relationship between worker and client and affect the extent to which other aspects can be achieved. Custodial officers who are used as case managers in prisons and expected to develop trusting relationships with individual prisoners are meant to achieve stronger involvement of the prisoners in decision-making and planning (McCallum and Furby 1999). Although some improvement in prison culture can result from more supportive relationships (Howells et al. 1999), it is unrealistic to expect more from the officers in a setting where their custodial capacity precludes the development of trust and the 'us against them' culture is firmly entrenched. Measures to track prisoners' progress are often quite indiscriminate in terms of their individual response to services and programs: merely their compliance and attendance at an anger management and/or drug education program are the outcomes that are measured. This has quite a debilitating effect on any aspirations for individualised service delivery.

Again, their position in the organisation and level of both felt and perceived authority is a factor in the frustration of some case managers trying to achieve more active participation from their clients in a social control milieu. As front-line workers, their involvement in decision-making and policy planning is often minimal or non-existent, and they are not handed the means to achieve anything that looks like a case management role. Even when case managers operating in institutional and community support settings ostensibly have more influence over service providers, they can still find it very difficult to achieve services for clients with problems that are perceived as notoriously difficult to manage and change. They are considered a poor risk in terms of outcomes to which the services are geared.

ADVOCACY IN SOCIAL CONTROL SETTINGS

To be influential in these settings, case managers need to be charged with the capacity to respond assertively to the needs of the homeless, the mentally ill, the criminal and Indigenous client groups. In many social control settings, the case management role begs reconstruction. The vestment of authority is essential to achieve more and different things and to advocate more successfully, or at all. Work should be directed purposefully towards building ability in the client group, collectively and individually, to speak for themselves and to be seen as more able. The cultivation of a more benevolent and optimistic attitude in the community and in industry settings, rather than focusing on relationships with individual clients, would diminish the role conflict inherent in working with Moxley's 'undesirables' (Moxley 1997).

Again, advocacy is the critical component, directly dependent upon the ability to influence and exert authority.

The ability to exert influence to improve client experience and outcomes in social control settings has emerged from different priorities. Suppression of the case management role in social control contexts needs to be countered to make advocacy viable. Workers in these settings must make a concerted effort to change how their roles are configured so as to play a more expansive part in their clients' care.

PRACTICE DIRECTED TO INCREASE CONSUMER CONTROL

Strictly speaking, there should be no limitations to the settings in which consumer-directed practice can be effected, although there are clients in some settings with whom the fostering of independence is not viable. When embarking on a course to enhance consumer control, the consumer–worker team operates strategically to counter an habitual service culture. Novel—almost radical—practice directions are triggered by contemplation of this component of case management.

This practice direction is viewed with optimism as a potential answer to some of the tensions and dilemmas surrounding current practice in most settings (Moxley 1997). It is an attractive, ideologically sound notion to foster independence in consumers by investing them with responsibility for their own care. For reasons such as practitioner hesitation to relinquish control, lack of opportunity and under-estimation of the role of advocacy, much current practice does not allow the involvement of consumers to the extent that is both possible and desirable (Stanley 1999). Dependence is increased in elderly clients when security and safety concerns prevail over attention to their levels of autonomy (Kunkel et al. 2000) and paternalistic attitudes curtail opportunities for those with physical disabilities to control their own care and live more independently (Tower 1994). The fundamental goal in consumer-directed practice is to make provision for consumers to control as fully as possible the planning and execution of their care. Achieving active participation on the part of consumers and their carers requires a fundamental shift in practice orientation: the case manager engages in different activities rather than gradually disengaging from responsibility. These decisions are based on an individualised service response to the client system which is in turn based on extensive assessment and collaboration. The delegation of responsibility is tailored to suit and sensitively managed. Workers aim to relinquish control and find the right balance between autonomy and risk for consumers.

EDUCATION, TRAINING AND CONSULTATION TO ENHANCE CONSUMER CONTROL

More articulate and confident clients and carers exercise choice more actively than those who are uncertain (Stanley 1999) and one of the two biggest challenges is to involve those more passive clients who resist getting involved and do not readily assume responsibility. Although the term 'consumer' is ubiquitously applied to represent any user of services, the distinction between users and consumers is made in this context on the basis of client involvement in the planning process (Stanley 1999; Kunkel et al. 2000). A key practice feature in the transformation of users to consumers is the preparation of the client system in terms of education, training and consultation (Friss 1993). The case manager is a resource, providing sufficient information about services to enable the client and their family, carers and others to decide how to use them to their best advantage. The proficiency of family members or informal carers who assume a case management role relates to proper training and opportunities to consult with a designated worker (Weil et al. 1985). Tower (1994, p. 195) links increased consumer autonomy with the ability of the worker to be a role model, advocating, teaching and coaching. Training goals should be articulated, linked to service goals and directed to the right people in the client's support network. Receptivity from the client system is reliant upon the development of a trusting and ongoing relationship with the case manager, not necessarily intense but definitively based on mutual trust, respect and the perception of the case manager as professional, impartial and knowledgeable.

Consumer-directed work evolves into an advocacy role when associated systems and service providers are resistant or prevent consumers from functioning as independent entities. The skills involved in development of the client system as an independent, whole unit are relatively sophisticated (it is usually easier to do it yourself than get others to do it), which may account for some worker resistance to this style of service delivery.

AVAILABILITY OF THE CASE MANAGER IN CONSUMER-DIRECTED PRACTICE

When families assume the case management role, their access to information about the services and options available to them has to be continuous (Woodside and McClam 1998) and they need ready access to unusual assistance from the case manager when there is a crisis. This relies heavily upon the availability of a very well-organised case manager who is deliberately, systematically relinquishing responsibility whilst maintaining accountability for the client system. The agency, of course, is responsible for ensuring that its case managers are at liberty to operate in this way. Consultation can be extensive and the onus is on the case manager to structure regular meetings and be available to talk, advise, help and step in when needed. Organisational and time management skills, plus the ability to work independently, are attributes that accompany this role. An elusive case manager cannot be a reputable consumer-directed practitioner.

DEVELOPMENT OF CONSUMER CONTROL IN DIVERSE SETTINGS

Limitations based on client capacity and potential for control are more relevant and beg definition to indicate responsiveness to this kind of intervention. The skills of the case manager are clearly tested when trying to work with those who have less resources and less functional levels of autonomy. O'Donnell et al. (1999) promote the use of consumer advocates to improve outcomes in terms of increased collaboration and participation in their care for mental health clients in the community. This strategy requires case manager time—more preparation time with individual clients and more time to train and develop consumer advocates. The other major challenge is to work alongside the more feisty consumers whose energy and commitment to their involvement need to be channelled and directed productively. Consumers such as adults with physical disabilities, the families of children with behavioural and physical disabilities and increasingly the aged can be impassioned about services and become vocal and politically active in bids to improve their circumstances. The case manager's imperative to inform, advise, support and encourage can be enacted with groups of consumers, at public meetings as well as with individual systems. The strong advocacy component can take many forms, especially in the manipulation of responses and reactions from service providers. Acting for groups of consumers with similar interests can take the case manager into corporate meetings and those conducted at various levels of government agencies.

ADVOCACY IN CONSUMER-DIRECTED PRACTICE

The concepts of advocacy and empowerment underpin approaches to enhance consumer control (O'Donnell et al. 1999), and Hyduck and Moxley (2000) highlight the practice challenge in their recognition of the need for advocacy in the context of work with older adults in the United States that seeks to empower the service user. A concerted focus on advocacy as a means to enable consumers to manage their own care more effectively, by improving how others communicate with and about the client, and to diminish barriers to the entrustment of responsibility is indicated. Effective advocacy is dependent upon a number of interweaving factors like authority and networking proficiency which dictate the level at which it can be pursued. Although advocacy is perceived as a critical component of all case management practice, it is recognised that oppressive contextual demands constantly narrow its application (Morales 1994; Rothman and Sager 1998). Stanley's (1999) observation of the lack of support for advocacy work in the United Kingdom reflects its general neglect in case management programs. The potential for consumer-directed applications to realise better outcomes is dependent upon organisational support and indisputably tied up with the development of more comprehensive, ambitious advocacy practice. Moxley (1997) emphasises how different advocacy needs to be to facilitate consumer control. Creativity is needed to draw on opportunities and ideas from the diversity of situations in which consumer-directed practitioners are engaged.

PRACTICE IMPERATIVE: CREATIVITY

It seems safe to conclude that a consumer-directed service approach releases the case manager from some organisational restraints, leaving more room for innovative practice. Moxley's (1997) optimism for the future of consumer-directed practice seems more realistic when creativity and innovation are factored into the process. Practitioners will have to think divergently to enact truly different models of advocacy–empowerment-based practice in this area of work. It is salutary to remind ourselves of the risk to consumers of responsibility being abdicated by the state in handing the problem back to them. Despite the rhetoric of strengths perspectives and client empowerment, it is relatively rare in today's case management world to find consumers being supported to more effectively manage their own situations. Progressive practitioners see consumers as the 'greatest resource' (Tower 1994, p. 191) for development. Consumers do currently have untapped potential and collective reservoirs of insight and strength, the realisation of which depends on a style of case management that manifests creative advocacy.

REFLECTION ON KEY PRACTICE DIMENSIONS

We have highlighted characteristic practice dimensions applied to particular settings which have led to a fallout of practice imperatives. As imperatives, they can be accepted as cornerstones of practice models developed to meet specific needs in specific contexts. It is crucial to develop programs of case management differentially 'to suit different user group needs' (Welch 1998, p. 23), adaptive to 'the existing culture and resources of the community' (Peterson et al. 1997, p. 249). Case management effectiveness is absolutely contingent upon role clarity (Conti 1999). The discussion in this chapter has led to a focus on the aspects of the process that are most pertinent and should be uppermost in the minds of those planning practice directions.

To an impressively large degree, each of the imperatives converges to a focus on worker authority and capacity to influence. Reflection on this critical dimension of practice continues in the next chapter, where we discuss some of the ethical dilemmas confronting case managers.

6

CRITICAL PRACTICE QUESTIONS AND ETHICAL DECISION-MAKING

The tensions associated with balancing incompatible needs and catering for the well-being of disparate parties with conflicting interests are inherent in health and human service work. There are few easy, one-dimensional problems to deal with in the management of people's lives. Professional judgment is required to arrive at the best solution or compromise position. Individual workers apply different reasoning in the decisions they make (Rothman 1998), based on their own values and attitudes. Critical reasoning skills are needed to manage the tensions and work through the issues that surround decisions to improve the health and social functioning of clients. Judgments are made in the context of a range of widely accepted human service practice principles and values about people and how they should be treated. These are reflected in various similar codes of practice that emphasise notions of acceptance, equality, justice, empowerment, self-determination and an holistic, environmental focus. In practice, most—if not all—of these principles have an ethical dimension (Loewenberg et al. 2000), which makes practice decisions so complex. Unless viewed flexibly, they can contort sensible decision-making. Assiduously avoiding client dependence, for instance, can impede client growth and development (Marschke and Freedberg 1997). As Trevithick (2000) reiterates, judgment can be clouded by fears of being judgmental and it is certainly confounded in practice by the idealism of a too fundamental or too literal commitment to the practice principles. Quite often, the pressure to arrive at decisions is unnecessarily conceived as a dilemma and described as problematic because of this lack of readiness to apply principles differentially.

It is up to individual workers to interpret and adapt the principles to their practice situations in a way that establishes a functional level of compromise. Dysfunction would be seen as either a clinging to the principles too slavishly and impeding progress, or disregarding them with consequent feelings of betrayal to themselves and clients. It is a worker's responsibility to establish that functional level of compromise, to analyse their situation and think carefully about what is the right balance for work with the clients in that setting. Operating within clearly defined parameters of acceptable work predicaments allows practitioners to isolate real dilemmas (those that are substantially ethical in nature and require rigorous analysis) more easily from routine practice decisions.

A DIFFERENT ETHICAL THRESHOLD FOR CASE MANAGEMENT

Decisions that occur in practice where professional judgment is applied as a matter of course and those provoked by a clash of values are sometimes hard to differentiate. The threshold separating them has to vary across different practice orientations. The pressures of the economic and contextual constraints that characterise case management approaches suggest that practitioners do have to define and adopt an ethical threshold that reflects the reality of the situation. Execution of judicious decisions can readily transform expected practice decisions into real dilemmas unless the diminished threshold of what is acceptable in terms of principled practice is clearly defined. It is not situational ethics that are being argued here but the application of a reasoning process to discern violations of an ethical stance from those that merely reflect the complexity of practice. Buffeted by competing demands, the overtaxed practitioner can misconstrue operational complexity and its origins. The counterperspective, espoused by Dominelli (1997), is that operational simplicity provokes misinterpretation of dilemmas. She argues that ethical considerations are being suppressed in increasingly bureaucratic procedures, leading case managers who have limited roles to 'technicalise' big problems (Dominelli 1997, p. 118). Both perspectives raise serious questions about how problems are conceived and analysed from an ethical perspective. Nurius et al.

Figure 6.1   Configuration of practice tasks and principles that create recurring dilemmas

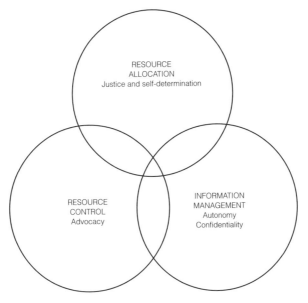

(1999, p. 13) declare that sound reasoning is dependent on 'the ability to recognize the signs of high-risk or problematic scenarios'. Refinement of the ethical threshold to elucidate practice dilemmas is crucial. The task now is to consider triggers to the dilemmas encountered by case managers and to present some strategies to contain them.

PERSISTENT PRACTICE DILEMMAS FOR THE CASE MANAGER

Provoked by the premises upon which case management is based, some themes central to practice dilemmas emerge. Addressed in various combinations in the literature, dilemmas are embroiled in issues surrounding the promotion of justice for clients, their autonomy, and their rights to privacy and advocacy (Kane 1992; Kane and Thomas 1993; Sheppard 1995; Rapp and Kisthardt 1996; Woodside and McClam 1998; Holt 2000). Decisions about how to acquire, distribute and control resources and manage information are governed—and usually confounded—by a practice orientation that upholds these principles.

The tasks and principles intertwine and affect all case managers in various combinations. Particular contextual pressures and priorities create different manifestations across practice settings, so it is a bit of a minefield to traverse for practice clarity. The configuration adopted in Figure 6.1 reflects some quite potent combinations, useful for illustrative purposes.

RESOURCE ALLOCATION IN CLIENT-CENTRED APPROACHES

Many crucial dilemmas that confront case managers in community-based, client-centred contexts hover around the concepts of fairness and equality when there are not enough resources to go around. Two themes emerge in discussions about the most pressing issues in relation to resource allocation. First, decisions about the allocation of services—the 'what, how much, for how long and from whom' questions fielded by Austin and McClelland (1996)—can be vexing for a practitioner striving to achieve justice for all. Second, decisions about consumer control and choice in a service environment of limited resources and unlimited need (Hugman 1991) fly constantly in the face of generalised client empowerment and self-determination principles (Sheppard 1995).

FAIRNESS AND CLIENT CONTROL IN A CONTROLLING SYSTEM OF CARE

Fairness is an elusive concept in a system that is perceived as fundamentally unfair by consumers dissatisfied with what they get and by case managers struggling with inadequate resources. In taking a dual focus on fairness to both clients and agency providers, Storl et al. (1999) find it the most challenging of the core practice principles for case managers. Judgments about the equitable, efficient and effective distribution of resources are based on an ethical decision-making process (Davies 1992) to identify what is essentially the best compromise position. Reamer (1998, p. 296) speculates on what criteria should be used to allocate limited resources and achieve 'distributive justice'. Everyday decisions about service provision can become very taxing when diverse perspectives impinge and the 'ism territory' (paternalism, ageism, sexism, etc.) is circumvented in the struggle to be fair.

The concept of client autonomy is intimately linked to that of fairness. Should workers target those clients who can be encouraged to take more control when this would mean neglect of others? Do not workers have to keep a tight rein on how much they involve clients in decision-making when there is little or no chance of client preferences being accommodated? Should workers support clients to take risks when that support is time-consuming? These are tricky questions. Front-line workers who are willing to assume some discriminatory power and embrace decisions to be made about how to allot their time wrestle with them. It is tempting to treat people as equally deserving, and not to discriminate in terms of potential for more autonomous function; and for some case managers, the pressure to take this route of providing basic services to all is insidious. Unequal distribution of resources can be viewed as the neglect of some clients in preference of others, so workers may opt for the conservative, middle road to avoid recrimination and treat all clients uniformly, suppressing any urge to distinguish merit. Martin et al. (1998) found that resource-starved case managers make a limited range of recommendations for children entering state custody in the United States, based on insufficient assessments. Sheppard (1995) highlights the associated tendency of workers facing complex situations to typecast people and selectively attend to predictable problems and situations that fall within familiar, established categories. Dominelli (1997) reinforces this point in bemoaning the loss of an holistic focus when care is packaged for delivery. As controlling tactics, they are all antithetical to notions of self-determination and consumer choice (Sheppard 1995). Lack of attention to idiosyncratic issues suppresses variety and potency of the service response. Although such blandness minimises certain dilemmas, it does raise others to do with client and worker potential.

It cannot be denied that some clients would blossom given the concerted attention of their case manager and access to an unusual range of services. It is also probably true that most case managers are able to identify whom amongst their clients would reap most benefit from preferential treatment. In most cases, it is likely that the benefit could be articulated in terms of increases in the client's support system and levels of control over their lives. To deny these clients the service commitment to realise such benefits can be seen at least as inefficient and at most as immoral, fuelling the argument to support active discrimination and targeting of those clients with most potential (Enos and Southern 1996).

Concomitantly, worker potential is suppressed in approaches characterised by a conservative orientation to flat, relatively equal distribution of resources. Dominelli (1997) uses the example of case managers who monitor the delivery of packaged care services as having little influence over the allocation of resources, becoming unconnected from individual clients about whom they have sparse detailed knowledge. The range of activities engaged in becomes limited—often to mostly brokerage tasks—while the more sophisticated activities, such as advocacy and development of resources, remain virtually untouched. There is an impact too on the extent to which the core functions are carried out: assessment, planning, implementing and evaluation are curtailed to fit the orientation so the worker's development in these areas is thwarted. It is not a big step to presume that the repetitive nature of this approach, which limits the range and depth of the case management task, leads to a loss of vitality and interest in the work. This creates dilemmas about professional identity and usefulness.

GUIDELINES TO DIMINISH DILEMMAS ABOUT FAIRNESS

Dealing with circuitous fairness dilemmas requires resolute effort to diminish the constraints imposed on practice activities. Practitioners themselves need to pursue an 'autonomous work style' that characterises the more 'entrepreneurial' practitioner (Raiff and Shore 1993, p. 25). Three ways come to mind for the practitioner to build a base from which to exercise more autonomy and become less susceptible to doubt and confusion.

Communication

First and most simply, workers must act on their responsibility to inform clients about the service restrictions they will encounter. Initial discussions with clients should, as a matter of protocol, include information about the state of play in relation to resource availability and access to their case manager. To have realistic expectations, clients need to know about the parameters of the exchange (Moxley 1996). Not only does this alleviate the anxiety and disappointment of unmet expectations for the clients, it also releases the case manager from stultifying levels of obligation that uninformed clients may impose. Clients with an awareness of the extent to which case management resources are stretched may demand less or make different, less oner-ous demands, or they may undertake more responsibility themselves. On a cautionary note, attempts to inform clients constructively in this way can easily deteriorate into complaint, system bashing and expres-sions of cynicism which are counter-productive. Workers, however disenchanted, should strive to inform clients objectively because it is their right to be given the facts of the situation rather than having their sympathy solicited. This latter ploy would contravene ethical practice.

Competence

The second way for practitioners to decrease the pressure is to pursue explicit and transparent practice with individual clients. Davies (1992) emphasises that precision in practice technology will enable practition-ers to pinpoint and define practice dilemmas more clearly. Sonntag (1995, p. 130) says simply that 'good listening and good understanding and a knowledge of the resources available' can help to protect client rights. If we know what we are doing and why we are doing it, then it is more likely that we will exercise good judgment and negotiate difficulties with impunity. Many of the dilemmas raised by the issues surrounding resource allocation can be addressed by improvements in practice technique, specifically in the formulation of individual client goals. An absolute priority is to link activities to discrete goals that form the basis of a plan set in place for a client (Rapp and Kisthardt 1996). Emboldened by a clarity of focus, workers are able to justify the decisions they make about how they will spend their time and distribute resources. As we emphasised in the earlier elaboration of the planning stage, action plans must be individually based, up-to-date, well documented and relevant. Confidence exudes from workers imple-menting an astute, coherent, logical and dynamic plan of action: they are able to justify their actions in concrete terms of what is to be achieved. Able to be quite categorical in relation to client goals and their associated activities, practitioners can exercise more independence of judgment with service providers and those from whom they seek assistance. If there is a lack of individual attention to clients in a regime of generalised, impersonal planning, it is much more difficult to discriminate need and resource allocation. Hence more ethical dilem-mas about resource distribution arise.

Organisational support

The third strategy is perhaps the most difficult because it depends upon the response from those who manage the agency context. Practitioners have to understand the implications created by the limitations of choice (Hugman 1991) and seek to develop strategies to accommodate them. These can only be developed from a position of knowledge and security. Practitioners need 'organizational guidance' to assume decision-making responsibility with clients (Holt 2000, p. 119) and resist working in an environment where policies that relate to contentious issues like confidentiality, service allocation and rights to self-determination are unclear (McClelland 1998). It is the responsibility of case managers to raise these questions of policy conscientiously, creating more awareness of the ramifications and seeking clear practice guidelines. Their responsibility is to influence the development of these as much as possible by ensuring that the principles they are struggling with are understood, that the client perspective is maintained and that decisions remain pragmatic.

The message in these three strategies is plain. Competent practice is intrinsically linked to the scale of ethical issues (Kane and Caplan 1993). Persistent practice dilemmas can be rendered less onerous by skilled practice and application of critical thinking.

THE QUESTION OF CLIENT AUTONOMY IN SYSTEM-DRIVEN APPROACHES

Referring to social care, Braye and Preston-Shoot (1995) discuss the dilemma for the practitioner operating from a traditional value base in contexts in which the prevailing language is of economy and value for money; and Reamer (1998) questions whether social workers can continue to practise ethically under significant cost constraints. The complexity and stress induced by cost containment must compromise effective case manager decision-making, as Nurius et al. (1999) suggest. They make the point too that the undermining of decision-making is increasingly expected in these practice environments—in this instance, in managed care environments in the United States (Nurius et al. 1999)—adding to the pressure on social workers. Current practice environments are not conducive to the exercise of sound reasoning by case managers.

The inference that care paths and plans in health care settings can easily override the clinical judgment of nurses is explicit in Daiski's (2000) analysis, while Storl et al. (1999) highlight the inherent difficulties for the case manager trying to strike a balance between clients' social welfare needs and medical treatments. The parallel balance when dealing with involuntary clients is finding the fulcrum that maintains discipline over client behaviour and transfers a level of responsibility they can handle (Enos and Southern 1996; Trotter 1999). At issue is the concept of client autonomy, both in the control of involuntary clients to protect society and in the treatment of health and social care clients in contexts grounded in decisions made by a parsimonious organisation. In their comparison of three decision-making models, Barnet and Taylor (1999, p. 332) opt for 'enhanced autonomy' over 'strong paternalism' and 'independent choice' models of case management in health care settings. Although not unique to managed care settings (Agich and Forster 2000), the question of autonomy here is somewhat different to the question of self-determination in community-based, client-centred approaches and the pressures on the case managers are different—or should be! Storl et al.'s (1999, p. 164) definition of the principle of autonomy rests partly on the notion of informed consent, of the client being 'neither manipulated nor coerced into making a given decision'. This is a quite murky area, especially in system-centred contexts where clients are more blatantly manipulated, and sometimes coerced to conform to prescribed treatment plans. The process of professional judgment taxes alternative priorities. The question being posed by workers is how much authority to exert over the behaviour of individual clients in order to ensure their safety and security, and that of others. Of course, these dilemmas confront case managers in every context. Sonntag (1995) illustrates the ethical conundrum for the community-based worker in deciding whether a client should be kept in hospital or released home to care for an abusive son with mental health problems. The client self-determination versus social control questions are brought sharply into focus. Arriving at an answer involves sound reasoning in identifying an ethical stance and assessing risk, and acceptance of 'the bottom line' of what is possible in that environment. These are uncomfortable decisions for the practitioner grounded in a culture of reverence for the notion of client self-determination.

ORGANISATIONAL SUPPORT TO DIMINISH DILEMMAS ABOUT
CLIENT AUTONOMY

Case managers can be forgiven for feeling scrutinised and monitored in business-oriented systems of care where care paths and rigid plans preside. As Gambrill (1990) suggests, it is characteristic that minimal attention is directed to the quality of their clinical decisions, or that they are valued. Nurius et al. (1999) call for the development of practice cultures that support rather than impede sound practice reasoning. If the demise of effective decision-making in case management contexts is accepted, then encouragement is needed for practitioners to exercise professional discretion. Storl et al. (1999) call for guidelines in health care settings to help case managers balance how to protect clients in care planning and foster autonomy by involving them in decision-making. Clarity about what the limits are, what is absolutely not negotiable and what can be manipulated to benefit a client is essential (Trotter 1999). Too hard or too soft a line taken by a case manager can create ethical dilemmas and be perceived as harsh, risky or idealistic. It is only worth pushing these limits if there is some chance of success and organisational support is needed to try.

THE DILEMMA OF CONFIDENTIALITY

Poor interpretation of the principle of confidentiality is responsible for many practice decisions that retard progress of treatment and plans in health and human service work. Confidentiality is often unwisely applied in quite heavy-handed ways to protect client privacy with debilitating consequences when access to information is denied those who need it to contribute their services and support. Care has to be taken, of course (Holt 2000), but Kane (1993, p. 157) warns against hiding behind 'a cloak of client confidentiality' to avoid accountability. A penchant for smothering debate or perhaps avoiding hard decisions can be suspected of practitioners who apply such a cloak indiscriminately. The dissection and integration of pertinent bits of information from a mass can be most influential and of great potential value to further a client's cause. Every practice situation requires critical analysis to decide how to discipline and manipulate the flow of client information most appropriately. For the case manager negotiating within a wide network of interested parties, the 'who needs to know', 'what do they need to know' and 'how to transfer it' questions can be onerous. Rothman and Sager (1998, p. 158) indicate how hard it is for the case manager who is 'the conduit of information to the client's whole network', especially when informal or volunteer workers are involved. Commonly, lack of analysis and understanding of confidentiality confound the process and its blanket use triggers unfounded dilemmas.

Implementation of confidentiality relates to the notion of authority. With clients in health settings and with involuntary clients in social care and control settings, the degree of confidentiality of the client–worker relationship is relatively shallow and often clumsily handled. Restrictions are imposed upon what is able to be kept private: any information of potential harm or threat to either the client or to others must be divulged. As we shall see later in the book, duty to report is not always unambiguous. Ethical dilemmas are easily provoked when the necessity to report restricts the relationship which otherwise would be a lot more therapeutic and beneficial to the client. The worker must mete out strict conditions and behave authoritatively to ensure that the limits remain steadfastly imposed.

Dilemmas also occur when a worker knows that to reveal a lot of information about a client's situation—not all of which is useful or needed by the service provider being solicited—will be influential in securing a service. For instance, securing subsidised housing for a woman and four children fleeing violence often entails disclosure of a range of personal details. The intent is to push the client's case ahead of others by escalating the perception of trauma and need. Clients can experience this as demeaning and are left more vulnerable by the revelations which they fear may be used to their disadvantage in the future. The dilemma that should confront the worker in this situation is how to balance the dual forces of a client's rights to privacy and their entitlement to better services (Glastonbury 1997). A worker with more authority to do so could influence the service provider in ways that do not contravene client privacy.

Contrarily, dilemmas arise for the worker from pressure not to release information which is pertinent. Take the worker trying to achieve supported accommodation in a boarding house for a client with mental health problems, just released from prison, with a poor track record of living amicably in the community. To reveal all in the referral process leads to refusal of accommodation, given the scarcity of available places. Proprietors with a vacancy will opt for the least risky boarder. The worker is faced with the dilemma of deciding whose interests to promote—the client's or the proprietor's—in the selection of which information to withhold. Essentially, this is a battle between the client's right to privacy and the proprietor's right to the information. Or take the nurse case manager trying to arrange the release from hospital of an obese, middle-aged stroke patient. In trying to instil confidence in the patient's wife in her ability to provide care at home, that nurse may well be tempted to withhold specific information about the patient's night-time bladder incontinence or aggressive refusal to get out of bed. Is this misconstrued or distorted confidentiality? Both the proprietor and the wife are misled by being given insufficient information.

ORGANISATIONAL AUTHORITY TO MANAGE CONFIDENTIALITY PARAMETERS

The professional judgment that comes into play in situations such as these relies on complex factors, and decisions are compounded by levels of desperation felt by workers making last-ditch efforts to find resources for 'undesirable' clients. Poor levels of accountability and limited authority may influence workers to move towards easier options; positions of authority within organisations enable practitioners to embrace more complex options. With clear procedures and lines of accountability and with the authority to influence proprietors and other service providers to accept clients who are seen as notoriously difficult, the dilemmas are less debilitating for case managers. Steyaert (1996) observes that individual autonomy and professional judgment are being eroded in current systems of service delivery, particularly in the way technology is implemented to benefit managers rather than practitioners.

INFORMATION TECHNOLOGY AND CONFIDENTIALITY

Despite persistent questions about the control of paper files and records (Steyaert et al. 1996), the use of computers to store and retrieve information is commonly viewed with even more distrust. 'Confidentiality used to be set within an environment of restrained disclosure but now is lost in a culture of information processing', writes Davidson (1998, p. 291) of managed care settings. Computers are now indispensable (Siefker et al. 1998; Nurius et al. 1999), but their advent has created a minefield, real or not, for workers concerned about controlling client information. The implications of client access to records is one factor. With access to electronic information more readily available to more people, the risk to client privacy and the potential for the misuse of information are greater (Hawkins et al. 1998). The ultimate quality care versus cost containment dilemma is reflected in the juggling of the requirement to store information that is necessary to ensure cost-effective, well-targeted services (Glastonbury 1997) and the need to minimise the potential for that information to be misused. Placing some types of information into a networked computer system can be perceived as direct contravention of the principle of confidentiality in the client–worker relationship. Although new systems claim better security and access provisions, and Hawkins et al.'s (1998, p. 176) rather alarming picture of 'an Orwellian scenario of control over personal choice' can be tempered, the control of privacy is nevertheless of concern to workers in some settings.

The suspicion that information is used most expediently for the organisation, rather than most beneficially for the client (Davidson and Davidson 1998), only exacerbates this concern. Information can be distorted at the point of entry (Glastonbury 1997) by the use of poorly structured tools and by workers keen to influence decisions, and distorted at the point of access to manipulate responses from those who bestow services. Coupled with the inflexibility of computers, which forces information into categories, this sort of 'massaging' of the data (Glastonbury 1997) has led to a lack of trust in computer information. It is seen as quite sterile.

Of concern, too, is the fact that many information systems are cumbersome and time-consuming to use, frustrating workers who think it is so much more important to spend the time interacting with and working directly for the client. Some systems are out of date, rendering information quite redundant. In the face of sophisticated developments in information technology, workers may feel vulnerable to what Dominelli (1997, p. 119) calls 'managerialist surveillance', and resent the time spent in front of a screen instead of with a client. The attitude of many workers to the process of recording can be defensive and/or dismissive, affecting both accuracy and diligence. On the other hand, some nurses are 'literally buried in paper' (Back 1999, p. 211) where more sensible use of technology could significantly reduce their recording time. There are some very real frustrations triggered by concerns about the availability and friendliness of computer technology. Ethical dilemmas are provoked when it is perceived that technology, or its lack, impedes the provision of good service.

GUIDELINES TO DIMINISH DILEMMAS ABOUT CONFIDENTIALITY

Management of verbal information: communication

To establish and maintain effective confidentiality parameters, frequent, direct discussions with clients about the confidentiality boundaries are important. Practitioners must communicate to a client when what they are saying contravenes the established boundaries with minimal disruption to the relationship and be very clear about the type of information that cannot be kept private. The ability to discriminate what has to be passed on and what need not is essential (Enos and Southern 1996; Trotter 1999). Nurses and custodial officers need particular skills to elicit information from a client who is threatening disruption or suicide and use professional judgment to discern the seriousness and worth of the threat in terms of how and to whom to report it. Decisions made about revelation of information must, of course, be communicated to the client as constructively and directly as possible.

Ethical communication is fundamental to the achievement of potential in relation to client autonomy and the preservation of confidentiality (Barnet and Taylor 1999). It is salutary to note Nurius et al.'s (1999) finding that workers are not actively involving clients in decision-making, the implication being that this is partly due to the increased 'technicalisation' of service delivery. Perhaps the relationship with their computers distracts workers to some extent from that with their clients! Clients who are informed about the context in which decisions are made, and who are privy to ongoing information from the worker about the pressures that are being brought to bear, are more actively involved in those decisions. This involvement effectively reduces the dilemmas and enhances the level of responsibility assumed by the client for the decisions made. An informed, involved client is more autonomous.

Management of documented information: competence

The standard of documentation and record-keeping procedures is critical to the notion of privacy, so workers are required to become competent and confident about their own use of information technology resources. Nurius et al. (1999, p. 16) emphasise how easy it is for information technology to confound reasoning and decision-making when systems are flawed and when 'workers . . . do not know how to critique and remedy the limitations of their information systems'. As well as being the base for decisions related to client care, accurate, comprehensive records of events, decisions and actions provide evidence or backing for aspects of a person's care that are in dispute (Aiken and Aucoin 1998). Callahan (1998) acknowledges the closer scrutiny of practice in managed care environments that the emphasis on documentation allows. Training and development in the formulation of action plans and in the maintenance of efficient running records are a top priority. Regular audits keep workers on their toes and development of structured documents or pro formas encourages efficiency of information entry and access. Workers should be actively engaged in the design and maintenance of appropriate methods to collect, store, retrieve and share information (Storl et al. 1999) that accommodate as far as is practicable the need to preserve client privacy and the client–worker relationship. Very clear guidelines about client access to filed information and their full awareness of how information is to be used are reflected in procedures that evidence accountability. Attention to these aspects would eliminate many of the actual difficulties encountered by workers and clear the way for recognition of critical dilemmas when and if they arise.

INFORMATION TECHNOLOGY AND ORGANISATIONAL SUPPORT

The process of reducing the extent of the ethical dilemmas associated with recording client information on computers involves two distinct tasks. First, it is essential for workers to reach a decision about best practice in terms of content and dissemination of information. This involves an analytical process—gathering the information needed to assess the situation, identifying the principles in question, determining what can be done and the consequences—in order to reach a decision. This needs to accommodate full knowledge and acceptance of workers' role as agents of the system in order to avoid idealism and impracticality. Every worker should know why information is collected and how it is used (Kane et al. 2000), and keep apace of developments in information technology which change how information and knowledge are affected (Belson 2000). Nurius (1995, p. 109) forecasts a trend for computers to be used more as 'a medium of thought and expression' in the human services, which would require reorientation and retraining. It is only with full awareness and computer literacy that decisions about appropriateness can be made. Second, advocating for change in data management is the worker's responsibility in order to address the imperative of client confidentiality (Davidson and Davidson 1998) and to diminish other dilemmas triggered by the use of information technology.

ADVOCACY AND CONSUMER CONTROL OF RESOURCES

A number of critical issues come into play when considering the rights of individual consumers to exert control over their care and manage their own resources. Previously we drew a distinction between those consumers with sufficient supports and the ability to articulate what they want, and those with less capacity to influence and fewer emotional and physical supports. Presuming a workload that precludes the ideal situation of being able to provide optimum service to everyone, how does the case manager decide who to support and advocate for to bring about maximum independence? Both activities require dedication and ongoing support—albeit support of a different nature. The ultimate dilemma, then, is the same fundamental decision about who receives the service and who does not. Essentially, the ethical dilemmas stem from incompatibility of core principles and the struggle to make decisions that bear allegiance to fairness and autonomy.

GUIDELINES TO DIMINISH DILEMMAS ABOUT ADVOCACY

The guidelines to alleviate anxiety about equitable distribution of resources that were suggested in our discussion of client-centred approaches apply here and need not be repeated. The requirement for the practitioner to arrive at a judgment about individual claims to service based on clearly established criteria highlights the skills of assessment and advocacy directed to encourage resource control in clients.

ASSESSING POTENTIAL

It is perhaps comparatively easy to decide the relative merits of individual clients in terms of their potential to control their own service provision when the pool of candidates is carefully selected. Proficient intake mechanisms ensure relevancy and subsequent assessment should address very specific criteria to preclude digression from the focus. Difficulties and inequities in allocation of service are significantly reduced by imposition of considered and sophisticated procedures. The development of protocols that focus on the ingredients needed for services exclusively geared to enhance consumer control over services is paramount.

BECOMING A COMPETENT ADVOCATE

Previously we established that advocacy is not practised sufficiently in nearly all case management contexts. Along with resource development, it is a neglected component of practice. It is indisputable that all clients would benefit from attention directed to redress inequities and discrimination in service availability and provision. Equally, it is indisputable that all case managers should be alert and responsive to opportunities to prevent paternalistic practice and increase client autonomy. These are triggers for the practice of advocacy, but for many workers their practice is inhibited by the boundaries of their work context (Tower 1994). The type of advocacy needed to encourage independence and control in consumers is different, as we have seen. It can be described as specialised. Sonntag's (1995) comment that case managers have the opportunity to operate uniquely is particularly relevant in this context for those case managers prepared to interpret the advocacy function differently. Readiness to take risks and diverge from comfortable practice methods would characterise the creativity that is essential to achieve results.

PROFESSIONAL SUPPORT

Workers embroiled in the intricacies of this type of work may find themselves working alone and in diverse settings, which brings to the fore another practice imperative: that of creating a professionally supportive context. Advocacy and decisions surrounding its effective execution are delicate, and are often difficult to initiate and manage alone. Being a member of a team (Holt 2000), able to share opinions and bounce off ideas, is tremendously encouraging and usually leads to the achievement of better outcomes for clients. Where there is no established, agency-based team of interested professionals, a team of individual, disparate case managers can be created as McClelland (1998) portrays, to meet regularly, pool concerns, and gain insight, momentum and the collective strength to lobby for change. Strategies such as this are rare but priceless in a range of habitually inward-looking practice environments. Issues brought to such forums move from being problems to becoming challenges and generate good resolve based on sound professional judgment.

ORGANISATIONAL SUPPORT

As a departure from more traditional approaches to client service, the mission to increase consumer control needs solid backing from the case manager's organisation and its affiliates. In a related study of consumers as workers, Mowbray et al. (1996, p. 66) conclude that the success of innovative programs that seek to develop new roles for consumers is contingent upon a 'reconfiguration' of organisational support. Strategic, persuasive tactics are probably needed to convince organisers and operators to invest in proposals for their case managers to depart from traditional directions in service delivery. Crucial to their success would be the establishment of plans that emphatically link worker activities to client goals and that are compatible with the organisation's enterprise and with funding.

SURVIVING CASE MANAGEMENT PRACTICE

Case management is a different approach that challenges health and human service practice traditionalism. Dogged adherence to core beliefs about the capacity of people to change and to values about how people are treated are still needed to protect clients, but case management practitioners must think very carefully about how to interpret these in practice. This is what makes case management relatively difficult. Orthodoxy about having to help everyone in need or providing equitable services has to be renounced in order to achieve a realistic perspective on what is possible. A conceptually clear, clinical approach is called for within defined parameters, reflecting a decisive practice orientation. Practitioners do not have to relinquish ingrained principles about how to treat people; the warmth, dignity and respect they show to clients are all undeniably important. It is the practice priorities that need to be rethought to reduce distress for workers and clients.

We have been at pains to highlight the need for practitioners to limit the ethical dilemmas by applying reason and imposing stricter control over what they allow to develop into problems. Competence does diminish ethical dilemmas by removing practice confusion and allowing a clearer focus on the moral uncertainties (Sonntag 1995; Kane et al. 2000). Skilled, informed practice ensures that dilemmas are kept in perspective. Clearer perceptions of role, contextual capacity and limitations, and how to direct energy for maximum client benefit, are needed to keep practice dilemmas in perspective for case managers.

In this chapter, we have tried to encapsulate how practitioners can embrace practice decisions more functionally as regular decisions rather than as problems. Certain practice predicaments become more pressing in some contexts than in others and we have used broad categories of case management approaches to highlight the pressures and formulate some guidelines. These can be viewed as a collective, with relevance but varying significance across diverse case management settings:

- Action should emerge from a deliberate reasoning process that considers the environmental context in which case management is being practised. Knowledge of how the case management process is best applied in particular contexts, and which aspects require emphasis, is needed.
- Articulation of role and preferred practice orientation to both clients and to administrative managers (those who formulate policy and agency direction) is required, in order to diminish unmet expectations and to provoke informed organisational decision-making.
- Skill development is essential in dedicated areas, pertinent to the work context.

The discussion has repeatedly led to four fundamental worker responsibilities:

- to understand how best to apply the case management process in the system in which they work;
- to think critically through the practice issues that trigger ethical discomfort;
- to minimise these through effective control and communication; and
- to operate strategically on behalf of clients to improve service delivery.

Diligence is required to maintain a functional level of compromise and ameliorate the frustration of wasted time and energy. It is a fact that there are disenfranchised, disconsolate and dismal health and human service workers who feel overwhelmed and paralysed by competing demands. Our discussion in this chapter has reinforced Gambrill's (1990) assertion that practitioners need to overcome both knowledge and attitudinal limitations to improve critical reasoning skills. Case managers need to analyse their situation to achieve awareness of how best to manage their tasks, and where and how to apply themselves to maximum effect. Raiff and Shore's (1993, p. 24) definition of exemplary practice as characterised by 'virtuosity, a knowledge-based practice and degree of professional autonomy' fits well with this conclusion. Clarity of purpose promotes a positive attitude to practice issues that arise so that decisions can be made without the complication of doubt and confusion about role. Developments such as these will help case managers to avoid the more covert ethical dilemma and professional dereliction—that of never becoming sufficiently involved.

We are, however, left slightly discomfited by what can be construed as blind optimism in our persistent message that practice can be rendered more tolerable and productive if the strategies are implemented to untangle practice dilemmas. For those case managers who still encounter crippling demands after conscientious development of their skills and influence, the message may feel like an empty one. When what is required is beyond reach, a more fundamental ethical question is raised. Organisations that set up unrealistic outcome demands and expect their workers to be superhuman by implementing an inappropriate service approach and impossible workloads with no organisational support are behaving immorally. Case managers facing this sort of onslaught are set up to fail and we resoundingly agree with McClelland et al. (1996, p. 275) that case managers 'are not miracle workers and cannot cure the ills of dysfunctional delivery systems'. Thus entangled, their perception of self as a dignified professional with integrity is at stake. The practice knowledge, organisational influence and wise targeting of skill and energy promoted in this chapter are ingredients of survival in the professional sense, but they may not add up to a solution.

PART III

CASE MANAGEMENT AS PROFESSIONAL BUSINESS

CHAPTER

7

THE MANAGEMENT IN
CASE MANAGEMENT

It will be evident from the earlier policy chapters that case management has been created and shaped in contexts where the social
dimensions of health and welfare, and the more recent economic
imperative of 'value-for-money', have operated. It will also be clear
that these forces combine in the practice arena to make complex, often
contradictory and burgeoning demands on health and human service
workers. Their job titles, employment conditions and work tasks are
evolving rapidly, and increasingly their world is being constructed
through the language of business. Management is an inherent component of business. The term 'management' produces a bewildering array
of paradoxes and contradictions in relation to case management.
Moxley (1997, p. 6) refers to the multiple meanings of management
in this context. Case management and case managers are certainly
products—and perhaps victims—of management thinking, processes,
language and structures which may be both liberating and oppressive
for workers and users of services alike. How can these things coexist?
What are the management facets of case management and what is their
significance for workers? What is being managed, by whom and why?

To start exploring these questions, we must detour briefly through
some material on management which is more abstract than that which
we have just left. However, it is particularly worthwhile—albeit in a
different register—because it helps to expose, clarify and validate
many of the often unarticulated tensions and paradoxes of case management practice and experience. It also explains the new language

which surrounds, shapes and embodies much contemporary case management work.

MANAGERIALISM AND CASE MANAGEMENT

The major approaches to the study of management over time are commonly described as classical, including Taylor's scientific management, bureaucratic, human relations, systems and more recently new managerialist (Coulshed and Mullender 2001). New managerialism is of particular relevance to case management because it throws light on both the context in which it takes place and on the phenomenon itself. New managerialism has emerged in response to the very complex, fragmented and diverse worlds in which management now happens and it has, according to Clarke and Newman (1997, p. 34), intersected with New Right ideologies to promote 'change', 'revolution' and 'transformation'. A relatively recent confluence of new managerialism and case management has seen the latter readily adopted or colonised as the tool through which transformations in health and human service delivery can be effected (Gursansky and Kennedy 1998). While several historical imperatives underpin case management, it is also both a creature of and an appropriation of new managerialism.

The origins and emergence of new managerialism and its attendant debates are fully explored in other places (e.g. Sheppard 1995; Clarke and Newman 1997; Considine and Painter 1997; Abbott and Meerabeau 1998; Exworthy and Halford 1999). In very simple outline, new managerialism—different from more traditional understandings of management—assumes that the solution to social problems can be found in the application of good business practices, inclusive of unfettered, entrepreneurial and visionary management. The authority and prerogative of managers is legitimated and all is possible if managers are 'let do their job' (Sheppard 1995, p. 61). The expertise of management in general is distinguished from other forms of expertise (Hugman 1998a), and takes precedence over all other forms of technical—including professional—expertise (Hugman 1991). The 'measure of all practice is the extent to which it fits with management structures and practice' and the manager is extolled as hero(ine) (Sheppard 1995, p. 61). Clarke's (1998, p. 239) overview of new managerialism claims that it covers an ideology in which managing for efficiency dominates, a calculative framework which attends to internal issues of efficiency and external issues of competitiveness, and a series of overlapping and often contradictory conversations about what and how to manage. That is, new managerialism is an ideology about the supremacy of management activity in society, an approach to practice for organisational efficiency and economic success, and also an academic discourse.

The ideology and the frameworks for efficiency are commonly characterised by the terminology of competition, markets, excellence, quality, human resources and customers—or what one of Hadley and Clough's community care interviewees in the United Kingdom described as 'MBA speak' (1997, p. 202). Yet Clarke and Newman's (1997, p. 92) analysis shows that calculative, affective, hard, soft, value driven and value neutral languages actually coexist in these frameworks. Each of these languages is represented, for instance, by terms like 'marketing strategy', 'customer care', 'devolved budget', 'collaboration', 'serving the customer' and 'workforce planning'. Similarly coexisting are both 'macho' or technical and feminised or relational images of management (Clarke and Newman 1997, p. 73). Workers experience conflicting messages and contradictory injunctions, argue Clarke and Newman (1997, p. 73), as traditional, competitive and transformational organisational orders, or regimes of power, coexist, ebb and flow. For example, many case managers will be familiar with contradictory instructions to keep 'customers' happy, curb client complaints and portray the agency as user responsive while limiting expenditure and time spent with clients. Similarly, they may be applauded for unorthodox organisational behaviour which produces a desired outcome while simultaneously being penalised for non-compliance with organisational procedures when things go wrong. They are exhorted to build collaborative relationships with workers in other services in the interests of integrated, customised service delivery and at the same time to meet the incompatible productivity demands of their own agencies.

Central among the debates of new managerialism are those concerning the relationships and conflicts between professionals and managers. This matter is vital for case management because, as we shall see, many case managers are both professionals and managers of individual service delivery, and thus straddle both groups. It is quite difficult to extract overarching conclusions about the professional–manager debates because, as Exworthy and Halford (1999) declare, commentators are considering different dimensions of relationships.

However, two main lines of interrelated arguments, which have particular relevance to case management, are briefly addressed here. The first line of arguments emphasises the degree of overlap between workers, inclusive of professionals, and managers. At its crudest, this is reflected in the populist joke that everyone is now a manager. Clarke and Newman (1997, p. 69) say of management that it 'is no longer the sole province of the most senior organisational tiers where men are generally to be found, but has cascaded down organisations to relatively low paid, low status service delivery functions'. It is not realistic to portray managers and professionals as entirely distinct groups because there is both conceptual argument and practical evidence about their interrelatedness and the instability of the connections between them. Managers often are appointed from the ranks of the professionals in probation (May and Annison 1998), more generally in social work (Sheppard 1995; Causer and Exworthy 1999; Coulshed and Mullender 2001) and across the social and health services (Clarke 1998). The two roles may actually be merging in practice in medicine (Causer and Exworthy 1999; Harrison 1999), in education (Menter and Muschamp 1999), and also in nursing (Causer and Exworthy 1999). Clarke and Newman (1997) have posited the managerialisation of social welfare through the integration into corporate structures of professionals like head teachers, ward and clinical managers and care managers by processes of delegation and devolved responsibility. It is also said (Exworthy and Halford 1999) that the metamorphosis of all staff into entrepreneurs controls them more effectively than any old-fashioned conflict between workers and managers could. Exworthy and Halford (1999) argue that it is not possible to know whether professionals are strategically embracing managerialism or managers are controlling the agenda, and they conclude that both things are likely.

The second line of arguments focuses on conflict between managers and professionals, and losses of autonomy and status experienced by the latter group. Deprofessionalisation is a recurring theme here. While Exworthy and Halford (1999, p. 6) argue that the patterns of discord between management and professionals are uneven across areas of service and professional groups, they do say that the new managerialism places public sector managers at least 'in a position of unparalleled power and authority' and that the traditional professional paradigm of authority and discretion is seriously threatened. This conclusion might be qualified by Flynn's (1999) opinion that professional work will always retain some of its necessarily discretionary and indeterminate nature and that, because of this, conflict between the two groups will, if anything, grow. However, the view that professionals are experiencing greater managerial control over their activities is commonly endorsed, with some provisos by others (Sheppard 1995; Dominelli 1997; Lymbery 1998; Hugman 1998a). It is even argued that social work, for example, is being taken over and compromised by management (Jones 1999). The study by Hadley and Clough (1997) of professionals in relation to managers in community care in Britain reports the former as feeling more controlled, less autonomous and more fearful of their managers than previously.

Whatever one's theoretical orientation within these debates, there is no doubt that the centrality and primacy of the role of professionals are being transformed or challenged both from within and without under new managerialist ideology and practice. Clarke (1998, p. 238) proposes three relevant tactics which reshape organisational meaning within managerialism: displacement, whereby the view of the 'customer' dislodges the previously predominant expert perspective of the professional; subordination, which requires that professional judgments be recast in terms of resource priorities instead of need; and co-option of professional 'home-ground' fundamentals like quality, service and good practice. A number of writers have noted that many professionals—social workers and nurses in particular—are caught in what Sheppard (1995, p. 77) calls a 'pincer movement' between the ascendancy of the consumer, Clarke's (1998) notion of displacement and the supremacy of management. The place where service and corporate concerns meet is an uncomfortable one and, when it is embodied in an individual worker, devolved stress is experienced and internalised (Clarke 1998). This awkward positioning and its consequences form a recurring theme in this part of the book.

So what does all this mean for case managers who, in title, are both managers and, as we will see in a later chapter, often also professionals? Case management in many ways epitomises the chaotic and contradictory picture outlined; it is located at that pivotal point where service and organisational tensions intersect. The presence of the word 'management' in its name and its validation of the centrality of the 'customer' are completely congruent with the spirit of new managerialism. Working at a distance from clients and engagement in tasks such as coordinating and monitoring are consistent with quasi-market conceptions of health and welfare (Hugman 1998b). So there is much about case management that can position the case manager strongly in relation to the new managerialist agendas. There is much about new managerialism which affirms—indeed, has even appropriated—some of the central characteristics of case management. On the other hand, many of the people working as case managers are the professionals described as increasingly subject to surveillance by their managers, pressure from clients and the dissonance of subordination and co-option. Moreover, many of these people, as will be discussed again later, have not been trained in management or administration, view management as an idea alien to their professional values (Lewis and Lewis 1983; Rapp and Poertner 1992) and feel powerless (Bar-On 1995; Moxley 1997; Coulshed and Mullender 2001).

Does this coverage of new managerialism bring the case management practitioner to an impasse? Not necessarily, because—although the picture might on the face of it look grim for the front-line worker—there are competing conclusions, neither managers nor professionals are homogeneous groups and change processes are uneven. At the very least, knowledge that conceptual debates about these issues exist can be illuminating and empowering; it can reduce a sense of isolation and embattlement; it can be surprisingly affirming; and it can lead to choices about where energies are put. As Clarke and Newman (1997, p. 93) say: 'Managerial discourses create the possibilities within which individuals construct new roles and identities, and from which they derive ideas about the logic of institutional change.'

On a less reductionist note, there is some agreement that there is—and will continue to be—a continuing core of autonomy for professionals (Sheppard 1995, p. 77; Flynn 1999, p. 35); we will revisit this point later. There are several reports that front-line workers are making sense of the new language and using it to enhance their own power in the purchase of services for clients (Clarke and Newman 1997, p. 97, quoting Mackintosh 1995). The language of new managerialism, which constitutes managers as active change agents in control of their own destinies (Clarke and Newman 1997), emphasises positive outcomes for clients and rejects the lack of accountability of much past health and human service practice, may well be attractive to many case managers. Sinclair (1997), writing from an organisational cultural perspective within the managerialist debates, presents a professional–managerial multicultural model which endorses a number of positions that might be useful to workers—for example, becoming knowledgeable about management in order to manage one's bosses, manage one's career and manage one's clients well so as not to validate historical claims of professional exploitation. This returns us to a more direct analysis of the role of the case manager.

THE CASE MANAGER AS THE MANAGER OF SERVICE DELIVERY

ARE CASE MANAGERS REALLY MANAGERS?

It is generally agreed that management involves planning, organising the necessary people and resources, commanding, monitoring and controlling, and evaluating. These functions, along with decision-making in unstable environments, were emphasised in Chapter 5. Many of these functions are not new to health and human service workers, but in combination and purpose they often are. Organising others to perform on behalf of a client and ensuring that they do so does add a new dimension to the responsibilities of many workers who become case managers. This is commonly referred to as 'getting work done through others' (Wolk et al. 1994, p. 157). It is argued that this is at the nub of many of the contradictions and inadequacies of case management practice, as it moves traditional approaches to work with service users out into more public and shared domains.

Social workers find this a challenge because they have been particularly acculturated to focus personally on clients directly and on disembodied targets like systems in their clients' interests (Orme and Glastonbury 1993). They are also said to devalue other providers (Bar-On 1995), and this claim can probably be made for all professional groups represented in case management. It has also been said (Challis and Davies 1986, p. 226) that the training of social workers in this instance produces in that profession the 'tyranny of individualisation' so that generalisations and predictions about cases are both neglected and inadequate. Again, a similar case could be mounted for nursing and other direct service helping professions where the traditional imagery accentuates emotionally satisfying, intimate and personalised service delivery.

Case managers may not see themselves as managers and they may not perform well as such, but they are managers. Why? Within a new managerialist framework, management functions are required of most workers and, more importantly, the notion of management is integral to the core conceptualisation of case management. Wolk et al.'s (1994) often-quoted study in which the work of chief executives over ten managerial roles was compared with that of case managers supports this assertion. Within the three interpersonal roles of figurehead, leader and liaison, there is no doubt that the last one is intrinsic to case management. Figurehead is also important in that the effective case manager is the visible orchestrator of client-related activity. Leadership is more vexed and exposes ever-present tensions between client and worker control over the case management process. However, we agree with Wolk et al.'s (1994) view that case managers should demonstrate leadership through modelling, motivating and building commitment; however, there is insufficient acknowledgment of the very real problems of case manager authority and we will return to this shortly. The informational roles of monitor, disseminator and spokesperson are critical to case management and a potential source of worker power—something we will also canvass later. In principle, the decision-making roles are extremely pertinent to case management, but they too require additional exploration in terms of legitimacy, authority and power.

WHAT IS BEING MANAGED AND FOR WHAT PURPOSE?

This question brings the controversy over the title case management on to centre stage. Under the preferred term 'care management' in the United Kingdom, Orme and Glastonbury (1993) emphasise that it is the care which is being managed, not the client. This position is contestable as, within a managerialist or even an idiomatic under-standing of the practicalities of health and human service work, mandates exist for the manoeuvring, leadership, even coercion and control of clients at times. It is naïve to think that a correctional or a clinical pathways case manager is not attempting to manage both a client and a service system. It is equally naïve to deny that there are elements of client management in a consumer-driven area of case management practice where the social control aspects are less apparent. Moxley's (1997, p. 6) commonsense approach to this whole topic is most compelling. He acknowledges that some are insulted by the name 'case management', apologises for offending them, but continues to employ the term because of its wide use in the literature and in practice. Whatever one's position on the actual target of management activity— and it may vary between and within 'cases'—we agree with Moxley

(1997) and Rapp and Poertner (1992) that the aim or purpose of case management should always be client-centred, that the case manager is a 'steward of the perspectives and desires of consumers' (Moxley 1997, p. 6) and that outcomes must primarily include benefit to the client.

CASE MANAGER POWER AND AUTHORITY

Having argued that case managers are managers, and having repeatedly stressed the importance of influence throughout the practice chapters, we are obliged to confront questions of case manager authority and power. These things must be considered in relation to peers, supervisors, clients and the general community. That is down, up and across in hierarchical terms.

The concept of power is the subject of extensive psychological and sociological theoretical work. This work is dealt with here only to the extent that it helps illuminate the case manager's role. Hugman (1991) describes two approaches to the study of power: power as an element of social action; and power as an aspect of social relationships. The first, more psychological, approach focuses on the capacity for action and the action itself, and is often criticised for implying that power is internally generated and operates in a social vacuum. The second, more sociological, approach acknowledges that power is 'exercised in the structuring of the social framework in which interests, ideas and issues are formed and known' (Hugman 1991, p. 35). That is, power must be understood in terms of its basis in social relationships. Hugman (1991) proposes that power involves an interplay between action and structure and that actions must be viewed in their social contexts. He canvasses à number of elements in which power is woven through the context and actions of the helping professions. These are hierarchy within professions, occupations as power structures in society, subordination of clients and construction of them as objects of occupations, and reproduction of racism and patriarchy. In other words, most aspects of helping professional life are imbued with power differentials and displays, many of them implicit but nonetheless all-pervasive.

We have introduced this apparent dichotomy in analyses of power for two reasons. One is to acknowledge the parameters of the social action or psychological approach, to which we turn later. The second, and perhaps more important, point is that no matter how powerless case managers may feel and no matter how limited their authority based on formal position (Hersey et al. 1996, p. 230), from a broader social standpoint power is an inherent part of their worlds and they are socially more powerful than the users of their services. In relation to case management in particular, Anderson's (2001, p. 168) recent US study found that welfare assistance recipients viewed their case managers 'as powerful actors who exerted considerable control over [them]' and who exercised their discretion autocratically and inconsistently. This power imbalance between clients and workers is the subject of extensive debate and documentation in other places (Hugman 1991; Braye and Preston-Shoot 1995; Sheppard 1995; Kane et al. 2000). However, it is not easily reconciled with the experiences of daily work life and commonly goes unaddressed in the practice world and in professional education.

Lipsky's (1980) inimitable notion of the street-level bureaucrat continues to have significance in any examination of relative power, despite its age and location in public service work. We have already seen that even the most gloomy prognoses of the new managerialist writers about professional autonomy have acknowledged that there is still some room for professional discretion. In fact, Lipsky (1991) himself has more recently affirmed the currency of the street-level bureaucrat by examining senior executives' needs to bring front-line worker actions more into line with policy objectives. He concludes that 'policy-makers and economists might wish it otherwise, but it seems clear that in the implementation of social welfare programmes there remains an irreducible extent to which worker discretion cannot be eradicated' (Lipsky 1991, p. 227). In brief, Lipsky (1980) argues that front-line workers make policy in that their aggregated daily decisions with and about clients add up to an overall agency response. In the face of ambiguous goals, insufficient resources, high workloads and reactive clients, workers create their own solutions and routines to manage their situations. They manipulate their own roles, influence who gets benefits, influence their own agencies and influence policy. For example, they find reasons for delaying responses to requests, provide only certain information, complete forms in particular ways, refer or do not refer on, define people in or out of eligibility and so on. The result is actual policy which may bear little resemblance to the official one. His conclusions are supported by Anderson's (2001) public welfare research which reveals just how potent the exercise of worker discretion is on clients' perceptions of the agency and the service they receive. It is vital that case managers appreciate their personal power in negatively and positively impacting on their organisations and the users of their services.

Moxley (1997) argues that there is a parallel between the history of case management and that of street-level bureaucracies. The former evolved as a buffer to the complexities, fragmentation and lack of responsiveness experienced by clients of the service system and yet these are the same forces which produce street-level bureaucracies. We will return in a later chapter to Lipsky's (1980) idea of front-line worker power because, while it can help explain the problems of many case management programs, it may also be a useful tool for assisting workers to analyse their place and influence in health and human service worlds.

To turn now to a more social action or psychological angle on power, French and Raven (1959) and Raven (1993) define social power as potential influence which derives from a number of sources, only one of which is formal organisational status or position. Raven's (1993) well-known categorisation of six power types, although socially decontextualised in Hugman's (1991) terms, is valuable for exploring possibilities and alternatives in terms of the way that case managers might think about themselves and their work. It outlines the basis or source of power that might be perceived in people by others. Of course, influencing others effectively will depend not only on the power base in operation but on the manner and techniques of its use which are not elaborated on here. The sources of power are outlined in Table 7.1.

Power can be a troubling issue, especially for front-line human service workers, accustomed to thinking of themselves at the bottom of the hierarchical pecking order. Case managers—in particular, social workers—are reported to often feel powerless (Dinerman 1992; Bar-On 1995; Moxley 1997; Coulshed and Mullender 2001), externally entrapped and controlled (McClelland et al. 1996) and uncomfortable with the notion of power (Bar-On 1995). For them, legitimate, reward, coercive and even expert power may be subjectively experienced as limited in relation to others in their own and other organisations, although Tanner's (1998) work on British care managers suggests that their power is increasingly rooted in administrative and management responsibility and less in professional autonomy and discretion. For many case managers, control of budgets and access to resources are restricted (Austin 1990, 1993; Rubin 1992), yet both may be critical in the exercise of power (Challis 1990), particularly legitimate and reward power. Case managers often work at the boundaries of

Table 7.1   Possible sources of power

Form of power	Source
Legitimate power	The origin of this power lies in formal position and authority, and in more subtle social debts owed through reciprocity, equity and responsibility.
Coercive and reward power	The basis of these two forms of power is found in the impersonal ability to apply both tangible rewards and threats, and also in the impact of one's personal approval or disapproval.
Expert power	This power is founded in attributed knowledge. It can be both positive and negative. In the latter case, the influencer will have the opposite effect to that intended or presumed in that the target of influence will do the opposite of what is hoped for by the influencer.
Referent power	This power is based on the ability to draw in or repel others such that they identify or disidentify with the would-be influencer. It can also be negative and positive.
Informational power	This power is founded in access to and use of data and in logical argument, and can be exercised directly and indirectly.
Connection power	This power base, posited by other writers (Hersey et al. 1996; Coulshed and Mullender 2001, p. 103), is based on perceived association with other people of significance.

organisational environments characterised by ambiguous procedures and imprecise intra- and inter-agency protocols (Rubin 1992), and this is likely to confound their attempted exercise of legitimate, reward and coercive, expert and informational power. The interaction between inadequate qualifications and low status in some areas of case management has been noted (Intagliata 1992; Moxley 1997; Walsh 2000), and it is probable that these factors also limit the expert power accorded many case managers.

Workers with little formal, structural or organisationally legitimate power—that is, authority—might easily become passive (in which case clients are disadvantaged) or seek other forms of influence (Rapp and Poertner 1992; Bar-On 1995). Influence can come from exploiting other relatively unused power bases or rethinking those assumed to be proscribed. Bar-On (1995), for example, describes otherwise resource-poor and power-constrained social work case managers engaging in what he calls 'moral suasion' with others on behalf of their clients— that is, 'impressing upon others their obligation on matters of general right and wrong' (1995, p. 74). This resonates with the social obligation component of legitimate power and may have some valency if applied strategically and with skill. However, it can easily be perceived as stereotypical, righteous carping and Bar-On himself acknowledges that it is insufficient for effective case management practice.

Gardner and Cary (1999), discussing case manager collaboration in community health where professional differentials are acknowledged to exist, advocate the development of what they call informal power, including goodwill, information-sharing and expertise. Their line of argument can be integrated with Raven's (1993) power categorisation and extended. Goodwill may be one dimension of a personal style which buttresses reward and positive referent power with other workers and clients. The absence of these style factors may equally underpin negative referent and coercive power. In crude terms, things such as courtesy and respect can be positively influential. There is no doubt that the personal style of the case manager is a potent force in clients' recorded experiences of case management (Gursansky and Kennedy 1998; Anderson 2001). We believe poor use of information and expert power to have been the less acknowledged saboteurs of much case management effort, and they are both to some extent within the control of the individual worker, even when information volatility and overload are endemic. Accurate and comprehensive information about services, facilities, policies and procedures, key staff in agencies and formal and informal resource possibilities is critical to good case management, as shown in earlier chapters, but it is not valued and cultivated by organisations and workers as much as it might be.

Similarly, as argued in Part II, critical thinking and record-keeping skills are essential. The ability to collect and assess information, and knit it into a logical and dispassionate argument, is potentially extra-ordinarily empowering (see Gambrill 1990). Social workers and other professional groups socialised to do and to feel, rather than to account for doing, often have resistance in this area. Others such as nurses may be competent with mechanical record-keeping but lack skills in integration and analysis of data. A worker who can develop, articulate and maintain a coherent and compelling argument based on accurate political, policy, procedural and practical information is not so easily ignored by those with equal or greater legitimate power. In fact, it may be perilous for the latter to ignore sound arguments which reveal flaws and limits in systems and procedures for which they have some formal responsibility. Expert power can be earned by individuals through other than formal qualifications. The development of particular practical skills, areas of knowledge and use of information power can all contribute to a case manager's ascribed expertise by other staff, managers and clients.

Knowing about various power bases is only part of what is needed to develop more influential practice. It is also important to understand that different power bases must be exercised in different circumstances and for different purposes (Hersey et al. 1996). Bar-On (1990) suggests that some social workers at least, perhaps unconsciously but not inappropriately, attempt to downplay their power with clients and inflate it with agency and other workers. Raven (1993) proposes the strategic use of power through a sequencing process akin to that of case management itself. He says that one must first determine motivation for attempting to influence, assess the power bases available, examine the costs of the attempt through each available base, prepare the scene, choose the mode, assess the effects of the influence attempt and incorporate feedback into further actions. This whole strategic planning process is in itself an exercise in critical thinking.

The idea of the conscious and purposeful exercise of power raises quite confronting personal and ideological issues for many case managers, and we will turn now to what all this material might mean for the individual worker.

MANAGING ONESELF AS A CASE MANAGER

This heading is in itself controversial as it implies acceptance, even internalisation, of managerialist rather than professional agendas. A pragmatic riposte is that case managers' job futures will increasingly depend on their managerial assets (Coulshed and Mullender 2001), so it is in their interests to be familiar with and exploit the prevailing language. Additionally, the complexities of their work environments mean that they really do need to cope with, or actively manage, change, diversity, time, superiors, perhaps resources and certainly information. Increasingly workers, in the face of casualised and contractualised work, have to think in terms of their own employment planning. A more weighty response is that the contradictions and pressures experienced by many case managers, supposedly themselves managers but with relatively little formal power in a managerialist world, are potentially very damaging to both workers and their clients unless dealt with in some way. There is no formula for how this might be done, but there is unlikely to be progress of any sort until, as Moxley (1997, p. 6) says, workers make personal sense of the word 'management'; we believe the precursor to this is knowledge. Confronting questions about the meaning of management and power might result in a decision to leave the health or human service sectors altogether, but for many workers this is not a realistic option. For some, it might prompt a move from case management into service provision. For others, it might encourage efforts to change how they or their organisations conduct case management. For some, it might liberate entrepreneurial talent and open up new business or employment options. For yet others, it might elicit only a modest desire for some level of personal reconciliation with the realities of the work world.

There is always a risk in pursuing this line of individualising the problems of generally unsatisfactory service systems, of blaming the case managers who may be victims of them, and we have acknowledged this in Part II. We agree with Dinerman's (1992, p. 4) blunt assertion that 'all the power in the world is useless if the requisite services do not exist'. This said, how can case managers survive personally and for their clients as good managers of service delivery?

There are linked conceptual and personal activities which might benefit workers in coming to grips with these issues. The first involves finding frameworks which assist in understanding where power at the front line is located, how it is used for good and bad and how it applies to the individual case manager. It is for this reason that we have briefly canvassed new managerialism and power and we will return in Chapter 9 to these ideas but mention here two practical examples. Iles (1997), writing of health, proposes that workers focus on the simple but hard things and exercise control over them. This requires discriminating between spheres of influence and spheres of concern and concentrating on the former which are within the purview of the worker. Spheres of concern are larger than spheres of influence and many dimensions of them are not within the worker's power to control.

Clinard (1989, p. 201) presents a more comprehensive model of personal power—or, as she calls it, 'succeeding with yourself'—in which understanding and action are combined. She explains interaction between thoughts, feelings and behaviour, all of which are passed through one's perceptual or programmed filter which sorts information about the external world. She proposes invaluable processes for analysing information and events which are troubling to an individual and for determining valid action in response to them.

The second activity entails assessing personal skills, power bases and public profile, making decisions about how to develop in chosen areas and recognising personal limitations. Professional and personal development plans, which may well have all the characteristics of a service plan for clients, can incorporate any number of informal and formal tasks inclusive of seeking additional qualifications. We will explore matters of professional identity and qualifications in the following chapters.

8

PROFILES OF CASE MANAGERS

As there is no single case manager identity, we must pursue a number of lines of inquiry to understand who these workers are, where they come from and how they interrelate. These matters are seldom fully considered despite their critical impact on the implementation of case management. Case managers are often amazed when faced with the scope, the diversities and the commonalities of the professional worlds in which their work is located. Again we argue that informed practitioners are potentially more powerful ones.

Comprehensive coverage of the contested conceptual terrain of what constitutes an occupation or a profession, and the process of professionalisation, are beyond the scope of this book. The term 'profession' is used here fairly loosely and does not signify a particular ideological or sociological position. For the sake of convenience, it refers to groups who identify themselves in this way, even though their claims may be challenged by others. In any analysis of case management and the professions, puzzling inconsistencies and contradictions soon become evident. This is largely because different voices are speaking. Burrage and Torstendahl (1990) say that there are four main actors involved in reference to professions: practising members, the state, consumers and universities. Meerabeau and Abbott (1998, citing Macdonald 1995) add professional bodies to this list. Thus, for instance, social workers or nurses practising as case managers may express opinions which are different from those of their clients, professional associations, their educators and relevant policy-makers. At any point in the following sections, any one of these five groups may be represented and, even within each of them, there may be a multiplicity of views.

WHO ARE CASE MANAGERS?

The short and simple answer to this question is that case managers are drawn from the health, human and social service employees of the past. Of course, a more comprehensive response invokes qualifications, employment trends and professional struggles and developments. These matters are explored in this chapter.

CASE MANAGERS WITHOUT HEALTH AND HUMAN SERVICE QUALIFICATIONS

Human service and health workforces are being restructured, either through or as a result of the shift to case management. Two significant features of the restructuring help explain more fully who case managers are and where they have come from. The first concerns those sections of workforces where professional-level education has traditionally not been a requirement for employment and where the introduction of case management has largely been motivated by an intention to professionalise or upgrade workforce knowledge and skills and to systematise existent intervention practices. In Australia and the United States for instance, large numbers of staff without formal qualifications in custodial corrections (Enos and Southern 1996; McCallum and Furby 1999) have now been redesignated as case managers. In Australia, the same situation has occurred in homelessness programs (Gursansky and Kennedy 1998; Wearing 1998).

In other areas of the human services in particular, the adoption of case management has resulted in the transformation of workers who were not originally employed as human service staff at all, and who are generally not university educated, into case managers. 'Clerks or lesser technicians' (Weil et al. 1985, p. 371) is one way of describing these people. For example, in the United States and in Australia, some income maintenance administrative staff and/or employment counsellors have been reclassified as case managers in labour market program reformation (Perlmutter and Johnson 1996; Gursansky and Kennedy 1998). Both these transmutations of formally unqualified staff are mirrored by literature which, although labelled case management, is largely an introduction to the ethical and practice fundamentals of professional intervention with clients (e.g. Enos and Southern 1996; Summers 2000).

It is impossible to quantify the numbers of case managers without formal health or human service qualifications, but there is no doubt that they exist in the United States (e.g. see Weil et al. 1985; Austin 1990; Burns et al. 1995; Rothman and Sager 1998; Pierre et al. 1999; Holt 2000), in Australia (Kennedy et al. 2001), in the United Kingdom (Sheppard 1995), in Canada (Fineman 1996) and in New Zealand (Northey 2000). Schindler and Brawley (1987), in detailing the growth of human services across the world and the attendant issues of training and professional relationships, show that what they refer to as para-professionals were, over a decade ago at least, the main providers of front-line services in most countries and were likely to be so for the foreseeable future. This conclusion still has validity for case management (e.g. see Anderson 2001), but it must be qualified. Case managers are not at all an educationally homogeneous group. If anything, in the United States at least, they inhabit a 'two-class system' in which qualifications for public program staff are being de-emphasised while private-sector programs provide 'a niche for workers with professional backgrounds' (Dill 1995, pp. 106–7).

There are competing forces which serve both to increase and reduce demand for formally qualified staff in the health and human services. Competition for desirable jobs and general increases in educational attainments, along with ideological shifts to reprofessionalisation in some fields (Wearing 1998), serve to raise the qualification levels of staff. However, deregulation of labour markets, anti-competition policies, contracting out of service delivery, cost factors and recognition of the importance of personal qualities can counteract educational requirements. This is illustrated by Senn et al. (1997, p. 137), who report on the shift from institutional to community residential care in the United Kingdom. They state that the demand for nursing staff has reduced, and 'increasing numbers of unqualified staff are providing care for people with mental illness'. Also in the United Kingdom, unqualified home helps are increasingly undertaking personal care work which was previously done by district nurses (Abbott 1998). Baer and Gordon (1996, p. 226) outline a movement in the United States— often managed by nurses working for consulting firms or as managers—to replace registered nurses with 'unlicensed assistive personnel'. Netting and Gordon (1996) similarly argue that, in managed care in the United States, social workers are finding themselves to be dispensable, while physicians are being replaced by nurses and nurses by aides.

CASE MANAGERS WITH HEALTH AND HUMAN SERVICE QUALIFICATIONS

The second feature of restructuring is the reassignment of professionally qualified workers as case managers. For example, in social services, corrections, mental health, acute health, disability and some parts of the aged care sectors, some traditionally qualified human service and health professionals are being converted—sometimes traumatically (Firth 1998/1999)—into case managers. This change has frequently been an integral part of the process of deinstitutionalisation in health and human services. Social workers and nurses are the two groups whose names are most commonly acknowledged in the case management literature (Lowery 1992; Kulbok and Utz 1999) and who are said to constitute the majority of case managers (Weil et al. 1985). Among the other groups frequently identified as case managers are psychologists, physicians, psychiatrists, rehabilitation and other counsellors, gerontologists and speech therapists. Netting (1992, p. 163) adds fiduciaries, and McClelland et al. (1996) include people with training in theology and education. More recently, occupational therapists have joined the list (Lohman 1999; Hafez 2000). Insurance specialists and paralegals (Murer and Brick 1997) have been mentioned along with physiotherapists (McClaran et al. 1998) and pharmacists (Ozanne et al. 2000). The implications of these professional transformations will be returned to in this and following chapters.

CASE MANAGEMENT EMPLOYMENT

Given the multiple approaches to case management and the wide range of settings and fields in which case management employment occurs, it is predictable that there are numerous relevant job titles. Care coordinator, service coordinator, care manager, options coordinator, discharge planner, rehabilitation counsellor and liaison worker are some of the more common titles which generally include case management functions. In relation to the human services in particular, we (Kennedy and Harvey 2001) and other Australian writers (McDonald 1999) have noted that, across the industry, employers are increasingly advertising generically titled rather than profession-specific jobs. The same pattern has been recorded for managed care in the United States (Davis 1998). This means that employers can establish more flexible hiring criteria with fewer professional restraints. However, as indicated earlier, social workers or other groups still employed and working under their professional titles may in fact be operating as case managers. A survey of the job titles of health care applicants for a specific case management credential in the United States found—not surprisingly—that half were called case manager, but among the fourteen other titles were nurse, social worker, medical doctor and occupational therapist (Murer and Brick 1997, p. 160).

Witheridge (1992, p. 107), describing hiring practices in a US mental health outreach program, says that '[they] focus on the person, not the degree'. Kane (1992, pp. 225–6) endorses this view by emphasising the ability to perform tasks rather than 'arbitrary training requirements'. Our own research on Australian job advertisements for case managers indicates that employers are giving greater priority to workers' attributes, qualities and experience than they are to qualifications (Harvey et al. 2001). The importance placed on personal qualities by employers in the hiring process is widely acknowledged (Lowery 1992; Friedman and Poertner 1995). Commentaries on the important personal qualities of case managers range from experimental, psychological approaches, such as that of Kirk (1995) on the importance of worker optimism, to lists of necessary attributes devised by practitioners (Lowery 1992; Quick 1997; Siefker et al. 1998). Quick's study, which required US case managers to identify their most important characteristics, articulated high levels of agreeableness, intellect (inclusive of creativity), conscientiousness and extroversion (inclusive of assertion), and low levels of emotionality. This list echoes many of the points raised in the previous chapter, as the ideal profile suggested by Quick's findings is of a considerate, assertive, resourceful, reliable, logical and composed person.

Case management work does not appear to be any more glamorous or well paid than the jobs or professional designations which predated or parallel it. It is said of the United Kingdom (Orme and Glastonbury 1993), and is certainly true for other countries, that career paths within case management are limited and that it lacks status and legitimacy, particularly when its clients are not socially valued—as, for instance, in corrections or unemployment work. Rothman and Sager (1998, p. 20) state that 'this is a professional task without glitter' and Moore (1998, p. 9 electronic) agrees: 'Case management is tough work and often takes place in hostile environments.' The relatively low salaries of many jobs in the United States have also been commented upon, along with the resultant loss of experienced staff (McClelland et al. 1996). However, we believe that there are more promising financial and prestigious opportunities for nurses in managed care in the United States and for senior nurse practitioners in private health in Australia. Self-employment and subcontracting in all countries are also areas of likely growth.

CASE MANAGEMENT AS CONTESTED PROFESSIONAL TERRITORY

In 1985, Weil et al. (p. 371) stated that 'none of the major helping professions yet claim[s] case management to be under [its] purview'. This was then a rather curious comment in view of contemporaneous reports about professional competition, especially between nurses and social workers (e.g. see Johnson and Rubin 1983; Berger 1996, p. 168). However, Weil et al. (1985) went on to acknowledge the existence of unqualified case managers and it is true that contestation about case management has focused on qualified and unqualified staff nearly as much as it has on inter-professional rivalry. We will return to this topic later. Suffice to say here that Weil et al. (1985) very wisely located their discussion about professional groups in the wider context of human service employment realities. Their statement has been succeeded by many assertions of professional territorial claims and debates for and about possession of case management—again mostly with reference to social work and nursing (e.g. see National Association of Social Workers 1992a; Vourlekis 1992; Berger 1996; McClelland et al. 1996; Netting and Williams 1996; Murer and Brick 1997; Hawkins et al. 1998). More recently, Netting and Williams (1996, p. 223) have said of case management: 'In actuality, no profession has a corner on this market.' A number of factors lie behind these ostensibly confusing but often-repeated declarations, in which claims of conflict are sandwiched between suggestions that case management is a professionally unoccupied space. As is so common with case management, commentators are often considering only parts of the picture and/or are engaging in rhetoric rather than analysis.

As to professional turf wars, several points are pertinent. Claims of custody or encroachment are more easily made when the concept being contested is as confused as case management can be. The fact that case management has been imposed on rather than generated by the professions has also contributed to ambiguity about its professional ownership. Firm professional territorial positions are often skirted in publicly accessible statements and tend to form the rumbling—but rather elusive—background noise to much writing and practice. A few writers do make unilateral declarations of professional primacy (e.g. for nursing see More and Mandell 1997) and professional associations incline this way (e.g. see National Association of Social Workers 1992a), but most writers, no matter how aligned, generally qualify their assertions.

Two important factors underpin the often-shifting world of interprofessional tensions. First, professional and disciplinary groups are notoriously insular and this is reflected in their writing. The case management literature is replete with articles and books written from within one professional perspective, and which do not so much deny the presence of unqualified staff and other professional groups in case management as completely ignore them. Assumptions about territorial imperialism can easily be drawn from what is not said as much as from what is said.

A second factor is the general acknowledgment that workers at the front line are jockeying for status, identity and scarce resources. In our experience, this is where many of the more shrill proprietorial claims are voiced. For example, Matorin (1998) says in respect of the health arena in the United States that consultants have set social workers against nurses in their recommendations for cost-effective and program-oriented staffing arrangements which give precedence to nurse managers. Similarly, Hawkins et al. (1998) argue that managed care in the United States is predicated on competition among providers such as social workers and nurses. The study by Netting and Williams (1996) shows that, when asked directly by researchers, front-line case managers with diverse backgrounds do report that their particular group is the one with the necessary expertise and skills to perform case management functions properly. The authors comment on the defensive survival concerns underpinning these responses.

NURSING AND SOCIAL WORK

Nursing and social work are two groups which warrant special comment in any analysis of professional ownership of case management because of their histories, prevalence and the alleged jostling between them. It is argued that both nursing and social work bring special skills, expertise and knowledge to case management, and there are obvious alignments between their declared professional intervention processes and that of case management. Both even claim to have been engaging in case management services for a hundred years (National Association of Social Workers 1992a, p. 21; More and Mandell 1997, p. xiii), although we have already seen in an earlier chapter that they often have not fully confronted the extent to which case management is different from traditional approaches to service delivery.

In the words of Austin (1990, p. 400) and Johnson and Rubin (1983, p. 53), social work brings to case management holistic 'person-in-environment practice theory'. It is said to be potentially best placed to 'construct and implement a client-driven, systems-impact paradigm for case management practice' (Rose 1992b, pp. v–vi) and that 'inherent in social work practice is the organization of resources to resolve immediate problems of society, community, family and the individual' (National Association of Social Workers 1992a, p. 23). Along with its contextual and resource knowledge contributions, it is claimed to have special skills in relationship-building and in sensitivity to the psychological dimensions of problems (Vourlekis and Greene 1992, p. xiii). While all these social work writers concede that they are not the only professional stakeholders in this area of practice, there are declarations that social work has provided, and should continue to provide, a leadership role (O'Connor 1988; National Association of Social Workers 1992a).

The nursing assertions about case management sound similar, if not more strident. It is contended that nurses 'have skills and knowledge that extend beyond the biophysical and pathological aspects of care, bringing an holistic perspective and knowledge base to . . . clients' (Bower 1991, p. 15). In the tradition of professional appropriation, it is said that 'the case management model of care exemplifies the core values of nursing as a profession' (Howe 1996, p. 149) and that 'case management is conceptually akin to the nursing process in that both are predicated on a model of problem solving' (More and Mandell 1997, p. xv). More and Mandell (1997, p. xiv) declare that 'nursing is without doubt the profession with the most appropriate knowledge base and skill base to prepare competent case managers'.

Certainly nursing and social work share many similarities, not least in their histories through which both have developed as low-status, predominantly female professions engaged in the socially devalued and controlled task of caring (Abbott and Wallace 1998), and inclined to construct themselves as victims (Hawkins et al. 1998). Both also have common historical experiences in community settings such as the settlement house movement in the United States (Hawkins et al. 1998) and Victorian charitable and other philanthropic endeavours in the United Kingdom (Abbott and Wallace 1998). Netting and Williams (1996) have also commented that both groups evidence undergraduate curricula concerned with human behaviour, social support and social and community change. Both groups, too, are returning to their community roots in many fields through the effects of deinstitutionalisation in health and human services.

While there are some recent reports of encouraging joint work between social work and nursing in managed community care (Hawkins et al. 1998), it is unclear what the longer term future for the relationship between these two groups in case management might be as the pressures to compete are both powerful and divisive. Abbott and Wallace (1998) argue that nursing has adopted new managerialism, and in our view it is professionally more entrepreneurial and vigorous in positioning itself in a changing world. Nursing has spearheaded the creation of the Case Management Societies in both Australia and the United States through smart corporate sponsorship arrangements. It has a pre-existing claim over social work in medical expertise; in community work it is familiar with devolved budgetary responsibility (Firth 1998/1999); and now it has developed valuable technical knowledge and skills through its experience with the processes of managed care. Nursing is perhaps additionally advantaged over social work in that it is accustomed to operationalising goals and working with protocols and cost caps (Caldwell 2000)—all desirable attributes in the health world and increasingly so in the human services.

PSYCHOLOGY AND MEDICINE

Psychologists, psychiatrists and physicians are consistently recognised in the health and human service literature as case managers. However, the acknowledgment is more commonly accorded by writers outside of these professional groups and seldom elaborated. Certainly these groups are peripheral in the debates about contested professional territory. Status factors may be operating here as the less influential and more insecure professional groups such as nurses and social workers, in health especially, vie for position. But let us pursue this a little further.

Neither the general case management literature nor, it would seem, the psychological or medical literature is characterised by much attention to case management itself, or these professions' preparation for and work in it. Psychiatrists like Kanter (1989) in the United States and Burns (2001) in the United Kingdom have certainly written extensively on practice approaches and on evaluation research respectively. Medicine has looked very closely at the role of the physician as the primary health provider, but how much this examination has extended to an analysis of the conceptual differences between case management and primary health care is unclear. Certainly there is evidence that physicians are responding with some interest to case management (McClaran et al. 1998) and their designation as case managers for the purposes of Medicaid in the United States (Hawkins et al. 1998) and their central role in Australian aged community care policies give them a formally mandated role. Those perhaps token medical writers included in more generic texts on case management commonly place themselves a little awkwardly to one side of the role. For example, Jones (1994) and Pearce and Morin (1998) concentrate on others that they will employ or connect with as case managers. The nursing writer Bower (1991) states that physicians only attend to the medical components of the work. This may in fact be appropriate, but exactly what it means and how the case management role may be professionally shared between medicine as the dominant profession and others warrants further scrutiny.

In relation to psychology, there appears to be a very loud silence indeed, both from within and from outside the profession, about its particular contributions and the implications of case management for it as a profession. The US social work writer Davis (1998) asserts, but does not elucidate, that psychology has been more proactive than social work, psychiatry, nursing and counselling in its educational and practice responses to managed care. It is likely that the claim is related to the private practice inclinations of US psychologists and the opportunities for them in managed care, and there are some psychology voices exploring how these opportunities might be even better realised by the profession (e.g. Knapp and Keller 2001; Reed et al. 2001). Certainly there is some research which indicates that psychologists, like nurses and social workers, are ethically exercised by the demands of managed care (Buckloh and Roberts 2001; Reed et al. 2001).

MORE ON PROFESSIONS AND CASE MANAGEMENT

NEW OPPORTUNITIES?

Professions, through their individual member, association or educational voices, have not been influential in the evolution and adoption of case management. Most professions have been confused about, actively resistant to or at least slow to respond to case management. The lamentations of the occupational therapist Hafez (2000) about her professional association's struggle to accommodate case management in its characterisation of practice is not unique. Obviously individual nurses, social workers, physicians and others, in the guise of or alongside policy-makers, planners, administrators and managers, have been in the vanguard of case management developments, but individual is the operative word. These individuals have stepped beyond, perhaps even rejected or been rejected by, a single professional identity and they are seldom endorsed spokespeople for their professions. However, there are signs of change.

There are some voices—perhaps still marginal—from within the professions which evidence enthusiasm about the possibilities presented by case management as an approach to service delivery. Orme and Glastonbury (1993) maintain that case management presents an almost too obvious but most significant mandated opportunity for professionals to work and learn together. Some social work writers, even more nursing writers and others with an eye to professional advancement suggest that case management may be the vehicle through which their profession might demonstrate leadership and enhance its power base. Lohman (1999, p. 113) says that case management will expand the 'field' of occupational therapy. The previously mentioned special claims of nursing and social work can be and are converted into valid statements of potential. In relation to social work, we have proposed in other places (Kennedy et al. 2001) that it could and should assume some leadership responsibility in the educational sphere at least. Orme and Glastonbury (1993) argue that social workers could become the assessment specialists in case management. However, motivating exhortations at professional conferences and in academic journals to critique or to seek leadership are not always accepted or easily translated into changed work structures, power relations and practice at the front line.

There is an alternative line of commentary which underscores the superficiality of any effort to equate case management with increased professional power. Daiski (2000), for example, argues convincingly that nursing aspirations for greater authority and improved quality of care through case management must be mediated by an appreciation that the goals of managed care are oriented to systems rather than patients. Thus managed care may offer opportunities to nurses but at the cost of profound ideological dilemmas. In a similar vein, Raiff and Shore (1993) observe social work's professional ambivalence with the neo-conservative aspects of case management. Firth's (1998/1999) study of the adjustment of staff to case management in the social services in the United Kingdom, which found increased accountability to the organisation rather than to service users, suggests similar challenges. There is, in fact, an academic debate in social work (Gordon and Kline 1997; Davidson and Davidson 1998) and in medicine (Agich and Forster 2000; Shapiro et al. 2000) about whether or not it is ethical to participate in managed care. Many related points have been canvassed in previous chapters and will again emerge in the later discussion about training and education.

DEPROFESSIONALISATION?

Concerns have been expressed by writers from different backgrounds about the potential for deprofessionalisation or deskilling under some manifestations of case management, and we have already mentioned a number of the pertinent managerial arguments. The concerns are located in the wider context of debates about the role and future of professions in society and, while these are not pursued here, one point must be made before we continue. Professions in society are already facing profound changes and perhaps deprofessionalisation through processes such as loss of cultural credibility, proletarianisation and/or internal combustion (Freidson 1994; Exworthy and Halford 1999). These things are not happening because of case management, although that phenomenon may in part reflect professions' loss of authority and at the same time exacerbate it. That said, the concerns about the deprofessionalising impact of case management take several forms.

One of them relates to the potentially conflicting aims of case management and professional practice. Daiski (2000, p. 77) concludes very forcefully that, in carrying out the technical tasks of care management, all participants including the case manager 'follow an algorithm for clinical decision-making. Therefore the primary goal of the case manager must be that the system is working smoothly, which is a management, not a nursing goal.' She adds that the management goal is inconsistent with holistic treatment of the individual, and that the managed care perspective does not support ethical professional nursing. Similarly, the British social work writer Lymbery (1998, p. 875) concludes that 'much of the work of the social worker within care management is limited by both time and resources . . . leading to a form of practice dominated by unimaginative, routinized, bureaucratic approaches . . . in fact, precisely the sort of practice which should no longer be considered as social work'.

A related set of concerns is founded on assumptions about professionals' exercise of discretion and independent functioning. The growth of procedural, technical and management controls over autonomous decision-making has been noted for nursing (Daiski 2000), social work (Sheppard 1995; Lymbery 1998; Firth 1998/1999) and medicine (Shapiro et al. 2000) in case management and particularly managed care. Firth (1998/1999) shows that social service staff in the United Kingdom, more than nursing staff, reported major role and accountability changes, loss of discretion, less enthusiasm and heightened anxiety after the introduction of case management.

However, professionals who rightly protest against technicalisation and the precedence of organisational needs often do not demonstrate that their practice under traditional service delivery arrangements was as autonomous and as client centred as they presume. In fact, as Austin (1993, p. 452) says, case management 'developed as a response to dysfunctional delivery systems' which were mostly orientated to provider and staff rather than client needs. Agich and Forster's (2000) analysis of the ethical dilemmas commonly asserted as inherent to managed care has some application in other areas of case management. They show that alleged conflicts between economic incentives and ethical obligations, assaults on patient and physician autonomy and erosion of the physician–patient relationship are not unique to managed care and not as serious as has been claimed. They posit that many aspects of these problems existed under the traditional fee-for-service approach to service delivery which was piecemeal, uncoordinated and where more service was equated with better service. Grusky (1997) similarly asserts that spending more on the client does not equate with better outcomes, yet some professional critiques of case management imply that budgetary control results in poorer service. While these points are quite compelling, they must not be allowed to mask the real problems of diminishing resources in health and human services.

Yet another connected concern about case management covers loss of intimacy with clients. Many people choose health and human service work in order to help people and this drive is commonly expressed through direct participation in the personal details of another's life. Heavy caseloads and case management models which shift problem-solving into the realm of inter-agency and system negotiation, and which emphasise outcomes rather than process, can separate workers from their perceived traditional sources of reward. Austin (1990, p. 403) says that the 'preference for more therapeutically oriented activities may not be fulfilled in many current case-management roles'. Of course, this hankering after intimacy with clients may reflect a flawed, nostalgic view of the helping world and it is also possible that some workers may be relieved at the distance now placed between them and the often dangerous, dirty and depressing lives of many clients.

It is also commonly alleged by professionals that case management dilutes professional identity and expertise. Joint training, removal of professional title, supervision by differently trained people, role blurring and regulation by organisational rather than professional codes and standards can trigger professional angst. Shapiro (2000), for instance, argues loss of clinical skills in medicine under managed care. However, the introduction of case management can be used unfairly as an explanation for all sorts of professional evils. For example, in Firth's (1998/1999) study mentioned above, one of the indicators which did not change for social service staff, relative to nursing staff, in the move to case management was role conflict because it was already high before the transition.

PARTICULAR CHALLENGES FOR SOCIAL WORK

For social work in particular, case management presents unique professional challenges, and there is debate within the profession about whether it can capitalise on or it is being attacked by case management (Payne 2000). Netting and Williams (1996) maintain that the question is not whether there are roles for social workers in case management, but whether or not they will perform them. This group is already recognised as well placed by its history and experience to approach case management confidently, yet it is perhaps most at risk from the phenomenon. Why is this? Comprehensive explanations for why social work is a 'fragile profession' (Abbott and Wallace 1998, p. 38) must be sought elsewhere, but we offer some comments about it in relation to case management. Social work has not engaged as forcefully and substantively as it might have with case management through its front-line work, professional association and education voices in particular. Its difficulties with the management aspect of the work have already been referred to and, while these are not unique to social work, they compound an already unpromising profile. At the front line, it sometimes assumes a pre-eminent role, rather than demonstrating special capacity, or it turns its face from such work altogether (Johnson and Rubin 1983; Austin 1990; Sullivan 1990).

An additional set of factors encumbers social work. It is a profession which, fairly or unfairly, commonly receives a poor press. Social work case managers are perceived by others as passive and insecure (Hawkins et al. 1998, p. 55) and/or unreliable, immature, gullible and unrealistic (Bar-On 1995, p. 70). Social work's areas of expertise remain ill-defined and easily trivialised (Abbott and Wallace 1998; Lymbery 1998), especially when they focus on process rather than outcomes. A number of British writers have argued that social workers have real difficulty in justifying their place now in social care because less qualified people are doing work that they once did and still do (Sheppard 1995; Abbott and Wallace 1998). In managed care in the United States, social work is said to be vulnerable because it is seen by administrators as an 'adjunct to the delivery of care' (Dzieglielewski and Holliman 2001, p. 132). Moreover, it is a profession readily 'misrepresented as cost ineffective' (Matorin 1998, p. 163), particularly in light of its adherence to notions of professional mentoring and supervision, which Matorin (1998, p. 163) refers to now as a 'luxurious antique'. Social work does have a traditional preoccupation with supervision which is now easily dismissed as indulgent and non-productive. However, the question of how to sustain good worker practice is very real and must not be lost. We will return to it in the next chapter.

In summary, social work has image problems and lacks an edge and a strategy for finding and implementing it in relation to case management. It is suggested that social work could capitalise on a previously and later mentioned perception that it is trained for case management work by developing and profiling the structure and content of its educational programs. It also has invaluable but poorly conceptualised and recognised potential in articulating and demonstrating skill in what Bar-On (1990, 1995) refers to as resource mobilisation. Dzieglielewski and Holliman (2001) advise social workers to become much more cost conscious in their work, more lateral in their thinking about their professional role possibilities, and better self-marketers and lobbyists.

A NEW PROFESSION OF CASE MANAGEMENT?

There are enthusiasts, mostly United States based, who assume or campaign for a new profession of case management. More often than not, they are prompted by a firm grasp of the magnitude, liability, financial commitment and business growth potential of case management activity in insurance-related areas such as managed care and workers' rehabilitation. The health care consultants Murer and Brick (1997, Foreword), for example, attempt to show that case management satisfies the traditional trait approach to classification of a profession. Their book mentions the need for new degrees for the 'evolving profession', and they draw attention to the existence of the Case Management Society of America as its representative body, to codes of ethics and to methods of self-regulation. Holt (2000), in a recent textbook, also refers to the evolving profession and Rossi (1999, p. 2) asserts that it is a 'profession [which] has been around for years'.

We do not agree that case management is a profession, whether one takes an idealised trait or other position on the term. Case management is an approach to or a methodology of service delivery. It concerns the way in which service is conceived of and structured. Case management functions are carried out by workers who may belong to groups which they or others consider to be professions. 'Case manager' obviously can be a job title, but we contend that it nominates approach to service delivery rather than type of worker. For this reason, we do not see sense in work towards a profession of case management, but we are realistic enough to concede that anything is possible in future if the cause has persistent and strategic supporters.

That said, two additional points are offered. Is case management work professional? Yes, very often, in the sense that it demands high levels of expertise, the exercise of discretion and adherence to standards of practice. But, as Moxley (1997) says, some case management approaches or functions involve relatively limited tasks which may not be described as professional. The critical issue is to have the chosen approach and its component parts so well conceptualised that particular people with the right knowledge and skills are matched against particular bits of the work.

If, as we argue, case management is not a profession in its own right, does it follow that it does not require specialist training? Are workers educated as nurses, social workers, psychologists and so on well prepared to carry out many of the components of case management work? Our answer is no, and this view will be supported in the next chapter.

CHOICES TO BE MADE

What a case manager makes of the positive, negative and often paradoxical forces outlined will be a function of professional identity, the particular model and organisation worked in and personal attitudes. In relation to the changes in community care in the United Kingdom and their impact on professional roles, Hadley and Clough (1997) state that workers are faced with making decisions about whether to hold course, exit the work, change their role or just survive. The same can be said of case management work and the necessity for personal decision-making reappears throughout this book. For some workers, case management may provide opportunities beyond traditional and often exclusive professional confines and/or open up private business possibilities. For others, perceived assaults by case management on professional identity and integrity may prompt work hibernation, passive resistance or retreat into familiar work habits where, despite the rhetoric, what is done resembles traditional forms of service delivery more than it does case management.

A more positive response to professional concerns calls for engagement with professional bodies and alliances with consumer groups in asking intelligent questions, publicising problems and lobbying for adaptation and change in programs. Informed workers are in a better position to make discriminating choices about the actual forms of case management work which best suit their professional skills, interests and futures. They may also be affirmed in their preference for direct service provision work and/or a single professional identity over case management. If this proves to be so, then they can seek alternative work positions in the full knowledge that they have made active choices based on a solid understanding of case management.

9

PREPARATION FOR CASE MANAGEMENT WORK

How have case managers been educated and trained for their work? The short answer to this question is generally 'not well'. The patterns of preparation for existing case managers reflect their varied backgrounds. In terms of education and training, nurses, social workers, occupational therapists, psychologists and other professionals functioning as case managers bring to the role their preservice profession-specific education with all its strengths and weaknesses, their profession-specific postgraduate education and, less commonly, a case management qualification. The formal educational qualifications of case managers in general range from school diplomas to doctorates (Intagliata 1992; Geron and Shassler 1994; Burns et al. 1995, p. 363), with overlays of work-based or agency-sponsored training and professional development.

In this chapter, university case management offerings which are profession and non-profession specific or generic are considered before work-based training and professional development. The terms 'education', in relation to universities, and 'training' for other possibilities, inclusive of on-the-job and vocational college activity, are used for convenience; the debate about the distinction between the two is not our focus. The categorisations utilised in this chapter are not entirely discrete, but they do stimulate exploration of a number of matters. Some university activity around case management, for example, may serve agency-sponsored training and/or professional development purposes. The profession-specific/non-specific distinction must also be qualified as an increasing number of offerings are claimed to embrace different professional groups. University options in case management range from fragments of material submerged in otherwise named and oriented subjects through to full programs which are directed specifically at case management practice and entitled 'case management'. These we tend to label loosely as formal offerings in case management.

PROFESSIONS AND CASE MANAGEMENT EDUCATION

Moxley (1997, p. 193) says of the United States that 'increasingly case management is seen as a core element of preservice preparation in social work, nursing, rehabilitation, and medical education'. Certainly, in Australia at least, employers seem to assume that graduates of social work and other human service degrees will have studied case management in their courses (Harvey et al. 2001). However, along with others (Weil et al. 1985; Witheridge 1992; Stroul 1995), we contend that the actual coverage of case management material at both undergraduate and postgraduate levels in most professional education is limited and unsatisfactory, both quantitatively and qualitatively. It is again within the ranks of social work and nursing that most of the discussion about professional education and training for case management occurs, and again normative assertions frequently coexist with evidence which suggests a different reality.

The US National Association of Social Workers (1992a, p. 23) claims that it is 'the only professional occupation that requires all practitioners to obtain professional education and training in the concepts of case management and to demonstrate an ability to apply these concepts successfully before recognition as social work professionals'. However, Austin and McClelland (1998) argue that social work courses in that country have been slow to embrace case management. Social work's educational deficiencies in relation to managed care have been noted too (Brooks and Riley 1998; Davis 1998). What case management education there is in social work in the United States is to be found mostly in undergraduate Bachelor of Social Work programs, although there are some reported examples of course activity at postgraduate level (Sullivan 1990; Moxley 1997). According to Raiff and Shore (1993), there has been little interest in developing graduate sequences in the United States because faculty members have been ill-prepared, they probably lack case management practice experience, and industry hiring practices do not commonly require Masters level applicants. Limited attention to case management in undergraduate and postgraduate social work education has been similarly and more recently acknowledged in Australia (Ozanne 1996; Kennedy et al. 2001).

In respect of the quality of social work education and case management, there appears to be a significant mismatch between what is done by case managers and the orientation and curriculum of preservice courses (Austin 1990; Bar-On 1990; Teare and Sheafor 1995; Hawkins et al. 1998; Wolk and Wertheimer 1999). In particular, the management issues discussed earlier pose significant challenges to existing curricula and teachers. The failure of preservice education to even scrutinise case management as an approach to service delivery, let alone canvass questions of worker influence, authority and resource mobilisation, has left many social workers ill-prepared to confront the demands of the role. At least in social work there has long been some recognition of these difficulties, and even suggestions that case managers may be better trained through undertaking public administration and business management courses (Gibelman 1983; Bar-On 1990).

Case management is also relatively new in nursing education (Haw 1995; Sinnen and Schifalaqua 1996; Hawkins et al. 1998). There are claims that it is not taught adequately in nursing generally in the United States (Genrich et al. 1999) and in mental health nursing in the United Kingdom (Thomas and Lovell 1999). It would seem, in contrast to social work, that most of the educational activity related to case management in nursing is at the postgraduate level. Haw's (1995) survey of US colleges revealed twelve programs or majors at postgraduate level and fewer (and a more muddied picture) at under-graduate level. That same 1995 study found that little research was being done by nursing faculty members around case management and that its inclusion in curricula was retarded by few nursing case manager role models, limited faculty expertise in the area and limited clinical placements.

Most of the criticisms made of social work and nursing education are relevant to other professions, but less acknowledged. Kanter (1989) asserted some years ago that social work, psychiatry, nursing and psychology in the United States all failed to systematically educate for case management work in preservice courses. The reasons for these educational inadequacies lie in faculty inexperience, concern about the theoretical and ideological integrity of the approach, lack of consensus about desirable backgrounds for case managers (Challis 2000) and the view canvassed earlier that case management is only a new title for old approaches to intervention and thus adequately covered in existing curricula. Professional education is often coupled with licensing and other accreditation requirements which complicate and retard responsive and innovative changes in courses, especially those which are 'interprofessional' (Mathias and Thompson 1997). In addition, pressures within universities compress the time, space and resources that disciplines need to cover traditional core curricula (e.g. for social work see Matorin 1998). In this sort of environment, tradition frequently prevails over new integrative and interdisciplinary material.

GENERIC CASE MANAGEMENT EDUCATION

Given that case management jobs have been in evidence for some years in many countries, generic university courses in case management might be expected to be flourishing, if not at preservice then at post-professional levels. The need for interprofessional or transdisciplinary training in the health area at least has been noted (McClaran et al. 1998). In fact, such courses have been slow to develop and most of the available options are postgraduate. The sluggish response to case management by profession-specific education has not been paralleled by a rapid expansion in generic courses. A few examples of generic university education in Canada and Australia (Ozanne et al. 2000; Kennedy et al. 2001), and in the United States in the health area in particular (McClaran et al. 1998), are reported. However, even the supposedly generic courses are commonly initiated and managed within the confines of one professional group such as nursing or social work, and thus evidence its orientation.

At a time when universities across the world are struggling to maintain income, it is curious that they have not seized at least the post-professional retraining or professional development opportunities presented by the adoption of case management in so many fields of practice. Why is this so? The answers lie in a complex amalgam of sociological and practical factors concerning the changing status and roles of education, the professions and health and human service work, some of which have already been mentioned in relation to case management.

Change in universities is generally a notoriously slow process as Meerabeau's (1998) analysis of nursing education in the United Kingdom shows so well. Her commentary on the power of disciplinary identity, abstract knowledge and boundary closure which has impeded the creation of academic disciplines in social work and nursing in particular applies even more to the hybrid creature that is case management. Case management is not the product of one disciplinary domain; it is rooted in practice and the 'female helping professions', and is thus a prime target for classic academic prejudices about what is intellectually and theoretically respectable and important. However, some academic caution is defensible.

We have argued elsewhere that case management practice is moving ahead of complementary theoretical work, largely through the relatively modest engagement by university faculties with case management (Kennedy et al. 2001). Partial and *ad hoc* course developments do not support intellectual activity of substance or vice versa. In these circumstances, the conceptual underpinnings of case management and the discourses necessary to challenge and improve practice remain underdeveloped. As Bricker-Jenkins (1992, p. 127) says of casework—though this is equally applicable to case management—much poor practice results from poor theory. Fortunately, current imperatives for universities to work in partnership with industry allow some optimism about the potential for joint teaching and research between practitioners and academics of the kind envisaged by Davidson (1998) in respect of case management, and demonstrated by several Canadian universities (Ozanne et al. 2000).

WORK-BASED TRAINING

Most of the case management training to date has occurred 'on the job', commonly through industry or government initiatives. This is reported for the United Kingdom (Hadley and Clough 1997; Gournay and Thornicroft 2000), the United States (Raiff and Shore 1993; Haw 1996), Japan, Canada and Australia (Ozanne et al. 2000). Among the reasons for this is the widespread adoption of whole-workforce enhancement policies. In Britain, the United States, New Zealand and Australia, governments have pursued general work-based assessment and recognition policies designed to improve workforce skills, flexibility and mobility. These moves have created what are known commonly in the United States and Australia as worker competencies (Bricker-Jenkins 1992; McCallum and Furby 1999), or in the United

Kingdom as National Vocational Qualifications (NVQs) (Mathias and Thompson 1997; Coulshed and Mullender 2001), and they emphasise output at work rather than input through formal qualifications. Thus, in many countries, programmatic, short, work-focused training is now contextually legitimated.

A number of the writers mentioned in earlier discussions of new managerialism see these developments as evidence of that very phenomenon (Hugman 1998a; Lymbery 1998; Jones 1999) because of their propagation of uncritical, formulaic descriptors of correct action. A more practical, but in no way inconsistent, reason for the prevalence of work-based training is that, as we have shown, case management has come to many workers once on the job. In the absence of formal qualifications, or in the presence of a non-uniformly qualified workforce, work-based training will be the obvious route through which new service delivery arrangements are introduced.

Before turning to the shape of work-based training, we require some assistance with the term itself. Payne's (1995, p. 226) schema which differentiates initial training, agency training and post-qualifying training provides useful headings for structuring further exploration of the topic.

A wide interpretation of initial training includes preservice professional education which has been, and will again be, considered, as well as preparation of workers for the introduction of new case management programs and agency–program induction of new workers. There is general consensus among commentators that the introduction of case management requires significant planning, resourcing, managing and the creation of appropriate structures for staged development of worker skill and agency effectiveness (Weil et al. 1985; Roberts-DeGennaro 1987; Rapp and Poertner 1992; Payne 1995; Rothman and Sager 1998) if it is not to be completely 'insufficient' (Gournay and Thornicroft 2000, p. 371). However, particularly for workers reassigned to case management roles, such training has been limited (Gursansky and Kennedy 1998; Matorin 1998; Rothman and Sager 1998). Kubisa (1990) argues that the cultural shift and training necessary to move a staff team to a new care management system takes two to three years to achieve. This timeline is generally inconsistent with current managerialist imperatives.

Payne (1995) contends that, as agency training targets experienced staff and commonly has an operational bias, it should be differentiated from post-qualifying training in which contextual and policy material, along with advanced skill development, are essential. He supports a planned and progressive approach to workforce knowledge and skill development. We endorse his position but find little evidence of it happening in practice. Rapp and Poertner's (1992, p. 167) concerns about training as a 'knee-jerk reaction to agency problems or a supposed panacea thrown at some organizational dilemmas' resonate with us a decade later. The resultant wasted resources, and more particularly the curdling of positive staff energy, are lamentable. If anything, the risk of superficial, variable quality agency-sponsored training is on the increase as educational consultants and providers—universities among them—compete for contracts with employers. The latter are themselves struggling to reconnoitre a most bewildering array of educational offerings and promises.

Four problems, in our experience, are conspicuous in the design and delivery of initial, agency and post-qualifying case management training.

POOR CONCEPTUALISATION OF CASE MANAGEMENT AND ROLES

The adoption of case management has not been accompanied by an adequate conceptualisation of the agency approach or the roles, authorities and relationships of the staff involved. Training is often contracted on a taken-for-granted basis as far as the form of the approach is concerned. Thus training easily degenerates into a debate about what case management actually is and/or a belated consultation on what it should be in that agency and/or protracted and generally unsatisfactory discussions about things like access to resources and client records, lines of management responsibility and location of decision-making.

CONSUMERS IGNORED

The clients–consumers–carers of the agency have been less prepared, or 'trained', for the introduction of case management than have the workers. We have elsewhere described bemused consumer responses to the introduction of a new case management service (Gursansky and Kennedy 1998) and in a previous chapter the problem of unmet expectations with ill-prepared clients was addressed. Confused and anxious clients and workers can very easily establish a mutually reinforcing cycle of resistance to changes in service delivery.

INADEQUATE CONTINUITY AND PROGRESSION

With frequent restructuring in organisations and high turnover of staff, corporate memory is poor. Decisions made about training are often ahistoric. Fragmented and repetitive, if not contradictory, training programs result. Thus staff skills and knowledge are not accumulating over time or being properly extended and evaluated in ways which are necessary for improved service delivery. Payne's (1995) vital sequence of operational training and advanced contextual and skill programs is frequently ignored. Staff unhappiness about training experiences in community mental health care in the United Kingdom has led to Senn et al. (1997) proposing that training budgets be allocated per worker, so that individually appropriate training programs can be constructed. There is a certain irony in concluding that principles about individualised service delivery, central to case management, are also applicable to human resource matters.

INAPPROPRIATE LEVEL AND PITCH

The level at which training is pitched is often unsuitable for the backgrounds and experience of the staff involved and inadequately integrated with their previous formal or likely future formal education. This is not surprising given the increasingly complex and diverse world of formal educational offerings, and the heterogeneity of many staff groups. There are two frequent outcomes of this problem. One is that all case managers, despite their backgrounds, are exposed to elementary material. Raiff and Shore (1993) have commented on the brief and introductory nature of much case management training. The second is that case managers do not receive appropriate credit for work training when they enrol in formal educational courses, because articulation negotiations between the sponsors of work-based training and educational providers have not taken place. However, there are some reports of commendable agency–university integrated approaches in child mental health in the United States (Weil et al. 1995) and in Canada (Fineman 1996), and it is likely that these will increase as universities become more entrepreneurial and workers more astute about their educational options.

HOW SHOULD CASE MANAGERS BE PREPARED FOR THEIR WORK?

This question raises a complex set of debates and paradoxes about case management, some of which have been discussed in earlier chapters. For example, is case management a profession or an extension of the traditional role of a pre-existing profession? Responses to these queries will shape views about the ideal educational preparation for case management. In this section, we canvass three issues: the juxtaposition of qualified and unqualified case managers; the level and disciplinary character of qualifications; and the essential elements of case management educational programs.

JUXTAPOSITION OF FORMALLY QUALIFIED AND UNQUALIFIED CASE MANAGERS

This issue has significant implications both for the future of case management itself and for those professional groups whose past and future is linked with it. These professions face serious dilemmas about leadership roles and about the risks of job competition in case management. However, any hint of a positive relationship between work performance and the absence of formal qualifications is often rejected out of hand by them. Abbott's (1998) work on the conflict between district nurses and home helps in frail aged community care in the United Kingdom is one instructive example of this professional denial. District nurses claimed that clients preferred them rather than unqualified home helps to perform personal care tasks. In fact, when asked, clients expressed greater satisfaction with home helps and described them as more friendly, approachable, willing and client-oriented than nurses. Studies such as these demand critical and strategic responses from the professional groups involved—in this case, nursing. Defensive reaction by the professions will result in the unattractive and futile 'occupational closure' depicted by Abbott (1998) and will not serve to save professional jobs.

There is little research on the sensitive matter of the relationship between qualifications and effectiveness. In 1985, Weil et al. (1985, p. 371) wrote on the question of who functions best as a case manager: 'These issues elicit strong feelings, but at present there is little research on which to base decisions.' Applebaum and McGinnis (1992, p. 13), in discussing the use of aides in home care in the United States, say 'a review of research in this area fails to identify even a single study that evaluated the effects of differential levels of training on worker quality'. These conclusions are not surprising given the diverse contexts and ways in which case management is carried out, varied criteria for effectiveness and the difficulties of comparing preparation, of which education is only one component, in any controlled way.

The juxtaposition of qualified and unqualified staff presents employers with difficulties in constructing staff development programs. For educational providers, it complicates the design of suitable curricula and the determination of eligibility for entry to the academy and at what level. Balancing educational appropriateness for unqualified but experienced workers and academic integrity is hard. Unqualified case managers themselves face particular issues of mobility and status, and associated personal decisions about professional development and employment futures. We will return to this point later.

The increasing interest in consumers, carers and parents as care managers (Stroul 1995; Moxley 1997) compounds the qualifications landscape. Many of these people are not formally qualified either in case management or in any other relevant professional area. While bringing essential attributes to the role—for example, they are reported to be more personalistic and flexible (Moxley 1989)—they must also be nurtured and to some extent protected. They are easily viewed as second-class workers in environments which value credentials (Mowbray et al. 1996), and this can undermine their effectiveness—to say nothing of their confidence. We advocate their use but, with others (Moxley 1997; Rapp 1998a), argue that they—like employee case managers—must be recruited and sustained with systematic organisational support and professional development programs.

Whatever one's position on qualifications, the fundamental importance of the case manager's personal qualities in combination with or independent of qualifications must again be recognised (Witheridge 1992). Rapp (1998a) reports a number of studies which found that consumers valued the interpersonal characteristics of their case managers much more than they did their credentials or consumer–non-consumer status. Witheridge (1992) doubts whether some aspects of the intensive case manager's role can be taught, and Rubin (1992) similarly wonders whether any type of preparation can adequately prepare a worker.

APPROPRIATE LEVELS AND DISCIPLINARY CHARACTER OF CASE
MANAGEMENT EDUCATION

There are two themes in the debate here. One concerns the level of entry, inclusive of qualifications, which is argued to be appropriate for case management work. The other relates to preferred professional qualifications. There is a general silence on the question of the value of generic compared with profession-specific case management education.

On the question of level of entry and qualifications, there are again two main, but overlapping areas, of deliberation. One concentrates on the advanced nature of the work and the other on matching qualifications to the type of work. A number of writers argue that case managers require postgraduate qualifications. Genrich et al. (1999) assert this for nurses and Siefker et al. (1998, p. 113) claim that case management in insurance rehabilitation is not a suitable 'entry-level occupation' for graduates. Raiff and Shore (1993) believe that their clinical case management approach requires a Masters or doctorate level qualification in interpersonal relations and psychopathology. This position on clinical case management is endorsed by others (Kanter 1989; Kanter 1992; Walsh 2000), who argue the need for Masters degrees in social work, psychology or nursing. Likewise, the highly technical demands of clinical pathways work are claimed to demand higher level qualifications (Moxley 1997). Murer and Brick (1997) declare for health case management that a Masters degree covering a range of health policy and regulation issues is desirable but seldom possible because the curriculum is not widely available. Their rider has more general application in that, no matter what is thought to be necessary in the way of qualifications, and even if they are available, the existent workforce may not possess them.

The more profitable line of discussion is that which emphasises congruence between type of case management program and level of qualification. Raiff and Shore (1993) differentiate between discrete case management tasks such as intake and referral, for which a Bachelors degree is appropriate, and psychosocial enhancement case management programs for which a Masters level degree in social work, psychology or nursing is necessary. Moxley (1997, p. 59) similarly argues that 'deprofessionalization can be useful when case management tasks are routine, high levels of clinical judgement are not required, and these case managers are provided good and timely supervision'. Challis (1990, p. 13) suggests that 'less professional staff' could undertake tasks of coordination and monitoring and Sheppard (1995) that some case management tasks can be done by people with vocational qualifications. Challis (1990), however, also argues that, in any system which allocates case management tasks among differently qualified staff, there is a risk of perpetrating a problem of social care whereby practical and psychological needs are separated, resulting in fragmented service for the consumer. Some US writers (Intagliata 1992; Rubin 1992) wonder whether highly qualified staff may be unwilling to undertake some of the more practical aspects of case management work—although this is disputed in Sankar and Brook's (1998) study of Master of Social Work qualified case managers—and whether they may be more prone to burnout. Intagliata (1992) argues that it is cost-effective to have paraprofessionals engage in linking and monitoring tasks. This position is arguable given the importance of the exercise of both discretion and authority in the monitoring task, especially if it spans multiple agencies.

As to which professional group is best educated for case management practice, the absence of adequate evaluative data is again evident, as are insular professional perspectives. Raiff and Shore (1993, p. 105) say in relation to social work that its claim for a special affinity in the preparation of case managers 'rests more on a theoretically defended than on a pragmatically demonstrated ground', and Challis (1990) argues that the relationship between care management and social work is insufficiently clarified. Social workers are perhaps more willing than many other groups to be self-critical about their preparation. For example, Challis (1990, p. 19), from within the profession, notes their deficiencies in clinical issues, negotiation and budget management, and Bar-On (1990) their lack of management and business acumen.

A few writers display a refreshing awareness of the range of professional groups actually involved in case management practice and even attempt some analysis of their comparative strengths and weaknesses. Weil et al. (1985), for example, describe which professional groups most commonly work in case management on the basis of field, target populations or function; their statements are consistent with the routine–clinical differentiations made earlier. Siefker et al.

(1998, p. 113) warn against the possible limitations of nurses compared with social workers in the non-medical aspects of rehabilitation cases, but also suggest that nurses, social workers and counsellors may not adjust well to case management in the insurance rehabilitation field because they are 'too client-advocacy orientated'. This declaration certainly reveals a position on the hegemony of the insurer! The same writers endorse the value of a business background for case management work in this area. Hawkins et al. (1998) argue that nurses and social workers have been better prepared for case management work through their broader scope of preservice training than have physicians. Orme and Glastonbury (1993) would allocate different workers to different stages of the case management process. They advocate that social workers carry out assessment functions and the person who has the necessary skills, whether unqualified or qualified, handles other phases of case management.

In summary, there is no consensus on the appropriate type and level of educational preparation for case management work (Rubin 1992; McClelland et al. 1996), and it is not useful to prolong debate about ideal forms. The enormous diversity in the fields, targets and functions of the work has been recognised now to the point where difference in preparation must also be formally acknowledged as both real and desirable. The case management discourse is mature enough to recognise that not all clients need case management, and as Orme (1993) argues, this point is interdependent with a similar appreciation of the variety in workers' backgrounds. The critical issue now is discriminating the skills and knowledge, supervision and support required by the particular case management program. Rapp's (1998a) recent conclusion that case managers should be selected as and when appropriate from a wide pool, including qualified and unqualified staff and consumers, is convincing. He adds that all of them must be well supervised and have easy access to necessary experts. Similarly, Rothman and Sager (1998) argue that, no matter who the workers are, they need access to expert consultants, solid supervision and—most important, we believe—adequate clerical backup.

IMPORTANT COMPONENTS OF CASE MANAGEMENT EDUCATION AND TRAINING

There is considerable agreement about necessary curriculum themes such as history and the policy context, and the stages of and worker skills required for the case management process. Management and entrepreneurial skills are also commonly and properly stressed (e.g. see Hawkins et al. 1998). A curriculum outline is not presented here because so much is dependent on education of whom, at what level and for what purpose. We do comment on a number of issues which recur to varying degrees in the literature and which we argue have applicability across all levels of education and training for all professional groups. We consider that all case managers require more than introductory exposure to the following material somewhere in their combinations of education, training activity and professional development experiences.

Competent management of diversity

The need for case managers to be culturally competent (Rogers 1995; Este 1996) goes almost without saying and has been alluded to earlier in the policy section. The reasons for and likelihood of case managers working with racial, religious, ethnic, Indigenous and other forms of diversity or cultural variability have been stressed for, among others, Canada and the United States (e.g. Rogers 1995; Este 1996), the United Kingdom (e.g. Cox 1997) and Australia (Harvey et al. 2001). In a three-year sample of Australian case management job advertisements, one-quarter of them required the worker to have knowledge and skills in working with Indigenous people and communities (Harvey et al. 2001). It is also generally agreed that most forms of preservice education or post-service training have not addressed this multifaceted area adequately (Rogers 1995; Este 1996; Cox 1997).

Rogers (1995, p. 62) defines cultural competence as the compilation of system or agency policies, and the personal attitudes, behaviours, skills and knowledge that are required for case managers to function effectively with people of diverse backgrounds and experiences. Rogers' inclusion of the agency is salient as it is easy to locate responsibility for effectiveness in the worker alone. The way in which the agency evidences its leadership, community consultation processes, program designs, resources and training relevant to cultural diversity will shape case manager attitudes and behaviour. Both Rogers (1995) and Este (1996) describe cultural competence as a developmental process, and this assertion—with which we agree—raises a number of points.

Competence with diversity must be emphasised beyond the more obvious issues of ethnicity and skin colour. Case management is characterised by diversity within and across staff and professional groups, within and across agency procedures and practices, and within client groups of similar ethnicity. Diversity, in fact, characterises many interdisciplinary teams and it is important that learning about difference and skills in dealing with it are generalised into all areas of work. Appreciating that 'a team's cognitive capability is related to its cognitive diversity' (Gardner and Cary 1999, p. 6) is vital.

Competence in managing diversity cannot be achieved through training and education alone. It is most unlikely to result from short inservice courses which lack follow-up and are not embedded in agency policies and practices. Evolutionary processes in educational programs and at work which require and encourage students and case managers to confront their own values and to open themselves progressively to different appreciations of the world are essential. It is timely for preservice professional educators in areas such as nursing and social work to develop joint qualifications with, for example, Indigenous studies, other language courses or health administration, and to encourage overseas student programs. Of course, personal characteristics including differential ability and willingness to expose oneself to diversity are also critical factors in these processes. Resistance to change and personal inflexibility in students and workers present the most vexing challenges for teachers and managers as confrontation must itself avoid any hint of cultural hegemony or harassment. Without in any way diminishing the importance of cultural competence, we believe that it should derive in both workplaces and educational programs from a broader philosophical commitment to unconditional courtesy, civility and tolerance.

Spanning and managing boundaries

It is generally agreed that training in multidisciplinary skills and practice is essential for case managers. We qualify this with two points. First, the term 'multidisciplinary' is narrow and suggests looking out or across from within professional groups. The wider phrase 'systems-spanning perspective' used by Vourlekis and Greene (1992, p. 181) is preferable because it can encompass awareness and action across boundaries and intersections other than just professional ones. It is relevant to boundaries and relationships within and between organisations, both government and non-government; between different levels of organisations and governments; between formal and informal service systems; and between workers and clients. At a personal level, the boundaries between thinking and doing and between teaching and learning especially must be understood and managed. Good case management education models good practice and reflects successful integration of boundaries between intellectual, emotional and practical spheres of activity. Schon's (1983) conception of the reflective practitioner is especially applicable to case management in its thrust for thinking across margins in problem-setting and action. In summary, perhaps the most fundamental requirements for case management practice are a perceptual set open to diverse values and structures and the skills in responding to them.

Second, the term 'multidisciplinary' lends itself to simplistic training program designs. In these, descriptions of different professional groups and exhortations to goodwill and collaborative practice can mask more complex matters of socialisation, power and authority, gender and the fact that collaboration is both a process and an outcome (Gardner and Cary 1999). It has been argued that insufficient attention is paid generally in professional and post-qualification education to 'role self-management', which is so essential in the team aspects of case management (Ovretveit 1993, p. 100). Hunter (1997) lists recurring team problems as the absence of care coordination, professional deskilling, contested role overlap between professionals, reduced role autonomy and role overload. Analysis of problems before solutions takes time and many training programs lack this. In addition, attention to problems runs counter to much of the managerialist discourse which has a strongly 'can-do' orientation and frowns upon so-called 'negative thinking'.

We agree with Moxley (1997) and Hawkins et al. (1998) that transdisciplinary approaches to education are desirable. That is, educators are selected on the basis of expertise rather than professional identity and there is recognition that working across traditional boundaries is in and of itself an area of special expertise which helps a team achieve more than just the sum of its component parts could. Transdisciplinary practice requires team members in the words of Raiff and Shore (1993, p. 95) to 'release' previously exclusive aspects of their professional roles to other groups, and to take on expanded roles as consultants. Casto et al. (1994) similarly explore the paradox of collaboration where conscious surrendering of power can produce very powerful practice. It is of course no mean feat to integrate this additional externally focused material while maintaining the integrity of core curriculum in any profession-specific program.

Multidisciplinary, and especially transdisciplinary, training and education are complex operations which generally require fundamental reorganisation of educational institutional structures. Staff readiness for this type of training first needs to be tested and developed (McClaran et al. 1998). The program itself must then recognise and challenge the professional socialisation which may have already taken place in the respective professional groups (Waugaman 1994). Boundary ambiguities and expectations between professional groups must be faced in training before it can and should move to joint activity and blurred roles (Bruhn et al. 1993; Payne 1995; Hawkins et al. 1998). Also relevant to the theme of different socialisation is acknowledgment that joint work or teamwork in case management demands some public performance and, while this can be exciting as Drake and Marlowe (1998) suggest, the resultant scrutiny can be extremely unnerving for groups like social workers who have been habituated in 'private' work with and for clients (Pithouse 1987).

Management of conflict in particular, and also decision-making, needs to be addressed (Ovretveit 1993). Gardner and Cary (1999, p. 5) say that 'many professions have not been socialized to understand the positive aspects of conflict and have great difficulty in dealing with it at any level'. Professions like social work have been acculturated in a consensual paradigm which implicitly characterises conflict as negative. Gardner and Cary assert that there will be no synthesis in team thinking and poor decision-making will occur unless these patterns are confronted and managed. If conflict is to be understood and handled, it is critical for theory and practice on the stages of team development to be covered. Dovetailing, or integrated and complementary work in teams, generally only comes after sequential periods of getting acquainted, competing and defending and then resolving operating norms (Hunter 1997, p. 211). In the same vein, promotion of the importance and 'ordinariness' of conflict, accepted and managed through arbitration and complaints processes within staff teams and for clients, is critical. Gardner and Cary's (1999) analysis of collaboration and conflict in professional groups characterised by power differentials provides a useful platform of knowledge for constructing educational programs for case managers.

A framework for making sense of the world

Perhaps one of the most central and difficult aspects of education in this area is assisting workers, in the face of often overwhelming evidence of the problems with case management, to avoid falling prey to cynicism and/or paralysis. Ideally, case management practice is founded on sound contextual information about history, policy development and implementation and evaluation, but this will expose workers to many of the damning conclusions addressed in previous chapters. How are these powerful conclusions to be acknowledged by the case manager while continuing to function effectively? How might the worker avoid the classic extremes of powerlessness which maintain the status quo, and the assumption of unrealistic responsibilities for outcomes that will never be effected, which leads to burnout (Taylor and Barnet 1999)? We have canvassed this most thorny question from other angles in previous chapters. There are no simple and single answers. However, we endorse Sheppard's (1995) view that adoption of a paradigm to help reconcile training for practice with the structural constraints of case management work is both necessary and possible.

A number of different ready-made approaches are available to educators; each may be useful in different circumstances and at different stages of professional life. For example, Daiski (2000) proposes a process of intellectual activity in which some adaptation to the system is combined with a change in perceptual sets on one's approach to the system and place in it. She suggests—as we have done previously in the interests of enhancing worker influence and impact—pursuing leadership, advocacy and alliances in and across practitioners and professional associations and amongst educators. Consumer groups can be added to this list, and Rothman and Sager (1998) promote interorganisational relationships. Schon's (1983) analysis of the reflective practitioner can also be useful for challenging and assisting workers to reframe their perceptions. Lipsky's (1980) notion of the street-level bureaucrat is potentially most helpful in assisting workers to see how they do influence and shape various aspects of their complex work worlds.

CASE MANAGEMENT AND PROFESSIONAL DEVELOPMENT

In any area of work, professional development is necessary if both organisations and workers are to adapt to changing conditions. By professional development, we mean any combination of supervision, work-based training, formal educational and professional extension activities which constitute individual and work group development plans. Case management raises a particularly challenging set of professional development responsibilities for both individuals and organisations. As case management has in many circumstances been imposed on an existing workforce which has limited or no relevant pre- or post-service training, what is expected of professional development may amount to almost full retraining. At the same time, opportunities for training have in many cases shrunk (Brooks and Riley 1998) and, as has been shown, the educational pathways in case management are patchy and non-uniform.

Employers bear major industrial and moral responsibilities for supervising, evaluating, challenging, supporting and developing workers in the interests of good practice. Without good management of workers, good management of service delivery by workers can neither be expected nor ensured. However, the interplay between individual and organisational factors in this area has long been recognised, and a range of other forces exist, which may well confront the individual with unwelcome and perhaps even inappropriate responsibilities. The problems of work-based training have already been discussed, and if an agency is not managing its training adequately, chances are it is not managing individual worker professional development well either. The process-oriented professional supervision traditionally expected by social workers in particular is less feasible and credible in new organisational and management arrangements. As has already been shown, an increasing number of case managers are, or can expect to become, subcontractors who do not fall within the sphere of responsibility of any agency. Other workers, still classed as employees, move relatively frequently between jobs, and their agency-sponsored training and professional development experiences may lack continuity and substance. On the whole, whether employees or self-employed, case managers are increasingly expected to have the capacity to 'get on with the job' with minimal external supports.

In summary, case managers often need to face professional development decisions and planning on two interconnected levels. One concerns life issues and the pursuit of survival strategies. This area has prompted a range of self-help and 'how-to' literature, which although often simplistic, at least recognises the complexity and demands of the case manager's role. Woodside and McClam (1998), for example, address tactics for preventing burnout, for evolving a healthy philosophy about case management work and for improving time management and assertion skills. Frager (2000) details what she refers to as the secrets of and answers to the difficulties of working with managed care organisations in the United States.

The second level of decision-making relates to professional identity, job mobility and formal qualifications. Individual workers face inconsistent, unreliable and rapidly changing data about what qualifications and experience they need for job competitiveness and mobility. In our experience, professional and educational parochialism and competition make it difficult for case managers to get objective advice from peers or educators about the necessity for professional or other qualifications, accreditations or affiliations in their personal career-planning processes. In devising a personal plan, all the assessment, resourcefulness, creativity and critical thinking skills required of a good client plan will be demanded of them. Strickland and O'Connell (1998), in reference to nursing in the United States, stress the opportunities as well as the challenges presented by fluid and dynamic work environments and tie together both personal and professional credential levels in their argument that case managers must shift to independent and entrepreneurial thinking about themselves. Their exhortation (1998, p. 8) that 'you need to see yourself as a talented, well credentialed individual with an extensive portfolio of skills, resources and experiences' is applicable to groups other than nursing. Some of these points are elaborated on in the next chapter.

CHAPTER

10

REGULATING CASE MANAGEMENT

The ways in which workers and their work are controlled, inhibited or regulated are always many and varied. For case managers in particular, the regulation backdrop is intricate, uncertain and often untested, because it crosses professional boundaries and covers new approaches to practice.

The notion of regulation, in its broadest sense, embodies a number of questions in health and human services. Who, if anyone, regulates and for what purpose? What are the regulators' sources of authority? What do they regulate? How formal is the regulatory system? Does the regulation work directly and/or indirectly on the target? How is compliance policed and what are the risks of detection for breaches? What are the penalties for breach? Does the existent regulatory system work to achieve the set purposes? Each of these questions is underpinned by an array of debates, driven by ideological, political, historical and methodological differences. In relation to case management, the debates are diffused and confused by the service delivery permutations across a range of fields of practice and by the involvement of different occupations and professions.

Regulation brings formal structural aspects of systems to mind—for instance, licensing and accreditation which directly impinge on access to practice and/or service provision rights. More indirect, but still formal, regulatory factors—such as civil law remedies—are less frequently acknowledged. Even less recognised as regulatory are the myriad other forces which shape and curb the behaviour of services and workers. Professional education—which we have already addressed—acculturates, moulds and prescribes workers' knowledge and behaviour. Management processes and practices, also previously discussed, by definition aim to control agency and worker behaviour and standardise service delivery. Human resource policies direct who is employed and how performance is monitored and rewarded. Funding sources command and prohibit agency and sometimes worker activity. Individual case managers' values are very insistent forces. These regulatory factors are not always obvious in that the relationship between them and control of service or behaviour is more circuitous and perhaps less immediate, but their impact is nonetheless significant.

It is important that the range and interplay of different levels of factors which can manipulate and monitor service delivery are appreciated because it is often the least obvious, informal and internal which can be the most compelling influences—for both good and bad. It is also important for case managers to understand the extent, source and type of constraints on their work because this knowledge can promote wider scope for independent action following assessment of the risks of compliance and non-compliance.

Figure 10.1 displays a range of interrelated targets and forces which might assist in an understanding of the landscape of case management regulation. The diagram is not comprehensive of all regulatory forces, targets and relationships, but it does underscore the scope and range of actors and influences involved. We have adapted Kane and Degenholtz's (1997) internal–external dichotomy from quality in home care because it encourages workers in particular to include locus of control when considering constraints on their work. As individual workers and agencies are two of the common targets of regulatory systems and processes, they are separated in the diagram. Examples of both formal and informal forces which can act on each of them are included. For instance, agencies and particular groups of workers may both require licensing under some form of state legislation before they can deliver a case management service. This force is formal in that it carries the weight of the state, has penalties for breach and is publicly documented. At the other end of the formality continuum, case managers' behaviour is regulated by their own beliefs, which are seldom public and for which breaches are a purely private matter. In the mid-range of the formality continuum are factors such as the impact of employer or agency requirements and professional codes of ethics on workers.

The sections which follow look more closely at licensing and

Figure 10.1 Range of regulatory influences on case management agencies and workers

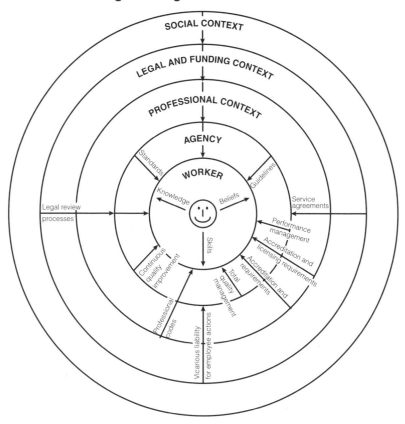

registration issues, other legal regulatory influences, accreditation, standards and guidelines for practice and codes of ethics, with a focus on the case manager.

LAW: LICENSING OR REGISTERING FOR CASE MANAGEMENT

A formal and direct form of regulation is evident when the state legislates to control aspects of service delivery, professional practices and/or the use of a professional title. Enos and Southern (1996, p. 218) define licensing in contrast to certification as 'a more highly regulated process. It is the formal and legal regulation of practice by statute law. In relation to individuals it functions to control access to both a title and to define the area of practice competency and jurisdiction.' It may also be directed at service provider agencies.

In relation to service provision and case management, there is a long legislative history which has been canvassed earlier in this book. Case management may be prescribed or at least acknowledged in the acts themselves, or in related regulations. In the United States, there is a legislative mandate in the areas of mental illness, child welfare, community-based long-term care, substance abuse and unemployment (Applebaum and Austin 1990; Austin 1993; Geron and Shassler 1994; Hagen 1994; Perlmutter and Johnson 1996; Austin and McClelland 1997) and in the United Kingdom such a mandate exists in long-term care (Payne 1995; Leutz 1999; Challis 2000). In Australia, case management has been enjoined legislatively in homelessness and labour market programs (Gursansky and Kennedy 1998; Wearing 1998). In Israel, case management had a central role in the legislative reorganisation of community aged care services in 1988 (Lowenstein 2000), as it has in Japan more recently (Ikegami 2000). The critical point is that, under all of these schemes—despite the different legislative agendas— case management as an approach to service delivery has formally received the imprimatur of a national government.

A multitude of other legislative systems and provisions may formally regulate the service program contexts in which case management, managed care or care management operate, even though these approaches may not be required by law. The manifestations of case management in these contexts will be moulded by the broader legal framework in which they operate. For example, legislative controls on agency performance may include requirements about worker qualifications and training (Geron and Shassler 1994), which will shape the character and style of the workforce. Hugman (1991) argues that there is a correlation between low levels of qualifications in social care areas, such as nursing homes in the United Kingdom, and greater pressures on governments to establish formal monitoring systems in those areas. If this position is combined with moves to deregulate workforces, it may be that regulatory systems in the human services in particular can be expected to concentrate more on service or agency performance indicators than on individual staffing qualifications.

However, at the individual worker level, states also do legislate to control the use of professional titles or practices. As yet, the title of case management is minimally regulated. In Japan, candidates for work in long-term aged care prepare themselves for an examination which must be passed before they can be employed as a case manager (Ikegami 2000). Elsewhere, anyone can call themselves a case manager (Kane 1992) and governments will not take action against them. This is not at all surprising, given the difficulties in defining case management and the countless numbers of differently prepared staff who work as case managers. However, states do commonly legislate to license or register many of the professional groups who work as case managers and require that they have met minimum qualification, and perhaps experience and supervision, criteria. For instance, physicians, psychologists, nurses and physiotherapists are universally licensed in some way. The picture with social workers is more complicated as they are licensed in the United States, in some provinces in Canada (Canadian Association of Social Workers 2001), but not in New Zealand (Connolly 2001) and not in any Australian state. Social work courses, rather than workers, are approved in the United Kingdom (Abbott and Meerabeau 1998). The United Kingdom is currently considering an innovative, comprehensive national scheme to register all staff who work in social care—which would, of course, cover most people working as care managers, regardless of their qualifications (Brand and Smith 2001). Case managers who happen to be licensed under one of these professional regimes are subject to all of that regime's requirements and penalties for non-compliance or malpractice, even if the legislation is completely silent on the topic of case management.

Debates about the effectiveness of the legislative regulatory processes just outlined are only mentioned here. While it is part of the dogma of professions and aspiring professions that regulation increases quality of service (e.g. see National Association of Social Workers 1992a), there are contrary voices which argue that extending credentialling approaches to case manager employment will guarantee increased costs but not higher standards of care (Kane 1992; Frager 2000). We endorse the view that regulatory systems and processes should be based on evidence of effectiveness in terms of improved service delivery to clients, rather than on ideological predilections (Applebaum and McGinnis 1992; Geron and Shassler 1994; Kapp 1999).

LAW: OTHER FACTORS RELEVANT TO
CASE MANAGEMENT

Case managers and their agencies ideally need to be aware of the range of other legislative, and perhaps common law, provisions which should inform practice but which do not relate directly to licensing of the agency, service or practitioner. Again, breaches of these provisions—if detected—will incur penalties imposed by the state or a court. These legal factors commonly only reveal themselves in response to crises when workers are at their most vulnerable. To add to the possible woes of the case manager and agency, Murphy (1999, p. 256) argues in relation to managed care at least that law lags behind rapid changes in service delivery arrangements and that it will 'be applied to current situations with sometimes unanticipated results'. Jurisdictions will differ in how and the extent to which they distinguish and respond to these legal factors which impinge on practice. In common law jurisdictions, they may be presented in a complex and dynamic configuration of legislative and common law constraints. Some of the most pertinent ones in common law jurisdictions are sketched here.

CONFIDENTIALITY

Confidentiality is a basic principle of fiduciary or professional relationships which are defined by trust and a responsibility to act in the best interests of another. As we have shown, it is often argued to be a particular challenge in case management because of the range of people, agencies and data storage and retrieval systems that may impact on a client. Two main and often conflicting legal problems of confidentiality impinge on case managers. One concerns the risks of attempting to maintain confidentiality and the other the risks of not maintaining it—or, in Ling's (1999) words, the protection of information and the need to know rule. These two conflicting imperatives often apply simultaneously and require practitioners to manage sophisticated balancing acts.

There are a number of legal factors which may compromise worker assumptions about their maintenance of confidentiality, not the least of which are the often implicit and contrary terms of the employment contracts between case managers and employers. Another major constraint on confidentiality is the limited professional legal privilege at common law possessed by most case managers. That is, their communications with clients are not protected by law and they or their notes are subject to court subpoena at any time. This is an unpleasant surprise to many health and human service practitioners who chant confidentiality as a mantra and believe their information about clients to be safe from scrutiny by any outside body. There are also various legal duties to report regardless of confidentiality, and we will return very soon to some of these. Confidentiality is only ever relative, and agency and worker procedures and practices around explanations of limits and informed consent must reflect this, as we have argued in the practice section. Knowledge of jurisdictional protections, if any, for professional privilege and of reporting obligations is important.

The second legal point is that case managers who do breach confidentiality are at risk of a prescribed penalty if legislation to cover their action exists—this could mean a civil suit under common law, or perhaps professional association sanctions under the relevant code of ethics. The success of a civil suit will depend on the arguments which the case manager and perhaps employer agency can mount about the structures in place to protect the client and the reasonableness of the breach in the circumstances. Whether or not the case manager will be personally liable for any damages awarded in a civil suit of this or any other type may depend on their employment and insurance status. In some jurisdictions, their employers may be vicariously liable for their actions. However, if they were engaged in misconduct, they will fall outside even their employers' protection. Self-employed case managers must rely on their professional indemnity insurance in the face of civil suits.

PROFESSIONAL NEGLIGENCE AND MALPRACTICE

Malpractice relates to professional misconduct which may be covered by applicable professional licensing legislation or even by criminal law. It may also include negligence. Negligence concerns a common law action against a worker or agency, commonly by a client, where it can be established that a duty was owed to the client, the duty was breached and damage was caused by the breach. The breach may lie in both an act or an omission to act and relies on proof that the behaviour alleged was inadequate. This is a difficult area in health and human services generally because it raises the vexed question of adequate standards of service delivery and practice. In relation to case management, performed by very differently experienced and qualified workers, it also raises the possibility of some of them being legally judged according to standards beyond their practice or competence scope.

The standards applied by courts would normally be those of reasonable and prudent case management in that area of practice. But how are these determined? The written documentation of and expertise from any pertinent accrediting body, professional association or agency are the expected sources of authority (More and Mandell 1997; Aiken and Aucoin 1998; Murphy 1999). However, written case management standards have not yet really been fully tested in courts and there are arguments about how the courts will apply them. It is claimed that the available standards are often so broad as to pose unusual risks in that they suggest that the case manager is responsible for everything, including care given by others (More and Mandell 1997). Murphy (1999), on the other hand, argues that the application by courts of lower standards of care is a possibility in managed care in the future if fiscal measures of reasonableness prevail over medical ones.

Negligence is especially a potential problem with case management because many workers may be working with one client, under a case manager's coordination. Who, then, is responsible for inadequate service? There is no simple answer to this question and all will hang on the facts of the particular case. The monitoring function of case management is thrown into stark relief by the possibility of this legal liability, as are our earlier emphasised points about good documentation. It is essential that confrontation and documentation of poor practice by others become part of normal case manager practice, not only in the interest of clients, but also for self-protection against legal liability.

Negligent misstatement is a sub-category of negligence which also has particular relevance to case management, as it covers wrong advice given to clients. If the advice is given by someone in a special relationship with the client who has competency to give advice, and if the advice is reasonably relied on to the detriment of the client, then the advice giver may be found liable. Case managers attempting to negotiate very complex and changing service worlds with and for their clients must be mindful of this possibility and constantly check and document information sources, currency and reliability.

DUTY TO REPORT

In most jurisdictions, there are laws which require specified workers to report particular things to authorities—for example, certain diseases or social security fraud or child abuse. Ignorance of the law will not protect a worker. However, case managers—more than many other health and human service workers—may face a wider scope of these duties as they move across and between service sectors and become privy to information beyond their own agency.

Some jurisdictions may legislate duties on workers to report threats of suicide and harm to others, intentions to commit offences, commission of offences and so on. The area of non-statutory duty to report threat and potential harm is more troubled and raises the possibility of counter-action for breach of confidentiality or even defamation. The US case of *Tarasoff* is frequently reported as imposing a duty on workers to warn of threats to others, but its application in other jurisdictions—for example, Australia—is less clear (McMahon 1992).

The question of reporting improper practice by others, including organisations, is likely to be of increasing legal significance as case managers interact with and use other services and workers. In general, the issue here is less likely to be one of imposed duty than of protection for speaking out. Some protection may be afforded the worker who reveals reprehensible practices under whistleblower legislation, and it is important for them to be apprised of the protective conditions which apply under any relevant piece of legislation.

CONTRACT LAW

For case managers in particular, knowledge of the basics of the common law area of contract is becoming increasingly important. Many case managers are contracting—whether they realise its legal implications or not—when they purchase or otherwise arrange services for their clients. They and their clients may be entering a contractual arrangement when a service plan is developed. A growing number of case managers are self-employed and enter into contractual agreements with funders to deliver services or are subcontractors of service agencies. Understanding and management of contractual processes are not within the experience of most health or human service workers—or, in fact, the agencies. However, without some level of competency in this area, workers are both ignorant of the risks to themselves of breach of contract claims, and also of potential leverage under contract law that they may have with those in the service world around them who do not behave or deliver as agreed.

CERTIFICATION AND ACCREDITATION FOR CASE MANAGEMENT

Certification generally refers to satisfaction of some qualification or assessment process. Enos and Southern (1996, p. 218) describe it as 'a type of regulation of professional practice that affords to the holder of a particular type of academic degree and/or educational preparation an exclusive and legally protected right to the use of a particular title'. As mentioned earlier, it is a less official process in that the state is generally not initiating and monitoring it. Certification requires a structure or body—commonly a professional association—to assess education and training programs and their graduates. Often this process overlaps with that of registration when a licensing authority relies on a professional association's recognition of a particular qualification in its determination of educational acceptability for registration.

'Accreditation' is a wide term referring to an authorised stamp of approval for performance in an identified field. According to Scrivens (1995, p. 12), the term is often used interchangeably with 'licensing', 'certification', 'authorising' and 'regulating', but is centrally characterised by submission to some form of external review. We do not precisely distinguish the terms 'certification' and 'accreditation' in our discussion as other writers tend to use them loosely. In relation to case management, both are most relevant when they are directed at an agency, an individual or an educational program. Both also seem to have an emerging purpose in the United States at least, in discriminating between individual practitioners like nurses who otherwise share indistinguishable educational licences and undergraduate educations (Holland 1999; Kulbok and Utz 1999).

Certification is a burgeoning and lucrative industry in the United States, although there is insufficient data to show that it results in better patient outcomes (Holland 1999; Frager 2000). It, like most regulatory processes, is attended by debate about its benefits and costs. For example, it is said to be costly, to conflict with and duplicate other professional ethical and accreditation requirements and to promote exclusivity, limited choices for consumers and medicalisation of problems (Rosen et al. 2000). On the benefit side, there are some US nursing and rehabilitation-based claims that possession of specialist certificates makes a case manager more marketable with employers (Case Management Advisor 1997).

Table 10.1 displays a range of case management certification or accreditation options for individuals in the United States. No other country at present offers such an array. Thomas and Lovell (1999) report one British possibility for mental health nurses and other professions through a charitable trust. There are no such options in Australia. While some agencies may encourage or give preference to employees and contractors who obtain certifications of the kind listed, it must be reiterated that there are generally no complementary state requirements about exclusive use of the general case management title or its practice. Case managers voluntarily offer themselves for these certification processes, they pay fees to do so, they meet criteria which focus on past achievements rather than actual work performance and there is no performance monitoring within certification periods. Number of years of work in a specific field and completion of a particular preservice degree are the common eligibility criteria. The examinations referred to generally involve short-answer questions. Even though the target groups shown, with the exception of the National Association of Social Workers (NASW) Certificate, are inclusive of different professions, it is nurses who mainly stand behind and utilise these certification options. There is acknowledgment that social service perspectives are under-represented in the Certified Case Manager (CCM) designation at least (Case Management Advisor 1997).

STANDARDS AND GUIDELINES FOR CASE MANAGEMENT

Standards typically refer to agreed or expected levels in some area, while guidelines, according to Geron and Chassler (1994, p. 95), serve a more educative function and 'refer to general objectives or principles of action'. Standards may cover structures, organisational functions and client-related functions (Ling 1999)—that is, the activities of care and outcomes—although the latter are generally quite crudely identified in many areas of case management. Guidelines may be more useful tools in helping to improve and shape service (Geron and Shassler 1994;

Table 10.1 US case management certification options (as at July 2001)

Certification and length	Certifying agency	Eligibility requirements	Primary industry identification	Professional targets
CCM Certified case manager 5 years	Foundation for Education and Research, Commission for Case Manager Certification	• Appropriate professional certification • Acceptable experience • Job description • Pass exam	Independent firms, hospitals, insurers, managed care companies	Any that promote physical, psychosocial and vocational well-being
A-CCC Continuity of Care certification advanced 5 years	National Board for Certification in Continuity of Care	• Bachelors degree • 2 years' full-time employment in continuity of care • Pass exam	Hospitals, managed care and others	Nurses, social workers, therapists, dieticians, physicians
CMC Care manager certified 3 years	National Academy of Certified Care Managers	• Specific case management and educational experience • Pass exam	Geriatric care	Nurses, social workers, mental health counsellors, psychologists
CRC Certified rehabilitation counselling 5 years	Commission of Rehabilitation Counselor Certification	• Completed or in process of completing Masters program • Acceptable experience • Pass exam	Rehabilitation	Counsellors
CDMS Certified disability management specialist 5 years	Foundation for Education and Research, Certification of Disability Management Specialists Commission	• Bachelors, Masters or Doctorate degree in certain disciplines • Acceptable experience • Pass exam	Disability	Anyone working with individuals with disabilities

Table 10.1 US case management certification options (as at July 2001) (cont.)

Certification and length	Certifying agency	Eligibility requirements	Primary industry identification	Professional targets
CRRN Certified rehabilitation registered nurse 5 years	Rehabilitation Nursing Certification Board	• Nursing licence • Experience in rehab. nursing • Pass exam	Rehabilitation	Nurses
CIRS Certified insurance rehabilitation specialist 5 years	Certification of Insurance Rehabilitation Specialists Commission	• Relevant licence and experience or qualification and experience combinations • Pass exam	Rehabilitation	Nurses, rehabilitation counsellors
CPHQ Certified professional in health care quality 2 years	National Association for Health Care Quality	• Relevant qualification, accreditation or nursing licence • Acceptable experience	All fields of health	Individuals working in health care quality, risk management and utilisation management
CSWCM and CASWCM Certified social work and advanced social work case manager 2 years	National Association of Social Workers	• NASW membership • Bachelor of Social Work • Acceptable employment and supervision • State social work licence or equivalent or CCM • Social work references	All fields	Social workers

Note: Adapted from Murer and Brick (1997, p. 160), with additional information from Kulbok (1999), National Association of Social Workers (2000), Case Management Advisor (1997) and More and Mandell (1997).

Bulger and Feldmeier 1998), as they can break practice down into more explicit units to enhance accountability.

Again, standards and guidelines may be directed at both agencies and workers, but their achievement will nearly always depend on both. For example, an agency standard which specifies that a particular assessment task will be finished within a set time after client contact is dependent on agency procedures, resource allocation, management and monitoring practices and on staff knowledge and compliance. Standards may be applied for different purposes at different levels of formality. They are commonly now built into service provision contracts for agencies and in areas such as managed care under different names like performance guarantees. Aimed at financial outcomes, they will have financial implications for the agency if they are not achieved (Frager 2000).

Standards and guidelines, like accreditation alternatives, emanate from a number of different sources of authority, such as government policy, agency policy and professional associations, and again there is no uniformity across all areas of case management practice. Bulger and Feldmeier (1998) note that there are no general national standards or guidelines in the United States for case management and argue the impracticality of such things at other than state or local level. There are no standards for care management with the elderly in the United Kingdom (Cox 1997), where it is commonly applied, although there are some general protocols under relevant legislation (Sonntag 1995). There are, however, an increasing number of organisations attempting to advance the practice of case management in the United States through promulgation of standards and guidelines (Geron 2000a, 2000b).

For example, the US National Council on Aging, the US National Association of Social Workers, the American Nurses Association (Bulger and Feldmeier 1998) and the Case Management Society of America (Smith 1995; Murer and Brick 1997; Kulbok and Utz 1999; Holt 2000) have all published inventories of standards which typically cover matters such as case manager qualifications, client focus, caseload sizes and care plan content. For example:

- Standard 9 of the National Association of Social Workers (1992b), which proclaims that: 'The social work case manager shall carry a reasonable caseload that allows that case manager to effectively plan, provide, and evaluate case management tasks related to client and systems', and the interpretative statement which follows outlines both agency and case management responsibilities in this area; and

- Part 111 of the CMSA Standards of Performance, clause B, which asserts: 'Case management requires a professional credential, education and experience' (Smith 1995, p. 12). It then goes on to list six measurement criteria that the case manager must work to meet. These cover qualifications, continuing education and experience.

The critiques of other regulatory processes apply also to standards and guidelines. Standards only technically pertain to those few workers who may be members of, or covered by, a particular promulgating body. As just shown, they are generally broad and static statements which do not specifically guide practice. Without quality methods attached to them and linkages with social justice indicators, standards are sterile (McGuire 1997). As Kane (1997) points out, they may be directed at the lowest common denominator and, in identifying minimal levels of required achievement, they do not act to upgrade performance. They also can act to stifle 'logical problem-solving, not to mention creativity' (Kane and Degenholtz 1997, p. 24). There is no evidence that the mere existence of standards or guidelines results in better outcomes for clients (Geron and Shassler 1994).

CASE MANAGEMENT AND CODES OF ETHICS

There are no general codes of ethics covering all case management. Codes are intrinsic to registration processes, groups that are attempting to portray themselves as professional, and sometimes agencies. Therefore some case managers with professional identities in, for instance, nursing or social work or psychology will be subject to the non-case management-specific codes of their particular professional association, if they happen to be a member of it, or their registering body if they are registered. These codes, however, do include aspirational principles for correct practice which are relevant to many of the fundamental dilemmas of case management where system and client interests appear to collide. For example:

- the American Nurses Association draft code (American Nurses Association 2000), clause 6.3 on responsibility for the health care environment, which says: 'Nurses should not remain employed in facilities that routinely violate patient rights or require nurses to severely compromise standards of practice or personal morality';

- the Australian Psychological Society code, which includes a statement under General Principle 111, Propriety that states: 'The welfare of clients and the public, and the integrity of the profession, shall take precedence over a member's self interest and over the interests of the member's employer and colleagues.' Five specific application clauses then follow; and

- the code of the British Association of Social Workers, which asserts: 'They will give precedence to their professional responsibility over their own personal interests' (British Association of Social Workers 1996, Principle 10, p. vi).

We are about to turn to the practicability of commands which confront the worker on a daily basis with choosing between their jobs and the rights/needs of their clients. The impact of professional codes is not only restricted by unfeasibility, generality and limited scope of authority, but also by practical problems of detection and enforcement. On a day-to-day level, they are probably more honoured in the breach than in the execution. Those codes designed to cross professional boundaries and cover interdisciplinary work (Casto et al. 1994) suffer even more from ineffectiveness and weak enforcement processes as they are seldom underpinned by authoritative mandates and by infrastructures of any sort. An increasing number of agencies are promulgating their own codes of ethics or good conduct and, while these may cover more staff than professional association codes and have more muscle through employer sanctions, they are often equally general.

We have canvassed issues of ethical practice in the practice section. Case managers do need to be familiar with any codes that may be pertinent to their practice, as transcendent principles can act as important beacons in the smog of daily work, and because they may be applied in legal negligence and malpractice actions. However, codes—like all components of a regulatory system—seldom supply a satisfactory answer to a worker's immediate dilemma and may be increasingly marginal at that level.

IMPLICATIONS FOR THE INDIVIDUAL CASE MANAGER

There are four main points which emerge from this complex, overlapping and often ambiguous regulatory milieu in which case management is conducted. First, case managers, depending on their professional title and their agency context, may be subject to dissimilar degrees of attempted control. We use the word 'attempted' because, whatever the extent of prescription, it generally does not get down to the detail of interactions with clients and it seldom includes procedures for actively seeking out problems and deficiencies. Even in the face of an apparent plethora of rules, a case manager is often very much alone and dependent on their own internal resources when it comes to making daily decisions. Self-reliance and personal support systems are essential in these demanding work worlds. We have previously mentioned ethics peer discussion groups described by McClelland (1998), and add here the strategic actions to challenge mind sets about the human costs of new service delivery recommended by Taylor and Barnet (1999), and based on a critical understanding of the new service environments. One critical skill which case managers do need to develop—for their own protection, if for no other reason—is the ability to assess the risk to themselves and their clients of all components of the regulatory systems in which they work. Estimating the risks of non-compliance with some prescription which they believe to work against their clients' best interests is as important as assessing the risks of reprisal that may be inherent in any form of relatively standard and commonly accepted procedure or action. Checklists of the kind provided by Ling (1999) can be useful tools for workers to use in sorting through the legal risks posed by any case management practice situation.

Kane and Degenholtz (1997), in arguing that formal regulatory systems are not synonymous with either compliance or quality, advocate for quality assurance programs which are structured to empower case managers to be a force for quality. So the second point is that organisations in particular, and workers too, face decisions about the extent to which they will take up this challenge. Even if the organisation evades the challenge, the individual worker can be a powerful force in clients' experiences of agencies and services and can make personal decisions about being forces for good. Kapp's (1999, p. 256) words are both trite and profound: 'Regulatory requirements may serve as a useful catalyst, but can never effectively substitute for that kindness and moral commitment [...] that, when all is said and done, will determine the rights and well-being of the patients whom the system is supposed to serve.' The notion of the street-level bureaucrat (Lipsky 1980) is again applicable.

Third, regulatory systems, whatever their many deficiencies, do inherently validate expectations about adequate performance and the right to protest against performance which is inadequate. The spirit behind these systems attests to the normalcy of complaint, even if the actual complaint processes are poor. This point is also both facile and profound, and for case managers it has two implications. One is that it poses a question to case managers about the extent to which they can or will open themselves up to scrutiny and feedback so as to improve their own practice. They have to decide how much they will resist or comply with genuine complaints processes and how much they will stimulate or extend limited, formulaic ones. The other is that service user criticism and complaint, if fostered and respected, can provide invaluable and often untapped sources of energy for change in service delivery. For workers, there is potential to harness or be harnessed by this energy in the interest of policy and service improvements. Complaints are often perceived by workers as threatening; their developmental possibilities are less well accepted.

The fourth and more pragmatic point is that case managers in many countries face a dearth of local accreditation options, while the United States presents a confusing range of possibilities for its citizens and overseas candidates. Once again, case managers face decisions about their professional competitiveness and profiles. Is a particular form of worker certification advantageous in their desired line of work; does the gain warrant the cost? In conclusion, workers not only need to negotiate complex regulatory regimes on behalf of their clients, but also in the interests of their own self-preservation and professional futures.

PART IV

REFLECTIONS

11

THROUGH THE LOOKING GLASS

W hat sense can we now make of this phenomenon called case management? We have pondered how we might bring this book to conclusion. Should attention be given to the issue of research and evaluation as a key to future practice and application? Certainly there would be much to commend this as a final theme, as many writers attest to the lack of systematic research and evaluation of the approach. Should we consider future directions for case management? This might suggest that we are taking a position that the approach will continue to develop in predictable ways. Over the past 30 years, case management has been adapted to many interests and as a result the concept has remained difficult to define and evaluate. Should we address the issue of credentialism so often presented as a way to ensure standards and consistency in practice? The argument for setting standards assumes greater homogeneity, both within practice and settings, than the evidence provides. The broad application of case management, its diverse forms, nomenclature and practice by human service professionals and other personnel poses significant barriers to such attempts to regulate practice. Should we focus on strategies to support the practitioner to address the contradictions that inevitably arise from this service delivery approach? Again, we have taken a particular position about the practice, arguing that the practitioner will draw on all their professional knowledge to undertake the case management task. We have deliberately avoided a focus on the detail of practice interventions and attended to the critical practice themes that are raised by the approach. So where does this leave us?

WHERE WE BEGAN

This book has been generated from our broad interests in service delivery and the nature of professional practice in the human services. Our curiosity about changes in service delivery and the implications for practitioners has exposed the breadth and diversity of application of case management. Like Alice in Wonderland, our journey of exploration has been 'curiouser and curiouser', alerting us to the dangers of over simplification or a search for consistency and coherence. What we have discovered are variations, diverse adaptations and multiple applications within practice settings, organisational contexts and across national boundaries. Perhaps the words of Lewis Carroll provide a justification for concluding with a chapter that alerts us to the key issues and conundrums generated from such diversity but incorporated under the rubric of case management:

> When you are describing
> A shape, or sound, or tint;
> Don't state the matter plainly,
> But put it in a hint;
> And learn to look at all things
> With a sort of mental squint.

So, adopting some refractive licence, some of the critical issues generated from the discussions in the preceding chapters are reviewed.

ALL PERVASIVE, YET ELUSIVE

Like so many of the writers acknowledged in this book (e.g. Austin and McClelland 1996, p. 1; Burns and Perkins 2000, p. 212), we would agree that case management is no longer an innovation in service provision. With a history of over 30 years, case management has become part of the established and international scene in the human services. Yet many of the debates about its value affirm the confusion and ambiguity associated with the approach, and the lack of consensus around definition and operationalisation. Some commentators (e.g. Lancet 1995; Marshall 1996; Reinhard 2000) would go so far as to assert that it is both ineffective and inadequately evaluated as a service delivery approach.

Does this mean that case management has had its day, that it was merely a fad or fashion? Is the brand name obsolescent? Has it lost its appeal for the human service professionals who were caught up in its development as it was incorporated into policy and program design? Will it be abandoned as a service delivery approach? After all, case management was paraded as an approach that would create more effective and cost-effective service responses for individual clients. The jury is still out on a decision about the achievements in these areas, in part because of inadequate evidence but also because the promise associated with case management is illusionary. As has been shown in a number of the preceding chapters, there are constraints on case management that compromise the realisation of its potential. However, the dilemma we wish to avoid is a state of 'paralysis' generated from analysis of case management that highlights limitations because of structural or organisational barriers. Constraints are an ongoing aspect of all practice in the human services and health sectors, and are not swept away by introducing a new service delivery approach such as case management.

In practice, we see a long and international history of case management. It is commonly applied to policy and program design with limited regard to its value and appropriateness. The adoption of the approach, for diverse agendas, has confirmed its expediency rather than increasing its wide professional endorsement. Roggenkamp and White (2001), in commenting on hospital case management, cogently illustrate case management as a rationalised myth that is implemented for a range of factors but in the absence of evidence supporting efficiency and effectiveness. Case management becomes self-perpetuating on the basis of such factors as institutional endorsement, competitors' adoption of the approach, where it becomes central to the dominant profession's activities and where it can be presented as responsive to wider health policy demands (in the United States this is managed care).

It may have provided new employment options for some professional groups such as nursing and social work, but others often see the demands of the case manager role as devaluing professional and clinical skills or as antithetical to scientific intervention. What is often neglected in discourses about case management is acknowledgment that the approach does not supersede service provision. Not everyone, nor every organisation, needs to be case managed or adopt the case management approach. Clients need services. Those services will not necessarily be provided best by a case manager or an organisation that offers case management. At times it is a disservice to offer case management. At times it is a disservice to offer case management without the complementary range of interventions that address particular needs.

Assuming that case management maintains a dominant position in human service provision, one of the challenges must be the question of how to get the best from the approach. Austin (2001) specified this as a key issue when she presented a paper on the question of who needs case management. Her retort to that question was 'it all depends'. In other words, whether case management is the appropriate response to an individual's service need will depend on many factors. The challenge is that we really know little about who it works for, under what conditions and for what cost (Summers 2000). We have demonstrated that case management has become a tool for reform, but not necessarily reform of service delivery *per se*.

Achieving best practice depends on our ability to determine the conditions for success, and for targeting the approach on the populations or individual circumstances that can be improved through a coordinated approach to service delivery. We already know from some detailed studies in the United Kingdom, Australia and Europe that not all outcomes for mental health patients are achieved through case management programs (Ford et al. 1996; Issakidis et al. 1999; Marshall and Creed 2000; Ziguras and Stuart 2000; Huxley et al. 2001). We need to continue to search for evidence to know how best to use case management. Is it for every prisoner, is it for every unemployed person or every complex family situation? The preoccupation with case management, and the all-encompassing nature of the concept, have led to other individualised service delivery interventions being devalued or recategorised to fit the case management label. Group work, family work, counselling and a range of therapeutic interventions (for example, assertive community treatment in mental health) may be more appropriate responses. But they are not case management *per se*. Within case management, these interventions may need to be used to respond to particular issues or problems for any given client situation. The key to best practice and positive outcomes in service provision is assessment and selecting appropriate responses for that situation (Burns and Perkins 2000). But this does not mean fitting every intervention under the banner of case management.

Without broadening the base of evaluation and searching for more understanding of how practice is shaped by the approach, we are without capacity to move towards best practice and relevant application. To date, the research has been extremely variable. Given the difficulty of defining case management, it is also difficult to know what program and policy fidelity is established for research purposes. Systematic research and evaluation require attention to why and what is to be evaluated. Kirkhart (1993) points out that the value framework of evaluation impacts on the orientation of the research, questions pursued and the informants used to build data. Summers (2000) draws attention to the need to establish frameworks for evaluation that can build data for cross-sectorial and discipline work. The questions about the strengths and limitations of case management will be achieved through inquiries that seek to 'drill down' and search for knowledge about what is done in practice (Reinhard 2000), examine how case managers pursue their tasks (e.g. Hromco et al. 1997; Grube and Chernesky 2001) and detail the 'nuts and bolts' of the service actually provided (Schmidt-Posner and Jerrell 1998; Bjorkman and Hansson 2000).

ABANDON CASE MANAGEMENT AND WHAT WOULD REMAIN?

Earlier in the book, we presented a statement of the principles under-lying the case management approach. The key words are listed here again to provide a basis for our final theme in this concluding chapter. We have argued that the principles are individualised and tailored service delivery that involves the client in planning the service mix, ensuring choice and contracted arrangements that maintain account-ability to the respective parties. The service arrangement for any given client is planned and established by drawing on a range of formal and informal service providers; it is not based on what can be offered from one organisation. The principles for the service plan are encapsulated in notions of boundary spanning, seamless service delivery and inte-grated services. Outcomes are specified and the case manager plays a critical role in monitoring and responding to changing circumstances to ensure timely, efficient and cost-effective service delivery. Finally, the approach carries with it promise of advocacy for individuals and in relation to system change.

The principles are fine in theory but, as we have discussed repeat-edly, the realities often do not match these expectations. Practitioners and clients alike witness the decline in tangible service delivery.

Inequalities in service access remain with the most vulnerable populations and the individuals having least opportunity to attain the standards of care promised in the rhetoric. Practitioners live with contentious ambiguities in their practice world as they attempt to make sense of an imposed approach for which they have been inadequately prepared and to which they may well have little commitment. Consumers remain bemused by new assertions of service arrangements but little change in their experience of services. Being case managed is of little value if the services are not adequate, appropriate and effective. As much as practitioners are ill-prepared for new practices, consumers are also given little information to negotiate in new conditions. The expectation of change agency through case management is as much illusionary as it has been in traditional service provision. Clearly these assertions do not apply evenly across all sectors or organisations, or to every practitioner. But the evidence suggests that the ambiguity about the approach and the consequent practice demands is pervasive, despite some exemplary data on particular initiatives.

ACKNOWLEDGING BOUNDARIES AND CHALLENGING BOUNDARIES

Despite the positives inherent in the rhetoric, it could be argued that the reforms promised through this new approach have not eventuated. The nomenclature is being challenged and the principles are viewed with increasing scepticism despite ongoing policy and program initiatives to introduce or maintain the approach. We may well see case management displaced as a favoured service delivery approach, but we would assert that many of the changes that it has heralded will be sustained—albeit under a different guise.

From the perspective of all stakeholders, the notions of integrated and individualised service delivery resonate with the demands of complex social and health needs, resource limitations and accountability. The experience of case management has promoted new demands on professional practice in the human services and new partnerships to facilitate the delivery of those services. The expectations of service providers have been recast through competitive and increasingly mixed market environments in the human services.

Moxley (1997) asserts that case management is entrenched in service provision for particular client populations. He sees the approach having particular application for the management of situations where control, costs and complexity are key issues for the community and policy-makers. We have argued that it is the underlying principles that are likely to be sustained whatever the nomenclature of the future. For these reasons and others proposed in this book, it is essential that we acknowledge the significance of the approach and pursue the challenges it poses as a vehicle that has promised different service delivery arrangements and practices in the human services.

REFERENCES

Abbott, P. (1998). Conflict Over Grey Areas: District Nurses and Home Helps Providing Community Care. In *The Sociology of the Caring Professions*. Eds P. Abbott and L. Meerabeau. London: UCL Press: 199–209.

Abbott, P. and L. Meerabeau (1998). Professionals, Professionalisation and the Caring Professions. In *The Sociology of the Caring Professions*. Eds P. Abbott and L. Meerabeau. London: UCL Press: 1–19.

Abbott, P. and C. Wallace (1998). Health Visiting, Social Work, Nursing and Midwifery: A History. In *The Sociology of the Caring Professions*. Eds P. Abbott and L. Meerabeau. London: UCL Press: 20–53.

Agich, G. J. and H. Forster (2000). Conflicts of Interest and Management in Managed Care. *Cambridge Quarterly of Healthcare Ethics* 9: 189–204.

Aiken, T. D. and J. W. Aucoin (1998). Legal Issues in Case Management. In *The Case Manager's Survival Guide*. Eds T. G. Cesta, H. A. Tahan and L. F. Fink. St Louis: Mosby: 159–66.

American Nurses Association (2000). Code of Ethics for Nurses. http://nursingworld.org/ethics/code9.htm [24 June 2001].

Anderson, S. G. (2001). Welfare Recipients' Views About Caseworker Performance: Lessons for Developing TANF Case Management Practices. *The Journal of Contemporary Human Services* 82(2): 165–73.

Applebaum, R. and C. Austin (1990). *Long-Term Care Case Management: Design and Evaluation*. New York: Springer.

Applebaum, R. and M. White, eds (2000). *Key Issues in Case Management Around the Globe*. San Francisco: American Society on Aging.

Applebaum, R. A. and R. McGinnis (1992). What Price Quality? Assuring the Quality of Case-Managed In-Home Care. *Journal of Case Management* 1(1): 9–13.

Austin, C. D. (1990). Case Management: Myths and Realities. *Families in*

Society: The Journal of Contemporary Human Services 71 (September): 398–405.

——(1992). Case Management in Long Term Care: Options and Opportunities. In *Case Management and Social Work Practice*. Ed. S. M. Rose. New York: Longman: 199–204, 210–18.

——(1993). Case Management: A Systems Perspective. *Families in Society: The Journal of Contemporary Human Services* (October): 451–59.

——(1996). Aging and Long-Term Care. In *Perspectives on Case Management Practice*. Eds C. D. Austin and R. W. McClelland. Milwaukee: Families International: 73–98.

——(2001). *Care/Case Management: Who Needs it? Does it Work?* 5th International Care/Case Management Conference, Vancouver, American Society on Aging.

Austin, C. D. and R. W. McClelland (1996). Introduction: Case Management—Everybody's Doing It. In *Perspectives on Case Management Practice*. Eds C. D. Austin and R. W. McClelland. Milwaukee: Families International: 1–16.

——(1996). *Perspectives on Case Management Practice*. Milwaukee: Families International.

——(1997). Case Management in the Human Services: Reflections of Public Policy. *Journal of Case Management* 6(3): 119–26.

——(1998). *Case Management Context in Bachelor of Social Work Education*. 4th International Conference on Long Term Care/Case Management, San Diego, California, American Society on Aging.

——(2000). Case Management in Contemporary Human Services. *Australian Journal of Case Management* 2(1): 4–7.

Austin, M. J. (1997). *Human Services Integration*. New York: The Haworth Press.

Back, V. D. (1999). Interdisciplinary, Collaborative Team Practice in Managed Care: The Provider Perspective. In *The Outcomes Mandate: Case Management in Health Care Today*. Eds E. L. Cohen and V. D. deBack. St Louis: Mosby: 207–14.

Baer, E. and S. Gordon (1996). Money Managers are Unraveling the Tapestry of Nursing. In *Ethics and Politics*. Eds S. Gordon, P. Benner and N. Noddings. Philadelphia: University of Pennsylvania Press: 226–30.

Baldwin, M. (2000). *Care Management and Community Care: Social Work Discretion and the Construction of Policy*. Aldershot: Ashgate.

Baragwanath, A. (1997). *Practical Implications of Case/Care Management—How Much Can We Do At Home?* Aged Care Australia Conference.

——(1999). Perspectives on Case Management as the Critical Link. *Australian Journal of Case Management* 1(1): 7–10.

Barnet, R. J. and C. Taylor (1999). The Ethics of Case Management: Communication Challenges. In *The Outcomes Mandate: Case Management in*

Health Care Today. Eds E. L. Cohen and V. D. deBack. St Louis: Mosby: 328–38.

Bar-On, A. A. (1990). Organizational Resource Mobilization: A Hidden Face of Social Work Practice. *British Journal of Social Work* 20: 133–49.

——(1995). Social Workers and Case Management. *Asia Pacific Journal of Social Work* 5(1): 63–78.

Bateman, N. (1995). *Advocacy Skills: A Handbook for Human Service Professionals.* Aldershot: Arena.

Bedell, J. R., N. L. Cohen and A. Sullivan (2000). Case Management: The Current Best Practices and the Next Generation of Innovation. *Community Mental Health Journal* 36(2): 179–94.

Belson, P. S. (2000). Case Management in a Windows World. In *Key Issues in Case Management Around the Globe.* Eds R. Applebaum and M. White. San Francisco: American Society on Aging: 60–6.

Berger, C. (1996). Case Management in Health Care. In *Perspectives on Case Management Practice.* Eds C. D. Austin and R. W. McClelland. Milwaukee: Families International: 145–74.

Bjorkman, T. and L. Hansson (2000). What Do Case Managers Do? An Investigation of Case Manager Interventions and their Relationship to Client Outcome. *Social Psychiatry and Psychiatric Epidemiology* 35: 43–50.

——(2001). Client Satisfaction with Case Management: A Study of 10 Pilot Services in Sweden. *Journal of Mental Health* 10(2): 163–74.

Blanch, J. R. O. (1999). Immigration Review Tribunal: Pilot Case Management Program to Ease Transition to the MRT. *Law Society Journal* 37(2): 26–7.

Bower, K. (1991). *Case Management by Nurses.* Washington: American Nurses Publishing.

Brand, D. and G. Smith (2001). Social Care Registration Project. Consultation paper on proposals for a draft registration scheme for the social care workforce. http://www.nisw.org.uk/gscc/index.html [28 March 2001].

Braye, S. and M. Preston-Shoot (1995). *Empowering Practice in Social Care.* Buckingham: Open University Press.

Brennan, J. (1996). Comprehensive Case Management with HIV Clients. In *Perspectives on Case Management Practice.* Eds C. D. Austin and R. W. McClelland. Milwaukee: Families International: 219–40.

Bricker-Jenkins, M. (1992). Building a Strengths Model of Practice in the Public Social Services. In *The Strengths Perspective in Social Work Practice.* Ed. D. Saleeby. New York: Longman.

Bridgman, P. and G. Davis (2000). *The Australian Policy Handbook.* Sydney: Allen & Unwin.

British Association of Social Workers (1996). The Code of Ethics for Social Work. http://www.basw.co.uk/pages/info/ethics/htm [20 March 2001].

Brooks, D. and P. Riley (1998). The Impact of Managed Health Care Policy on Student Field Training. In *Humane Managed Care?* Eds G. Schamess and A. Lightburn. Washington: NASW: 455–64.

Bruhn, J. G., H. G. Levine and P. L. Levine (1993). *Managing Boundaries in the Health Professions*. Springfield: Charles C. Thomas.

Bryson, L. (1992). *Welfare and State: Who Benefits?* Houndmills, Basingstoke, Hampshire and London: Macmillan.

Buckloh, L. M. and M. C. Roberts (2001). Managed Mental Health Care: Attitudes and Ethical Beliefs of Child and Pediatric Psychologists. *Journal of Pediatric Psychology* 26(4): 193–202.

Bulger, S. and C. Feldmeier (1998). Developing Standards and Quality Measurements for Case Management Practice. *Journal of Case Management* 7(3): 99–104.

Burch, H. A. (1999). *Social Welfare Policy Analysis and Choices*. New York: The Haworth Press.

Burns, B. J., E. A. Gwaltney and G. K. Bishop (1995). Case Management Research: Issues and Directions. In *From Case Management to Service Coordination for Children with Emotional, Behavioural, or Mental Disorders: Building on Family Strengths*. Eds B. J. Friesen and J. Poertner. Baltimore: Paul H. Brookes: 353–72.

Burns, T., M. Fiander, A. Kent, O. Ukoumunne, S. Byford, T. Fahy and K. Kumar (2000). Effects of Case-Load Size on the Process of Care of Patients with Severe Psychotic Illness—Report from the UK700 Trial. *British Journal of Psychiatry* 177 (November): 427–33.

Burns, T., A. Fioritti, F. Holloway, U. Malm and W. Rossler (2001). Case Management and Assertive Community Treatment in Europe. *Psychiatric Services* 52(5): 631–6.

Burns, T. and R. Perkins (2000). The Future of Case Management. *International Review of Psychiatry* 12(3): 212–18.

Burrage, M. and R. Torstendahl (1990). *Professions in Theory and History*. London: Sage.

Caldwell, B. (2000). Case Managers are Conduit Between Patients, Providers in Quest for Quality, Cost-Effective Care. *Employee Benefit Plan Review* 54(7): 12–14.

Callahan, J. (1998). Documentation of Client Dangerousness in a Managed Care Environment. In *Humane Managed Care?* Eds G. Schamess and A. Lightburn. Washington: NASW Press: 299–307.

Cambridge, P. (1992). Case Management in Community Services: Organisational Responses. *British Journal of Social Work* 22: 495–517.

Campbell, G., C. David, B. Jellie, S. Podger and H. Raik (1994). *Case Management: Maintaining the Balance*. Melbourne: Australian Government Publishing Service.

Canadian Association of Social Workers (2001). http://www.casw-acts.ca/legislation.htm [20 March 2001].

Carson, E., R. Kennedy, D. Gursansky and K. Oxenberry (1996). *Women,*

Case Management and Labour Market Programs. Adelaide: University of South Australia.

Case Management Advisor (1997). Scrambling for CM Certification? Here's What to Know About 6 Choices. *Case Management Advisor* 8(1): 1–5.

Cass, B. (1995). *Unemployment and Active Employment Policies: An Australian Perspective—The Way Forward.* The National Summit on Employment and Case Management, Sydney: Australian Catholic Social Welfare Commission.

Casto, R. M., M. C. Julia, et al. (1994). *Interprofessional Care and Collaborative Practice.* Pacific Grove, California: Brooks/Cole.

Causer, G. and M. Exworthy (1999). Professionals as Managers Across the Public Sector. In *Professionals and the New Managerialism in the Public Sector.* Eds M. Exworthy and S. Halford. Buckingham: Open University Press: 82–101.

Challis, D. (1990). Case Management: Problems and Possibilities. In *Care Managers and Care Management.* Ed. I. Allen. London: Policy Studies Institute supported by The Joseph Rowntree Memorial Trust: 9–29.

——(2000). Care Management in the United Kingdom. In *Key Issues in Case Management Around the Globe.* Eds R. Applebaum and M. White. San Francisco: American Society on Aging: 50–9.

Challis, D., R. Chessum, J. Chesterman, R. Luckett and K. Traske (1990). *Case Management in Social and Health Care.* Kent: Personal Social Services Research Unit.

Challis, D., J. Chesterman, R. Darton and K. Traske (1993). Case Management in the Care of the Aged: The Provision of Care in Different Settings. In *Community Care: A Reader.* Eds J. Bornat, J. Johnson, C. Pereira, D. Pilgrim and F. Williams. London: Macmillan in association with Open University Press: 184–203.

Challis, D., R. Darton and K. Stewart (1998). Emerging Models of Care Management for Older People and Those with Mental Health Problems in the United Kingdom. *Journal of Case Management* 7(4): 153–60.

Challis, D. and B. Davies (1986). *Case Management in Community Care: An Evaluated Experiment in the Home Care of the Elderly.* Aldershot: Gower.

Challis, D., B. Davies and K. Traske (1995). Community Care: Immediate Concerns and Long-term Perspectives. In *Community Care: New Agendas and Challenges from the United Kingdom and Overseas.* Eds D. Challis, B. Davies and K. Traske. Kent: PSSRU.

Chi, I. and G. Wong (2001). *Demonstration Project of Case Management for Dementia Care in Hong Kong.* 5th International Care/Case Management Conference, Vancouver, American Society on Aging.

Clarke, J. (1998). Doing the Right Thing? Managerialism and Social Welfare. In *The Sociology of the Caring Professions.* Eds P. Abbott and L. Meerabeau. London: UCL Press: 234–54.

Clarke, J. and J. Newman (1997). *The Managerial State: Power, Politics and Ideology in the Remaking of Social Welfare*. New Delhi: Sage.

Clay, C. (1999). Case Management in a Female Prison: Where Have We Been, Where Are We Now, Where Are We Going? *Case Management: The Coming of Age and the Getting of Wisdom*. Melbourne: Case Management Society of Australia.

Cleak, H. and K. Serr (1998). Case Management in Action: An Examination of Two Cases in the Area of Alcohol Related Brain Damage. *Australian Social Work* 51(1): 33–8.

Clinard, H. H. (1989). *Winning Ways to Succeed with People*. Winston-Salem: Effectiveness Training and Consulting.

Cnaan, R. A. (1994). The New American Social Work Gospel: Case Management of the Chronically Mentally Ill. *British Journal of Social Work* 24(5): 533–57.

Cohen, E. L. and T. G. Cesta (1994). Case Management in the Acute Care Setting: A Model for Health Care Reform. *Journal of Case Management* 3(3): 110–28.

——(1997). *Nursing Case Management: From Concept to Evaluation*. St Louis: Mosby.

Cohen, E. L. and V. deBack, eds (1999). *The Outcomes Mandate: Case Management in Health Care Today*. St Louis: Mosby.

Compton, A. and M. Ashwin, eds (2000). *Community Care for Health Professionals*. Oxford; Butterworth Heinemann.

Connolly, M., ed. (2001). *New Zealand Social Work: Context and Practice*. Auckland: Oxford University Press.

Considine, M. and M. Painter, eds (1997). *Managerialism: The Great Debate*. Melbourne: Melbourne University Press.

Conti, R. M. (1999). The Broker Model of Case Management. In *The Outcomes Mandate: Case Management in Health Care Today*. Eds E. L. Cohen and V. deBack. St Louis: Mosby: 122–31.

Coulshed, V. and A. Mullender (2001). *Management in Social Work*. Palgrave: Hampshire.

Cox, C. (1997). Case Management: An American's Observations of Community Care in Britain. *Journal of Case Management* 6(3): 88–94.

Craig, T. K. J. (1998). *Models of Case Management and their Impact on Social Outcomes of Severe Mental Illness*. Eds K. Mueser and N. Tarrier. Boston: Allyn and Bacon: 355–71.

Daiski, I. (2000). The Road to Professionalism in Nursing: Case Management or Practice Based in Nursing Theory? *Nursing Science Quarterly* 13(1): 75–9.

Davidson, J. R. and T. Davidson (1998). Confidentiality and Managed Care: Ethical and Legal Concerns. In *Humane Managed Care?* Eds G. Schamess and A. Lightburn. Washington: NASW: 281–92.

Davies, B. (1992). *Care Management, Equity and Efficiency: The International Experience.* Canterbury: PSSRU, University of Kent.

——(1994). Improving the Case Management Process. In *Caring for Frail Elderly People: New Directions in Care.* Paris, OECD Social Policy Studies 14: 111–43.

Davis, G. (1997). Implications, Consequences and Futures. In *The New Contractualism?* Eds G. Davis, B. Sullivan and A. Yeatman. Melbourne: Macmillan Education: 224–33.

Davis, K. (1998). Managed Health Care: Forcing Social Work to Make Changes. In *Humane Managed Care?* Eds G. Schamess and A. Lightburn. Washington: NASW Press: 409–24.

Denney, D. (1998). *Social Policy and Social Work.* Oxford: Clarendon Press.

Dill, A. (1995). Case Management as Cultural Practice. *Advances in Medical Sociology* 6: 81–117.

Dinerman, M. (1992). Managing the Maze: Case Management and Service Delivery. *Administration in Social Work* 16(1): 1–9.

Diwan, S. (1999). Allocation of Case Management Resources in Long-Term Care: Predicting High Use of Case Management Time. *The Gerontologist* 39(5): 580–90.

Dominelli, L. (1997). The Institutional Parameters of Social Work. In *Sociology for Social Work.* Ed. L. Dominelli. Houndmills: Macmillan: 113–20.

Drake, R. E. and N. Marlowe (1998). Case Managers and Boundaries. *Community Mental Health Journal* 34(3): 319–20.

Dzieglielewski, S. F. and D. C. Holliman (2001). Managed Care and Social Work Practice: Implications in an Era of Change. *Journal of Sociology and Social Welfare* 38(2): 125–39.

Eardley, T. and M. Thompson (1997). *Does Care Management Help Unemployed Job Seekers?* Sydney: Social Policy Research Centre, University of New South Wales.

Edwards, M. (2001). *Social Policy, Public Policy: From Problem to Practice.* Sydney: Allen & Unwin.

Enos, R. and S. Southern (1996). *Correctional Case Management.* Cincinnati: Anderson Publishing Co.

Erdmann, Y. and R. Wilson (2001). Managed Care: A View from Europe. *Annual Review of Public Health* 22: 273–91.

Este, D. (1996). Cultural Competency of Case Managers. In *Perspectives on Case Management Practice.* Eds C. Austin and R. McClelland. Milwaukee: Families International: 241–56.

Everitt, A. and P. Hardiker (1996). *Evaluating for Good Practice.* London: Macmillan.

Exworthy, M. and S. Halford (1999a). Assessment and Conclusions. In *Professionals and the New Managerialism in the Public Sector.* Eds M. Exworthy and S. Halford. Buckingham: Open University Press: 121–39.

——(1999b). Professionals and Managers in a Changing Public Sector: Conflict, Compromise and Collaboration? In *Professionals and the New Managerialism in the Public Sector*. Eds M. Exworthy and S. Halford. Buckingham: Open University Press: 1–17.

Exworthy, M. and S. Halford, eds (1999). *Professionals and the New Managerialism in the Public Sector*. Buckingham: Open University Press.

Fern, P. and E. Marks-Gordon (2001). *Unfinished Business: Clinical Issues in Providing Care Management to Holocaust Survivors*. 5th International Care/Case Management Conference, Vancouver, American Society on Aging.

Fineman, L. (1996). Developing a Formal Educational Program for Case Managers: One Canadian Experience. *Journal of Case Management* 5(4): 158–61.

Firth, H. (1998/1999). Accountability, Role Change and Adjustment to Care Management. *Social Work and Social Sciences Review* 8(1): 42–58.

Flynn, R. (1999). Managerialism, Professionalism and Quasi-markets. In *Professionals and the New Managerialism in the Public Sector*. Eds M. Exworthy and S. Halford. Buckingham: Open University Press: 18–36.

Ford, R., P. Ryan, P. Norton, A. Bladsmoore, T. Craig and M. Muijen (1996). Does Intensive Case Management Work?: Clinical, Social and Quality of Life Outcomes from a Controlled Study. *Journal of Mental Health* 5(4): 361–8.

Frager, S. (2000). *Managing Managed Care: Secrets from a Former Case Manager*. New York: John Wiley & Sons.

Free, R. (1995). *Employment Policy: The Solutions to Unemployment in Partnership*. Sydney: National Summit on Employment Opportunities and Case Management.

Freidson, E. (1994). *Professionalism Re-Born: Theory, Prophecy and Policy*. Oxford: Policy Press.

French, J. and B. Raven (1959). The Bases of Social Power. In *Studies in Social Power*. Ed. D. Cartright. Ann Arbor: Research Centre for Group Dynamics, Institute for Social Work, University of Michigan: 150–67.

Friedman, C. R. and J. Poertner (1995). Creating and Maintaining Support and Structure for Case Managers: Issues in Case Management Supervision. In *From Case Management to Service Coordination for Children with Emotional, Behavioural, or Mental Disorders: Building on Family Strengths*. Eds B. J. Friesen and J. Poertner. Baltimore: Paul H. Brookes: 257–74.

Friss, L. R. (1993). Family Caregivers as Case Managers. *Journal of Case Management* 2(2): 53–8.

Gaebler, T. (1996). Reinventing Government. In *New Ideas, Better Government*. Eds P. Weller and G. Davis. Sydney: Allen & Unwin: 11–18.

Gambrill, E. (1990). *Critical Thinking in Clinical Practice: Improving the Accuracy of Judgements and Decisions About Clients*. San Francisco: Jossey-Bass.

Gambrill, E. and R. Pruger, eds (1997). *Controversial Issues in Social Work Ethics, Values and Obligations*. Needham Heights: Allyn and Bacon.

Gardner, D. B. and A. Cary (1999). Collaboration, Conflict and Power: Lessons for Case Managers. *Family and Community Health* 22(3): 64–77.

Genrich, S. J., P. S. Karns and J. Neatherlin (1999). Off the Beaten Track: MSN Education for a Changing Health Environment. *Journal of Case Management* 1(3): 175–80.

Geron, S. M. (2000a). Care Management in the United States. In *Key Issues in Case Management Around the Globe*. Eds R. Applebaum and M. White. San Francisco: American Society on Aging: 10–21.

——(2000b). Measuring the Quality and Success of Care Management. In *Key Issues in Case Management Around the Globe*. Eds R. Applebaum and M. White. San Francisco: American Society on Aging: 159–75.

Geron, S. M. and D. Shassler (1994). The Quest for Uniform Guidelines for Long-Term Care Case Management. *Journal of Case Management* 3(3): 91–7.

Gibelman, M. (1983). Social Work Education and the Changing Nature of Public Agency Practice. *Journal of Education for Social Work* 19(3): 21–8.

Gil, D. S. (1992). *Unravelling Social Policy: Theory, Analysis and Political Action Towards Social Equality*. Vermont: Schenkman Books.

Glastonbury, B. (1997). The Implications of Information Technology in Social Care. In *Community Care: A Reader*. Eds J. Bornat, J. Johnson, C. Pereira, D. Pilgrim and F. Williams. London: Macmillan in association with Open University Press: 287–92.

Glettler, E. and M. G. Leen (1996). The Advanced Practice Nurse as Case Manager. *Journal of Case Management* 5(3): 121–6.

Goffman, I. (1961). *Asylums*. Harmondsworth: Penguin.

Goodin, R. E., B. Headey, R. Muffels and J. Dirven (1999). *The Real Worlds of Welfare Capitalism*. Cambridge: Cambridge University Press.

Gordon, R. and P. M. Kline (1997). Should Social Workers Enrol as Preferred Providers with For-profit Managed Care Groups? In *Controversial Issues in Social Work Ethics, Values and Obligations*. Eds E. Gambrill and R. Pruger. Needham Heights: Allyn and Bacon: 52–62.

Gournay, K. and G. Thornicroft (2000). Comments on the UK7000 Case Management Trial. *British Journal of Psychiatry* 177 (October): 371.

Graham, J., K. J. Swift and R. Delaney (2000). *Canadian Social Policy: An Introduction*. Ontario: Prentice-Hall.

Gray, L. (2000). Care Management: The Care Planning Process and International Perspectives. In *Community Care for Health Professionals*. Eds A. Compton and M. Ashwin. Oxford: Butterworth Heinemann: 88–99.

Greene, R. (1992). Case Management: An Arena for Social Work Practice. In *Social Work Case Management*. Eds R. Greene and B. Vourlekis. New York: Aldine de Gruyter.

Grube, B. and R. H. Chernesky (2001). HIV/AIDS Case Management Tasks and Activities: The Results of a Functional Analysis Study. *Social Work in Health Care* 32(3): 41–63.

Grusky, O., D. Podus, C. Webster and A. Young (1997). Measuring the Cost and Outcome Effects of Case Management Teams. *Research in the Sociology of Health Care* 14: 305–25.

Gursansky, D. and R. Kennedy (1998). Discourses of Case Management: A Labour Market Program Analysis. *The Australian Journal of Career Development* 7(2): 17–21.

Hadley, R. and R. Clough (1997). *Care in Chaos: Frustration and Challenge in Community Care*. London: Cassell.

Hafez, A. (2000). Case Management Practice. *American Journal of Occupational Therapy* 54(1): 114–15.

Hagen, J. L. (1994). JOBS and Case Management: Developments in 10 States. *Social Work* 39(2): 197–205.

Halevy-Levin, S. (2001). *Creating a Caring Geriatric Community in a University Hospital Setting*. 5th International Care/Case Management Conference, Vancouver, American Society on Aging.

Halfon, N., G. Berkowitz and L. Klee (1997). Development of an Integrated Case Management Program for Vulnerable Children. *Child Welfare* LXXII(4): 379–96.

Harrison, S. (1999). Clinical Autonomy and Health Policy: Past and Futures. In *Professionals and the New Managerialism in the Public Sector*. Eds M. Exworthy and S. Halford. Buckingham: Open University Press: 50–64.

Harvey, J., R. Kennedy and D. Gursansky (2001). Case Management and Employment Trends in the Human Services: Discerning that Employers Really Want Artists, Scientists and Superhumans. In *Case Management: Art or Science?*. Melbourne: Case Management Society of Australia.

Hassett, S. and M. J. Austin (1997). Service Integration: Something Old and Something New. In *Human Services Integration*. Ed M. J. Austin. New York: The Haworth Press: 9–29.

Havas, E. (1998). Managed Care: Business as Usual. In *Humane Managed Care?* Eds G. Schamess and A. Lightburn. Washington: NASW Press: 75–84.

Haw, M. A. (1995). State-of-the-Art Education for Case Management in Long-Term Care. *Journal of Case Management* 4(3): 85–94.

——(1996). Case Management Education in Universities: A National Survey. *The Journal of Care Management* 2(6): 10–23.

Hawkins, J. W., N. W. Veeder and C. Pearce (1998). *Nurse Social Worker Collaboration in Managed Care: A Model of Community Case Management*. New York: Springer.

Healey, K. M. (1999). Case Management in the Criminal Justice System. In *National Institute of Justice: Research in Action*. Washington: US

Department of Justice, Office of Justice Programs, National Institute of Justice: 1–12.

Heffernan, J. and G. Shuttleworth and R. Ambrosino (1997). *Social Work and Social Welfare: An Introduction.* 3rd edn. Minneapolis/St Paul: West Publishing Co.

Henderson, M. G. and A. Collard (1992). Measuring Quality in Medical Case Management Programs. In *Case Management and Social Work Practice.* Ed. S. M. Rose. New York: Longman: 170–84.

Hepworth, D. H., R. H. Rooney and J. Larsen (1997). *Direct Social Work Practice: Theory and Skills.* Singapore: Brooks/Cole: 194–229.

Hersey, P., K. Blanchard and D. Johnson (1996). *Management of Organizational Behavior: Utilizing Human Resources.* Englewood Cliffs, New Jersey: Prentice-Hall.

Hill, M. (1993). *Understanding Social Policy.* Oxford: Blackwell.

Hill, M. and G. Bramley (1986). *Analysing Social Policy.* Oxford: Blackwell.

Holland, D. E. (1999). Determining the Relevance of a Certification Exam to Home Health Care Nursing Practice. *The Journal of Long Term Home Health Care* 1(3): 197–201.

Holt, B. J. (2000). *The Practice of Generalist Case Management.* Needham Heights: Allyn and Bacon.

Howe, S. (1996). Nurse Case Management and Long Term Care. In *Nurse Case Management in the 21st Century.* Ed E. Cohen. St Louis: Mosby: 119–55.

Howells, K., G. Hall and A. Day (1999). The Management of Suicide and Self-harm in Prisons: Recommendations for Good Practice. *Australian Psychologist* 34(3): 157–65.

Hromco, J. G., J. S. Lyons and R. Nikkel (1997). Styles of Case Management: The Philosophy and Practice of Case Managers. *Community Mental Health Journal* 33(5): 415–28.

Huber, D. L. (2000). The Diversity of Case Management Models. *Lippincott's Case Management* 5(6): 248–55.

Hudson, H. (1994). Case Management: The EPIC model. A Case of Not Grasping the Nettle. In *Community Care: New Agendas and Challenges from the United Kingdom and Overseas.* Eds D. Challis, B. Davies and K. Traske. Aldershot: Arena.

Hugman, R. (1991). *Power in Caring Professions.* Basingstoke: Macmillan.

——(1998a). Social Work and De-professionalisation. In *The Sociology of the Caring Professions.* Eds P. Abbott and L. Meerabeau. London: UCL Press: 178–98.

——(1998b). *Social Work and Social Value.* London: Macmillan.

Hunter, A. (1997). Teamwork. In *Quality Care for Elderly People.* Eds P. Mayer, E. Dickinson and E. Sandler. London: Chapman and Hall Medical: 199–215.

Huntt, D. C. and B. S. Growick (1997). Managed Care for People with Disabilities. *The Journal of Rehabilitation* 63(3): 1–15.

Huxley, P., S. Evans, T. Burns, T. Fahy and J. Green (2001). Quality of Life Outcome in a Randomized Controlled Trial of Case Management. *Social Psychiatry and Psychiatric Epidemiology* 36: 249–55.

Hyduck, C. A. and D. P. Moxley (2000). Challenges to the Implication of Personal Advocacy for Older Adults. *Families in Society: The Journal of Contemporary Human Services* 81(5): 455–66.

Ikegami, N. (2000). The Development of Care Managers in Japan and the Impact of the New Public Long-term Care Insurance. In *Key Issues in Case Management Around the Globe*. Eds R. Applebaum and M. White. San Francisco: American Society on Aging: 43–9.

Iles, V. (1997). *Really Managing Health Care*. Buckingham: Open University Press.

Inciardi, J. A., S. S. Martin and F. Scarpitti (1994). Appropriateness of Assertive Case Management for Drug-Involved Prison Releasees. *Journal of Case Management* 3(4): 145–9.

Intagliata, J. (1992). Improving the Quality of Community Care for the Chronically Mentally Disabled: The Role of Case Management. In *Case Management and Social Work Practice*. Ed. S. M. Rose. New York: Longman: 25–55.

Issakidis, C., K. Sanderson, M. Teesson, S. Johnston and N. Buhrich (1999). Intensive Case Management in Australia: A Randomised Controlled Trial. *Acta Psychiatrica Scandinavica* 99(5): 360–7.

Ivantic-Doucette, K. A. and G. Maashao (1999). Huduma Kwa Wagonjwa: An African Perspective on Case Management. In *The Outcomes Mandate: Case Management in Health Care Today*. Eds E. L. Cohen and V. deBack. St Louis: Mosby: 276–85.

Jack, R., ed. (1998). *Residential versus Community Care: The Role of Institutions in Welfare Provision*. Basingstoke: Macmillan.

James, A. (1994). *Managing to Care: Public Service and the Market*. New York: Longman.

Johnson, N. (1987). *The Welfare State in Transition: The Theory and Practice of Welfare Pluralism*. Sussex: Wheatsheaf Books.

Johnson, P. J. and A. Rubin (1983). Case Management in Mental Health: A Social Work Domain? *Social Work* 28(1): 49–55.

Jones, C. (1999). Social Work: Regulation and Managerialism. In *Professionals and the New Managerialism in the Public Sector*. Eds M. Exworthy and S. Halford. Buckingham: Open University Press: 37–49.

Jones, J. (1994). The Psychiatrist's Perspective. In *Clinical Case Management*. Ed. R. Surber. Thousand Oaks: Sage: 194–207.

Kane, R., K. Freda and L. Heikoff (2000). Ethics, Power and Case Management. In *Key Issues in Case Management Around the Globe*. Eds

R. Applebaum and M. White. San Francisco: American Society on Aging: 120–36.

Kane, R. A. (1992). Case Management: Ethical Pitfalls on the Road to High-Quality Managed Care. In *Case Management and Social Work Practice*. Ed. S. M. Rose. New York: Longman: 219–28.

——(1993). Uses and Abuses of Confidentiality. In *Ethical Conflicts in the Management of Home Care: The Case Manager's Dilemma*. Eds R. A. Kane and A. L. Caplan. New York: Springer: 147–57.

Kane, R. A. and A. L. Caplan, eds (1993). *Ethical Conflicts in the Management of Home Care: The Case Manager's Dilemma*. New York: Springer.

Kane, R. A. and H. Degenholtz (1997). Case Management as a Force for Quality Assurance and Quality Improvement in Home Care. *Journal of Aging and Social Policy* 9(4): 5–28.

Kane, R. A., J. D. Penrod, G. Davidson, I. Moscovice and E. Rich (1991). What Cost Case Management in Long-Term Care? *Social Service Review* 65 (2 June): 280–303.

Kane, R. A. and C. K. Thomas (1993). What is Case Management, and Why Does it Raise Ethical Issues? In *Ethical Conflicts in the Management of Home Care: The Case Manager's Dilemma*. Eds R. A. Kane and A. L. Caplan. New York: Springer: 3–6.

Kanter, J. (1989). Clinical Case Management: Definition, Principles, Components. *Hospital and Community Psychiatry* 40(4): 361–8.

——(1992). Mental Health Case Management: A Professional Domain. In *Case Management and Social Work Practice*. Ed. S. M. Rose. New York: Longman: 126–30.

Kapp, M. (1999). Home Health Regulation: Is it Good for the Patient? *The Case Management Journal* 1(4): 251–7.

Kennedy, R. (1985). *Charity Warfare: The Charity Society in Colonial Melbourne*. Melbourne: Hyland House.

Kennedy, R., D. Gursansky and J. Harvey (2001). The Response by Australian Universities to Case Management. *Australian Social Work* 54(4): 29–38.

Kennedy, R. and J. Harvey (2001). Advertised Jobs in the Human Services: Advice to Prospective Employees. *Journal of Career Development* 10(2): 28–33.

Kennedy, R., J. Harvey and D. Gursanky (1998). Educating Human Service Workers in Case Management: A Black Box? In *Case Management: The Critical Link. Melbourne: Case Management Society of Australia.*

Kirk, S. A. and G. F. Koeske (1995). The Fate of Optimism: A Longitudinal Study of Case Managers' Hopefulness and Subsequent Morale. *Research on Social Work Practice* 5(1): 47–61.

Kirkhart, K. E. and M. C. Ruffolo (1993). Value Bases of Case Management Evaluation. *Evaluation and Program Planning* 16: 55–65.

Kirner, J. (1995). *The Employment Services Regulatory Authority and its Role in 1995: The Contracted Case Management System.* Sydney: National Summit on Employment Opportunities and Case Management.

Kisthardt, W. E. and C. A. Rapp (1992). Bridging the Gap Between Principles and Practice: Implementing a Strengths Perspective in Case Management. In *Case Management and Social Work Practice.* Ed. S. M. Rose. New York: Longman: 112–25.

Knapp, S. and P. A. Keller (2001). Professional Associations' Strategies for Revitalizing Professional Psychology. *Professional Psychology: Research and Practice* 32(1): 71–8.

Korr, W. S. and L. Cloninger (1991). Assessing Models of Case Management: An Empirical Approach. *Journal of Social Service Research* 14(1/2): 129–46.

Kubisa, T. (1990). Care Manager: Rhetoric or Reality. In *Care Managers and Care Management.* Ed. I. Allen. London: Policy Studies Institute supported by The Joseph Rowntree Memorial Trust: 1–8.

Kulbok, P. A. and S. W. Utz (1999). Managing Care: Knowledge and Educational Strategies for Professional Development. *Family and Community Health* 22(3): 1–11.

Kunkel, S. R., L. Duffy-Durham and M. Scala (2000). Consumer Direction and Traditional Case Management: Common Ground or Contested Terrain? In *Key Issues in Case Management Around the Globe.* Eds R. Applebaum and M. White. San Francisco: American Society on Aging: 104–12.

Lancet (1995). Case Management: A Disastrous Mistake. *Lancet* 345: 399–401.

Leff, J. (1997). The Future of Community Care. In *Care in the Community: Illusion or Reality?* Ed. J. Leff. Chichester: John Wiley and Sons: 203–10.

Lemire, A. and L. Mansell (2001). *Implementing a Coordinated Access Model for Continuing Care Services in Alberta, Canada.* 5th International Care/Case Management Conference, Vancouver, American Society on Aging.

Leutz, W. N. (1999). Five Laws for Integrating Medical and Social Services: Lessons from the United States and the United Kingdom. *The Milbank Quarterly* 77(1): 77–110.

Levin, P. (1997). *Making Social Policy: The Mechanisms of Government and Politics, and How to Investigate Them.* Buckingham: Open University Press.

Lewis, J. and H. Glennerster (1996). *Implementing the New Community Care.* Philadelphia: Open University Press.

Lewis, J. and M. Lewis (1983). *Management of Human Service Programs.* Pacific Grove: Brooks/Cole.

Libassi, M. F. (1992). The Chronically Mentally Ill: A Practice Approach. In *Case Management and Social Work Practice.* Ed. S. M. Rose. New York: Longman: 77–90.

Ling, C. (1999). *Case Management*. Englewood: Linda Skidmore-Roth.

Lipsky, M. (1980). *Street-Level Bureaucracy: Dilemmas of the Individual in Public Services*. New York: Russell Sage Foundation.

——(1991). The Paradox of Managing Discretionary Workers in Social Welfare Policy. In *The Sociology of Social Security*. Eds M. Adler, C. Bell, J. Clasen and A. Sinfield. Edinburgh: Edinburgh University Press: 212–28.

Loewenberg, F. M., R. Dolgoff and D. Harrington (2000). *Ethical Decisions for Social Work Practice*. Itasca, Illinois: F.E. Peacock.

Lohman, H. (1999). What Will it Take for More Occupational Therapists to Become Case Managers? Implications for Education, Practice and Policy. *American Journal of Occupational Therapy* 53(1): 111–15.

Loomis, J. F. (1992). Case Management in Health Care. In *Case Management and Social Work Practice*. Ed. S. M. Rose. New York: Longman: 160–9.

Lowenstein, A. (2000). A Case Management Demonstration Project for the Frail Elderly in Israel. *Journal of Case Management* 2(1): 5–14.

Lowery, S. (1992). Qualifications for the Successful Case Manager. *Case Manager* 3(4): 66–8, 70–1, 73–6.

Lymbery, M. (1998). Care Management and Professional Autonomy: The Impact of Community Care Legislation on Social Work with Older People. *The British Journal of Social Work* 28(6): 863–78.

Marschke, J. and S. Freedberg (1997). Is it Unethical for Professional Helpers to Encourage or Allow Clients to Become Dependent on Them? In *Controversial Issues in Social Work Ethics, Values, and Obligations*. Eds E. Gambrill and R. Pruger. Needham Heights: Allyn and Bacon.

Marshall, M. (1996). Case Management: A Dubious Practice. *British Medical Journal* 312: 523–4.

Marshall, M. and F. Creed (2000). Assertive Community Treatment—Is it the Future of Community Care in the UK? *International Review of Psychiatry* 12(3): 191–6.

Martin, L. M., C. L. Peters and C. Glisson (1998). Factors Affecting Case Management Recommendations for Children Entering State Custody. *The Social Service Review* 72(4): 521–44.

Mathias, P. and T. Thompson (1997). Preparation for Interprofessional Work: Trends in Education, Training and the Structure of Qualifications in the United Kingdom. In *Interprofessional Working for Health and Social Care*. Eds J. Ovretveit and P. Mathias. Houndmills: Macmillan.

Matorin, S. (1998). The Corporatization of Mental Health Services: The Impact on Service, Training and Values. In *Humane Managed Care?* Eds G. Schamess and A. Lightburn. Washington: NASW: 159–70.

May, T. and J. Annison (1998). The De-professionalisation of Probation Officers. In *The Sociology of the Caring Professions*. Eds P. Abbott and L. Meerabeau. London: UCL Press: 157–77.

McCallum, S. and J. Furby (1999). Case Management for the Northern Territory Correctional Services. *Australian Social Work* 52(4): 45–9.

McClaran, J., Z. Lam and L. Snell and E. Franco (1998). The Importance of the Case Management Approach: Perceptions of Multidisciplinary Team Members. *Journal of Case Management* 7(3): 117–26.

McClelland, G. (1998). Case Managers Meeting to Discuss Ethics. *Generations* 22(3): 96–7.

McClelland, R. W. (1996). Managed Care. In *Perspectives on Case Management Practice*. Eds C. D. Austin and R. W. McClelland. Milwaukee: Families International: 203–18.

McClelland, R. W., C. D. Austin and D. Schneck (1996). Practice Dilemmas and Policy Implications in Case Management. In *Perspectives on Case Management Practice*. Eds C. D. Austin and R. W. McClelland. Milwaukee: Families International: 257–77.

McDonald, C. (1999). Human Service Professionals in the Community Services Industry. *Australian Social Work* 52(1): 17–25.

McGuire, L., ed. (1997). Service Delivery Contracts: Quality for Customers, Clients and Citizens. In *The New Contractualism*. Eds G. Davis, B. Sullivan and A. Yeatman. South Melbourne: Macmillan Education Australia: 102–18.

McMahon, M. (1992). Dangerousness, Confidentiality, and the Duty to Protect. *Australian Psychologist* 27(1): 12–16.

Means, R. and R. Smith (1994). *Community Care*. Basingstoke: Macmillan.

Meerabeau, L. (1998). Project 2000 and the Nature of Nursing Knowledge. In *The Sociology of the Caring Professions*. Eds P. Abbott and L. Meerabeau. London: UCL Press: 82–105.

Meerabeau, L. and P. Abbott (1998). Reflections. In *The Sociology of the Caring Professions*. Eds P. Abbott and L. Meerabeau. London: UCL Press: 255–63.

Mehr, J. (1995). *Human Services: Concepts and Intervention Strategies*. Boston: Allyn and Bacon.

Menter, I. and Y. Muschamp (1999). Markets and Management: The Case of Primary Schools. In *Professionals and the New Managerialism in the Public Sector*. Eds M. Exworthy and S. Halford. Buckingham: Open University Press: 65–82.

Midgely, J. (1997). *Social Welfare in Global Context*. Thousand Oaks: Sage.

Miley, K. K., M. O'Melia and B. Dubois (1998). *Generalist Social Work Practice: An Empowering Approach*. Needham Heights: Allyn and Bacon.

Mishra, R. (1984). *The Welfare State in Crisis: Social Thought and Social Change*. Sussex: Wheatsheaf Books.

Montevilla-Vargas, G. (2001). *Elder Abuse: Struggling to Establish a Community Case Management Model in Bolivia*. 5th International Care/Case Management Conference, Vancouver, American Society on Aging.

Moore, S. (1992). Case Management and the Integration of Services: How

Service Delivery Systems Shape Case Management. *Social Work* 37(5): 418–23.

Moore, S. T. (1998). Organizational and Managerial Supports for Service Quality in Health and Human Services. *Family and Community Health* 21(2): 20–30.

Morales, C. E. (1994). Advocacy and Case Management. In *Clinical Case Management: A Guide to Comprehensive Treatment of Serious Mental Illness*. Ed. R. W. Surber. Thousand Oaks: Sage: 121–35.

More, P. and S. Mandell (1997). *Nursing Case Management*. New York: McGraw-Hill.

Mowbray, C. T., D. P. Moxley, S. Thrasher, D. Bybee, N. McCrohan, S. Harris and G. Clover (1996). Consumers as Community Support Providers: Issues Created by Role Innovation. *Community Mental Health Journal* 32(1): 47–67.

Moxley, D. (1989). *The Practice of Case Management*. Newbury Park: Sage.

——(1996). Teaching Case Management: Essential Content for the Preservice Preparation of Effective Personnel. *Journal of Teaching in Social Work* 13(1/2): 111–40.

——(1997). *Case Management by Design: Reflections on Principles and Practices*. Chicago: Nelson-Hall.

Murer, C. G. and L. L. Brick (1997). *The Case Management Sourcebook: A Guide to Designing and Implementing a Centralised Case Management System*. New York: McGraw-Hill.

Murphy, E. K. (1999). Managed Care: Legal and Policy Issues. In *The Outcomes Mandate: Case Management in Health Care Today*. Eds E. L. Cohen and V. deBack. St Louis: Mosby: 256–67.

Murphy-Berman, V. (1994). A Conceptual Framework for Thinking About Risk Assessment and Case Management in Child Protective Service. *Child Abuse and Neglect* 8(2): 193–201.

Naleppa, M. J. and W. J. Reid (2000). Integrating Case Management and Brief-treatment Strategies: A Hospital-Based Geriatric Program. *Social Work in Health Care* 31(4): 1–23.

National Association of Social Workers (1992a). Case Management in Health, Education, and Human Service Settings. In *Case Management and Social Work Practice*. Ed. S. M. Rose. New York: Longman: 21–4.

——(1992b). Standards for Social Work Case Management. http://www.naswdc.org/practice/standards/casemgmt.htm [30 January 2001].

——(2000). *Speciality Certification in Case Management*. Baltimore: Speciality Certifications.

Netting, F. E. (1992). Case Management: Service or Symptom? *Social Work* 37(2): 160–3.

Netting, F. E. and F. G. Williams (1996). Case Manager–Physician Collaboration: Implications for Professional Identity, Roles and Relationships. *Health and Social Work* 21(3): 216–24.

——(1999). Geriatric Case Managers: Integration into Physician Practices. *The Case Management Journal* 1(1): 3–9.

Newell, M. (1996). *Using Case Management to Improve Health Outcomes.* Maryland: Aspen Publishers.

Nocon, A. and H. Qureshi (1998). *Outcomes of Community Care for Users and Carers: A Social Services Perspective.* Buckingham: Oxford University Press.

Northey, R. (2000). The New Zealand Framework for Disability Support Services: A South Pacific Model. In *Key Issues in Case Management Around the Globe*. Eds R. Applebaum and M. White. San Francisco: American Society on Aging: 34–42.

Nurius, P. S. (1995). Critical Thinking: A Meta-Skill for Integrating Practice and Information Technology Training. In *Human Services in the Information Age*. Eds J. Rafferty, J. Steyaert and D. Colombi. New York: The Haworth Press: 109–26.

Nurius, P. S., S. P. Kemp and J. Gibson (1999). Practitioners' Perspectives on Sound Reasoning: Adding a Worker-in-Context Component. *Administration in Social Work* 23(1): 1–27.

O'Connor, G. G. (1988). Case Management: System and Practice. *The Journal of Contemporary Social Work* (February): 97–106.

O'Connor, I., J. Wilson and D. Setterlund (1998). *Social Work and Welfare Practice*. Sydney: Addison Wesley Longman.

O'Donnell, M., G. Parker, M. Proberts, R. Matthews, D. Fisher, B. Hohnson and D. Hadzi-Pavlovic (1999). A Study of Client-focused Case Management and Consumer Advocacy: The Community and Consumer Service Project. *Australian and New Zealand Journal of Psychiatry* 33(5): 684–93.

Offe, C. (1984). *Contradictions of the Welfare State*. London: Hutchinson.

Orme, J. and B. Glastonbury (1993). *Care Management: Tasks and Workloads*. Houndmills: Macmillan.

Ovretveit, J. (1993). *Coordinating Community Care: Multidisciplinary Teams and Care Management*. Buckingham: Open University Press.

Ozanne, E. (1990). Reasons for the Emergence of Case Management Approaches and their Distinctiveness from Present Service Arrangements. In *Community Care Policy and Practice: New Directions in Australia*. Eds A. Howe, E. Ozanne and C. S. Smith. Clayton: Public Sector Management Institute, Monash University: 186–94.

——(1996). Case Management Applications in Australia. *Journal of Case Management* 5(4): 153–7.

Ozanne, E., D. Gursansky, N. Ikegami, A. Joshi and C. Austin (2000). Education and Training: International Perspectives. In *Key Issues in Case*

Management Around the Globe. Eds R. Applebaum and M. White. San Francisco: American Society on Aging: 146–58.

Patterson, J. (2000). *Good Practice in Multi-Agency Linkages: Report on Coordinated Service Responses for Homeless People with Complex Needs*. Adelaide: Department of Human Services Linkages and Protocols for Homeless People Advisor Group: 1–81.

Payne, M. (1995). *Social Work and Community Care*. London: Macmillan.

——(2000). The Politics of Case Management and Social Work. *International Journal of Social Welfare* 9: 82–91.

Pearce, C. W. and C. J. M. Morin (1998). Physicians Learn New Roles for Managed Care: Modernising the Caduceus. In *Nurse Social Worker Collaboration in Managed Care: A Model of Community Case Management*. Eds J. W. Hawkins, N. W. Veeder and C. W. Pearce. New York: Springer Publishing Company: 150–64.

Perlmutter, S. and R. Johnson (1996). Case Management in the Public Welfare System. In *Perspectives on Case Management Practice*. Eds C. D. Austin and R. W. McClelland. Milwaukee: Families International: 166–201.

Peterson, G. A., I. D. Drone and M. Munetz (1997). Diversity in Case Management Modalities: The Summit Model. *Community Mental Health Journal* 33(3): 245–50.

Pierre, R. G. S., J. I. Layzer, B. Goodson and L. Bernstein (1999). The Effectiveness of Comprehensive Case Management Interventions: Evidence from the National Evaluation of the Comprehensive Child Development Program. *American Journal of Evaluation* 20(1): 15–35.

Pierson, P. (1994). *Dismantling the Welfare State? Reagan, Thatcher, and the Politics of Retrenchment*. Cambridge: Cambridge University Press.

Pilisuk, T. and H. Sullivan (1998). Designing an Automated Services Tracking System for a Caregiver Support Program. *Journal of Case Management* 7(1): 18–23.

Pithouse, A. (1987). *Social Work: The Social Organisation of an Invisible Trade*. Aldershot: Avebury.

Polinsky, M. L., C. Fred and P. Ganz (1991). Qualitative and Quantitative Assessment of a Case Management Program for Cancer Patients. *Health and Social Work* 16(3): 176–83.

Quick, B. (1997). The Relationship Between Personality Traits and Job Satisfaction for Case Managers. *The Journal of Care Management* 3(5): 78–82.

Rafferty, J., J. Steyaert and D. Columbi, eds (1995). *Human Services in the Information Age*. New York: The Haworth Press.

Raiff, N. R. and B. K. Shore (1993). *Advanced Case Management: New Strategies for the Nineties*. New Delhi: Sage.

Rapp, C. A. (1998a). The Active Ingredients of Effective Case Management: A Research Synthesis. *Community Mental Health Journal* 34(4): 363–80.

——(1998b). *The Strengths Model: Case Management with People Suffering*

From Severe and Persistent Mental Illness. New York: Oxford University Press.

Rapp, C. A. and W. Kisthardt (1996). Case Management with People with Severe and Persistent Mental Illness. In *Perspectives on Case Management Practice.* Eds C. D. Austin and R. W. McClelland. Milwaukee: Families International: 17–45.

Rapp, C. A. and J. Poertner (1992). *Social Administration: A Client-centered Approach.* New York: Longman.

Rapp, L. A., C. N. Dulmus, J. Wodarski and M. Feit (1998). Integrated Human Service Delivery System: Public Welfare Model. *The Journal of Applied Social Sciences* 22(2): 151–60.

Rapp, R. C., C. W. Kelliher, J. Fisher and F. Hall (1994). Strengths-based Case Management: A Role in Addressing Denial in Substance Abuse Treatment. *Journal of Case Management* 3(4): 139–44.

Raven, B. (1993). The Bases of Power: Origins and Recent Developments. *Journal of Social Issues* 49(47): 227–51.

Reamer, F. G. (1998). Managed Care: Ethical Considerations. In *Humane Managed Care?* Eds G. Schamess and A. Lightburn. Washington: NASW Press: 293–8.

Reed, G. M., R. F. Levant, C. Stout, M. Murphy and R. Phelps (2001). Psychology in the Current Mental Health Marketplace. *Professional Psychology: Research and Practice* 32(1): 65–70.

Reinhard, J. (2000). Limitations of Mental Health Case Management: A Rational Emotive and Cognitive Therapy Perspective. *Journal of Rational–Emotive and Cognitive–Behavior Therapy* 18(2): 103–17.

Rife, J. C., R. J. First, R. Greenlee, L. Miller and M. Feichter (1991). Case Management with Homeless Mentally Ill People. *Health and Social Work* 16(1): 58–66.

Roberts, C. S., C. Severinson, C. Kuehn, D. Straker and C. Fritz (1992). Obstacles to Effective Case Management with AIDS Patients: The Clinician's Perspectives. *Social Work in Health Care* 17(2): 27–40.

Roberts, J., G. Browne, A. Gafni, M. Varieur, P. Loney and M. De Ruitter (2000). Specialised Continuing Care Models for Persons with Dementia: A Systematic Review of the Research Literature. *Canadian Journal on Ageing* 19(1): 106–26.

Roberts-DeGennaro, M. (1987). Developing Case Management as a Practice Model. *Social Casework: The Journal of Contemporary Social Work* 68 (October): 466–70.

Roessler, R. T. and S. E. Rubin (1998). *Case Management and Rehabilitation Counseling: Procedures and Techniques.* Austin: Pro-ed.

Rogers, G. (1995). Educating Case Managers for Culturally Competent Practice. *Journal of Case Management* 4(2): 60–5.

Roggenkamp, S. D. and K. R. White (2001). Is Hospital Case Management a Rationalized Myth? *Social Science and Medicine* 53: 1057–66.

Rose, S. M. (1992a). Case Management: An Advocacy/Empowerment Design. In *Case Management and Social Work Practice*. Ed. S. M. Rose. New York: Longman: 271–301.

——(1992b). Introduction: Case Management and Social Work Practice—History and Context. In *Case Management and Social Work Practice*. Ed. S. M. Rose. New York: Longman: v–x.

Rose, S. M. and V. L. Moore (1995). Case Management. In *Encyclopedia of Social Work*. Eds R. L. Edwards, J. G. Hopps, L. D. Bernard et al. Washington: NASW Press: 335–40.

Rosen, A. L., E. B. Gross, E. Young, M. Smolenski and D. Howe (2000). To Be or Not to Be? Credentials for Case/Care Management. In *Key Issues in Case Management Around the Globe*. Eds R. Applebaum and M. White. San Francisco: American Society on Aging: 93–103.

Rosenberg, G. (1998). Social Work in a Health and Mental Health Managed Care Environment. In *Humane Managed Care?* Eds G. Schamess and A. Lightburn. Washington: NASW Press: 3–22.

Rossi, P. (1999). *Case Management in Health Care*. Philadelphia: W. B. Saunders Co.

Rothman, J. (1991). A Model of Case Management: Toward Empirically Based Practice. *Social Work* 36(6): 520–8.

Rothman, J. and J. S. Sager (1998). *Case Management: Integrating Individual and Community Practice*. Boston: Allyn and Bacon.

Rothman, J. C. (1998). *From the Front Lines: Student Cases in Social Work Ethics*. Needham Heights: Allyn and Bacon.

Rubin, A. (1992). Case Management. In *Case Management and Social Work Practice*. Ed. S. M. Rose. New York: Longman: 5–19.

Ryan, P., R. Ford, A. Beadsmoore and M. Muijen (1999). The Enduring Relevance of Case Management. *British Journal of Social Work* 29(1): 97–125.

Saleebey, D., ed. (1992). *The Strengths Perspective in Social Work Practice*. New York: Longman.

Sankar, S. and D. Brooks (1998). Social Work Case Management: Challenges for Social Work Education and the Profession. In *Humane Managed Care?* Eds G. Schamess and A. Lightburn. Washington: NASW Press: 378–86.

Saunders, P. (2000). Global Pressures, National Responses: The Australian Welfare State in Context. In *Contemporary Perspectives on Social Work and the Human Services: Challenges and Change*. Eds I. O'Connor, P. Smyth and J. Warburton. Melbourne: Pearson Education: 12–29.

Scannapieco, M. and R. L. Hegar (1995). Kinship Care: Two Case Management Models. *Child and Adolescent Social Work Journal* 12(2): 147–56.

Schamess, G. and A. Lightburn, eds (1998). *Humane Managed Care?* Washington: NASW Press.

Schindler, R. and E. Brawley (1987). *Social Care at the Front Line*. New York: Tavistock.

Schmidt-Posner, J. and J. M. Jerrell (1998). Qualitative Analysis of Three Case Management Programs. *Community Mental Health Journal* 34(4): 381–92.

Schon, D. (1983). *The Reflective Practitioner*. New York: Basic Books.

Scrivens, E. (1995). *Accreditation: Protecting the Professional or the Consumer?* Buckingham: Open University Press.

Senn, V., R. Kendal, L. Willetts and N. Triem (1997). Training Level and Training Needs of Staff. In *Care in the Community: Illusion or Reality?* Ed. J. Leff. Brisbane: John Wiley and Sons: 137–44.

Shapiro, R. S., K. A. Tym, J. L. Gudmundons, A. R. Derse and J. P. Klein (2000). Managed Care: Effects on the Physician–Patient Relationship. *Cambridge Quarterly of Health Care Ethics* 9: 71–81.

Sheafor, B. W., C. R. Horejsi and G. A. Horejsi (2000). *Techniques and Guidelines for Social Work Practice*. Needham Heights: Allyn and Bacon.

Sheppard, M. (1995). *Care Management and the New Social Work: A Critical Analysis*. London: Whiting and Birch.

Siefker, J. M., M. B. Garrett, A. Van Genderen and M. Weiss (1998). *Fundamentals in Case Management: Guidelines for Case Managers*. St Louis: Mosby.

Silin, P. (2001). *Gay Men and Lesbians: Special Issues in Care/Case Management*. 5th International Care/Case Management Conference, Vancouver, American Society on Aging.

Sinclair, A. (1997). After Excellence: Models of Organisational Culture for the Public Sector. In *Managerialism: The Great Debate*. Eds M. Considine and M. Painter. Melbourne: Melbourne University Press: 134–51.

Sinnen, M. and M. Schifalaqua (1996). The Education of Nurses: Nurse Case Managers' View. In *Nurse Case Management in the 21st Century*. Ed. E. Cohen. St Louis: Mosby: 55–62.

Smith, D. (1995). Standards of Practice for Case Management. *The Journal of Care Management* 1(3): 6–16.

Solomon, P. (2000). Precipitants of Case Management from an International Perspective. *International Journal of Law and Psychiatry* 23(3–4): 419–28.

Solomon, P. and J. Draine (1994). Family Perceptions of Consumers as Case Managers. *Community Mental Health Journal* 30(2): 165–76.

Sonntag, J. (1995). A Case Manager's Perspective. In *Elder Mistreatment: Ethical Issues, Dilemmas, and Decisions*. Ed. T. F. Johnson. New York: The Haworth Press: 115–30.

Stanley, N. (1999). User–Practitioner Transactions in the New Culture of Community Care. *British Journal of Social Work* 29(3): 417–35.

Steering Committee for the Review of Commonwealth/State Service Provision

(1997). *Reforms in Government Service Provision*. Melbourne: Commonwealth of Australia, Industries Commission.

Steyaert, J., D. Colombi and J. Rafferty, eds (1996). *Human Services and Information Technology: An International Perspective*. Aldershot: Arena.

Storl, H., B. DuBois and J. Celine (1999). Ethical Decision-making Made Easier. *Journal of Case Management* 1(3): 163–9.

Strickland, D. and O. C. O'Connell (1998). Saving Your Career in the 21st Century. *Journal of Case Management* 7(2): 47–51.

Stroul, B. (1995). Case Management as a System of Care. In *From Case Management to Service Coordination for Children with Emotional, Behavioural or Mental Disorders: Building on Family Strengths*. Eds B. J. Friesen and J. Poertner. Baltimore: Paul Brookes: 9–25.

Stuart, A. and K. Thorsen (1996). *Quality and Client Rights in Market Based Reforms: The Case of Employment Services*. 3rd National Conference of Unemployment, Queensland University of Technology, Brisbane.

Sullivan, W. P. (1990). Becoming a Case Manager: Implications for Social Work Educators. *Journal of Teaching in Social Work* 4(2): 159–72.

Sullivan, W. P. and B. J. Fisher (1994). Intervening for Success: Strengths-based Case Management and Successful Ageing. *Journal of Geontological Social Work* 22(1/2): 61–74.

Summers, M. (2000). Facilitating Comparisons Between Evaluations of Case Management Programs. *Journal of Case Management* 2(2): 87–92.

Summers, N. (2000). *Fundamentals of Case Management Practice: Exercises and Readings*. Albert Complex: Wadsworth/Thomson Learning.

Sunley, R. (1997). Advocacy in the New World of Managed Care. *Families in Society: The Journal of Contemporary Human Services* 78 (January/February): 84–94.

Tanner, D. (1998). Empowerment and Care Management: Swimming Against the Tide. *Health and Social Care in the Community* 6(6): 447–57.

Taylor, C. and R. Barnet (1999). The Ethics of Case Management: The Quality Cost Conundrum. In *The Outcomes Mandate: Case Management in Health Care Today*. Eds E. Cohen and V. deBack. St Louis: Mosby: 27–36.

Teare, R. J. and B. J. Sheafor (1995). *Practice-sensitive Social Work Education: An Empirical Analysis of Social Work Practice and Practitioners*. Alexandrina, Virginia: Council on Social Work Education.

Thomas, B. and K. Lovell (1999). Mental Health Nursing and Case Management in Great Britain. In *The Outcomes Mandate: Case Management in Health Care Today*. Eds E. Cohen and V. deBack. St Louis: Mosby: 112–21.

Tower, K. D. (1994). Consumer-centred Social Work Practice: Restoring Client Self-determination. *Social Work* 39(2): 191–6.

Trevithick, P. (2000). *Social Work Skills: A Practice Handbook*. Buckingham: Open University Press.

Tripp, R. (1976). *The International Thesaurus of Quotations*. Middlesex: Penguin Reference Books.

Trotter, C. (1999). *Working with Involuntary Clients: A Guide to Practice*. Sydney: Allen & Unwin.

Vandivort-Warren, R. (1998). How Social Workers Can Manage Managed Care. In *Humane Managed Care?* Eds G. Schamess and A. Lightburn. Washington: NASW Press: 255–67.

Vourlekis, B. S. (1992). The Policy and Professional Context of Case Management Practice. In *Social Work Case Management*. Eds B. S. Vourlekis and R. R. Greene. New York: Aldine de Gruyter: Chapter 1, 1–9.

Vourlekis, B. S. and R. R. Greene (1992). Mastering the Case Manager Role. In *Social Work Case Management*. Eds B. S. Vourlekis and R. R. Greene. New York: Aldine de Gruyter: 181–90.

Vourlekis, B. S. and R. R. Greene, eds (1992). *Social Work Case Management*. New York: Aldine de Gruyter.

Walsh, J. (2000). *Clinical Case Management with Persons Having Mental Illness: A Relationship-based Perspective*. Singapore: Brooks/Cole.

Waugaman, W. (1994). Professionalization and Socialization in Inter-professional Collaboration. In *Interprofessional Care and Collaborative Practice*. Eds M. Casto and M. Julia. Pacific Grove: Brooks/Cole: 23–31.

Wearing, M. (1998). *Working in Community Services: Management and Practice*. Sydney: Allen & Unwin.

Weed, R. O., ed. (1999). *Life Care Planning and Case Management Handbook*. Boca Raton: CRC Press.

Weil, M., J. M. Karls and Associates (1985). *Case Management in Human Service Practice*. San Francisco: Jossey-Bass.

Weil, M., I. Zipper and S. Dedmon (1995). Issues and Principles of Training for Case Management in Mental Health. In *From Case Management to Service Coordination for Children with Emotional, Behavioural or Mental Disorders*. Eds B. Frieson and J. Poertner. Baltimore: Paul H. Brookes.

Welch, B. (1998). Care Management and Community Care: Current Issues. In *Community Care, Secondary Health Care and Care Management*. Eds D. Challis, R. Darton and K. Stewart. Aldershot: Ashgate.

Weller, P. (1996). The Universality of Public Sector Reform: Ideas, Meanings and Strategies. In *New Ideas, Better Government*. Eds P. Weller and G. Davis. Sydney: Allen & Unwin: 1–10.

Willems, D. (1996). The Case Manager in Holland Behind the Dikes: A Hole Filler or Bridge Builder. *Journal of Case Management* 5(4): 146–52.

Williams, F. (1989). *Social Policy: A Critical Introduction*. Cambridge: Policy Press.

Wilmot, S. (1997). *The Ethics of Community Care*. London: Cassell.

Witheridge, T. F. (1992). The Assertive Community Treatment Worker: An Emerging Role and its Implications for Professional Training. In *Case*

Management and Social Work Practice. Ed. S. M. Rose. New York: Longman: 101–11.

Wolk, J. L., W. P. Sullivan and D. Hartmann (1994). The Managerial Nature of Case Management. *Social Work* 39(2): 152–9.

Wolk, J. L. and M. R. Wertheimer (1999). Generalist Practice vs. Case Management: An Accreditation Contradiction. *Journal of Social Work Education* 35(1): 101–13.

Wood, G. G. and R. R. Middleman (1989). *The Structural Approach to Direct Practice in Social Work.* New York: Columbia University Press.

Woodside, M. and T. McClam (1998). *Generalist Case Management: A Method of Human Services Delivery.* Pacific Grove: Brooks/Cole.

Yarmo, D. (1998). Research Directions for Case Management. *Journal of Case Management* 7(2): 84–91.

Ziguras, S. and G. Stuart (2000). A Meta-analysis of the Effectiveness of Mental Health Case Management Over 20 Years. *Psychiatric Services* 51(11): 1410–21.

Zlotnik, J. L. (1996). Case Management in Child Welfare. In *Perspectives on Case Management Practice.* Eds C. D. Austin and R. W. McClelland. Milwaukee: Families International: 47–72.

INDEX